ELEVEN YEARS
IN
CEYLON

ELEVEN YEARS

IN

CEYLON

COMPRISING

SKETCHES OF THE FIELD SPORTS

AND

NATURAL HISTORY OF THAT COLONY

AND AN ACCOUNT OF ITS

HISTORY AND ANTIQUITIES

MAJOR FORBES

IN TWO VOLUMES

VOL. II

ISBN : 978-93-5324-359-3 (Set)

ISBN : 978-93-5324-361-6 Vol. 2 (HB)

First Published, London, 1840

Published, 2020

Published by

Facsimile Publisher
12 Pragati Market
Ashok Vihar, Ph-2
Delhi-110052
E-mail: books@facsimilepublisher.com

Printed at: G. Print Process, Delhi.

Eleven Years in Ceylon

Major Forbes

ELEVEN YEARS IN CEYLON.

COMPRISING

SKETCHES OF THE FIELD SPORTS

AND

NATURAL HISTORY OF THAT COLONY,

AND AN ACCOUNT OF ITS

HISTORY AND ANTIQUITIES.

BY MAJOR FORBES, 78TH HIGHLANDERS.

A land of wonders! which the sun still eyes
With ray direct, as of the lovely realm
Enamour'd, and delighting there to dwell.

THOMSON.

IN TWO VOLUMES.

VOL. II.

LONDON:
RICHARD BENTLEY, NEW BURLINGTON STREET,
Publisher in Ordinary to Her Majesty.
1840.

CONTENTS

OF THE SECOND VOLUME.

CHAPTER I.

ANCIENT FORTRESS OF SIGIRI.

CHAPTER II.

TO TRINKOMALEE.

CHAPTER VI.

COLD PLAINS. — NUWARA ELLIA.

CHAPTER VII.

HORTON PLAINS.

CHAPTER VIII.

TO THE ANCIENT CITY OF MÁGAM.

CHAPTER IX.

RELIGION OF CEYLON.

CHAPTER X.

BUDDHA'S TOOTH IN THE PALACE OF KANDY.

CHAPTER XI.

HISTORY OF THE PORTUGUESE IN CEYLON.

CHAPTER XII.

HISTORY OF THE DUTCH IN CEYLON.

CHAPTER XIII.

THE CINGALESE LANGUAGE AND LITERATURE.

CHAPTER XIV.

HISTORY OF THE ISLAND PRIOR TO THE CINGALESE CONQUEST, B.C. 543.

APPENDIX.

TRANSLATIONS OF INSCRIPTIONS.

A

RESIDENCE IN CEYLON.

CHAPTER I.

ANCIENT FORTRESS OF SIGIRI.

A little while, along thy saddening plains,
The starless night of desolation reigns.—CAMPBELL.

Rock of Sigiri. — Ancient Fortress. — Kásyapa the Parricide. — Fate of the King Daasenkellia. — His Cruelty. — Remains of a Gallery. — Ascent to the Summit now impracticable. — Dilapidated Rock Temple. — Ceylon Leopards, — how destroyed. — Encounter of a Kandian with a Leopard. — Tank of Sigiri. — Sigiri to Dambool. — Andagalla Pass. — Nalande. — Elephants.

WE returned from Polannarrua by Minneria and Paecolom; and from thence struck off to the right to search for the ruins of Sigiri, an ancient capital of the island, hitherto unnoticed by Europeans. From Paecolom, after riding four miles,—part of our way lying along the embankment, and part in the bed of a large tank,—the morning mist suddenly cleared away, and we found ourselves on the verge of a piece of water, reflecting from its unruffled surface the large forest-trees around, with the bare overhanging sides and brushwood-covered summit of the rock of Sigiri,* which appeared to have started from the plain, and to frown defiance over the scanty fields and far-extending forests of the surrounding plain.

From the spot where we halted I could distinguish massive stone walls appearing through the trees near the base of the rock, and now felt convinced that this was the very place I was anxious to discover. Although the appearance and situation of such a rock must have attracted the attention of those who formed the earliest strongholds of Ceylon, yet its hard substance and impracticable ascent do not seem to have been completely overcome until A.D. 478; at which time it was made the seat of Government, and became the capital of

* Sikhari signifies a mountain-stronghold or hill-fort, but so simple a derivation and so appropriate a designation is rejected; and the learned natives derive its name from Siha or Singha, (a lion), and giri (a rock), and assert that it was so called from the number of lions sculptured on different parts of the fortress. Their derivations, always fanciful and often absurd, are not supported in this instance by any remains which we discovered; it is one of the very few places of consequence in which I have not found lions sculptured in various attitudes.

the island, in the reign of Sigiri Kasoomboo the First, who is also called Kásyapa the Parricide, in consequence of his having attained to the throne by the murder of his father Daasenkellia. The minister and son-in-law of this King was also an accomplice in the crime. After a reign of eighteen years the Parricide was defeated in battle, by forces which his younger brother Moogallána had raised on the continent. The action took place in the neighbourhood of Sigiri, and Kásyapa anticipated his fate by killing himself on the field of battle; but the minister, and upwards of one thousand of those who were cognizant of the crimes or participated in the success of Kásyapa, suffered death by order of the victor. The murder of his father, and the usurpation of the throne by Kásyapa, are thus related in Turnour's literal translation of the Mahawanso, a Cingalese history written immediately after these events, or nearly fourteen hundred years ago.

"He (the King Daasenkellia, called also Dhátuséno,) had two sons, born of different but equally illustrious mothers, named Kassapo, and the powerful Moggallana. He had also a daughter as dear to him as his own life. He bestowed her, as well as the office of chief commander, on his nephew. This individual caused her to be flogged on the thighs with a whip, although she had committed no offence.

The Raja, on seeing his daughter's vestments trickling with blood, and learning the particulars, furiously indignant, caused his nephew's mother (the King's own sister) to be burned naked. From that period (the nephew), inflamed with rage against him, uniting himself with Kassapo, infused into his mind the ambition to usurp the kingdom; and kindling at the same time animosity in his breast against his parent, and gaining over the people, succeeded in capturing the King alive. Thereupon Kassapo, supported by all the unworthy portion of the nation, and annihilating the party who adhered to his father, raised the Chhatto.* Moggallana then endeavoured to wage war against him; but, being destitute of forces, with the view of raising an army repaired to Jambudipo.†

"In order that he might aggravate the misery of the monarch, already wretched by the loss of his empire, as well as the disaffection of his son and his own imprisonment, this wicked person (the nephew) thus inquired of the Raja Kassapo: 'Raja, hast thou been told by thy father where the royal treasures are concealed?' On being answered 'No:' 'Ruler of the land, (observed the nephew,) dost thou not see that he is concealing the treasure for Moggallana?' This worst of men, on hearing this remark, incensed, despatched messengers to his father

* Chhatto, canopy of royalty. † The continent of India.

with this command, 'Point out the treasures!' Considering that this was a plot of that malicious character to cause him to be put to death, (the deposed King) remained silent; and they (the messengers) returning reported accordingly. Thereupon, exceedingly enraged, he sent messengers over and over again (to put the same question). (The imprisoned monarch) thus thought: 'Well, let them put me to death, after having seen my friend, and bathed in the Kálawápi tank;' and made the following answer to the messengers, 'If ye will take me to the Kálawápi tank, I shall be able to ascertain (where the treasures are.') They, returning, reported the same to the Raja. That avaricious monarch, rejoicing (at the prospect of getting possession of the treasures), and assigning a carriage with broken wheels, sent back the messengers.

"While the sovereign was proceeding along in it, the charioteer who was driving the carriage, eating some parched rice, gave a little thereof to him. Having eaten it, pleased with him, the Raja gave him a letter for Moggallana, in order that he might (hereafter) patronize him, and confer on him the office of 'Dwáranáko' (chief warden).

"Thus worldly prosperity is like the glimmering of lightning! What reflecting person, then, would devote himself to the acquisition thereof?

"His friend, the Thero, having heard (the rumour)

'The Raja is coming!' and bearing his illustrious character in mind, laid aside for him some rice cooked of the 'masa' grain mixed with meat, which he had received as a pilgrim; and saying to himself, 'The King would like it,' he carefully preserved it. The Raja, approaching and bowing down to him, respectfully took his station on one side of him. From the manner in which these two persons discoursed, seated by the side of each other, mutually quenching the fire of their afflictions, they appeared like unto two characters endowed with the prosperity of royalty. Having allowed (the Raja) to take his meal, the Thero in various ways administered consolation; and, illustrating the destiny of the world, he abstracted his mind from the desire to protract his existence.

"Then repairing to the tank, diving into and bathing delightfully in it, and drinking also of its water, he thus addressed the royal attendants: 'My friends, these alone are the riches I possess.' The messengers, on hearing this, conducting him to the Raja's capital, reported the same to the monarch. The sovereign, enraged, replied, 'As long as this man lives, he will treasure his riches for his (other) son, and will estrange the people in this land (from me);' and gave the order, 'Put my father to death.' Those who were delighted (with this decision) exclaimed, 'We have seen the back (the last) of our enemy.' The enraged monarch, adorned in all the insignia of royalty, repaired to the (imprisoned) Raja, and kept walking to and fro in his presence. The (deposed) King, observing him, thus meditated: 'This wretch wishes to destroy my mind in the same manner that he afflicts my body; he longs to send me to hell: what is the use of my getting indignant about him? what can I accomplish?' and then benevolently remarked, 'Lord of statesmen, I bear the same affection towards thee as towards Moggallana.' He (the usurper), smiling, shook his head. The monarch then came to this conclusion: 'This wicked man will most assuredly put me to death this very day.' (The usurper) then stripping the King naked, and casting him into iron chains, built up a wall, embedding him in it, exposing his face only to the east, and plastered (that wall) over with clay.

"What wise men, after being informed of this, would covet riches, life, or prosperity!

"Thus the monarch Dhátuséno, who was murdered by his son in the eighteenth year of his reign, united himself with (Sakko) the ruler of Déwos."

As the Mahawanso was written by a priest, we find that, in its pages, Kings are judged, and their actions are recorded and commented on, more with regard to the prospective benefits of Buddhism and its teachers, than to fulfil those higher objects which give the principal value to modern history. Mahanámo, its author, wrote in the fifth century of the Christian era: he was the uncle and religious instructor of the murdered King Dhátuséno; and, in speaking of him, exclaims, "Who is there who is able, by a verbal description alone, to set forth in due order all his pious deeds!" Yet the historian mentions the wanton death of a priest by command of this pious King, and accounts for his subsequent misfortunes as "the retribution manifested in this life for that impious act." At the same time Mahanámo seems to forget that, in the portion of the narrative above quoted, he had recorded the real cause of the loss of his kingdom, and the miserable death of Dhátuséno, to be in consequence of the persevering hostility of the King's nephew. This person, who was also son-in-law of the King and chief commander of his forces, was roused to vengeance by the death of his mother (the King's own sister), who had been stripped naked and burned to death by order of the royal monster whose piety is so lauded by the priestly historian.

To form the lower part of the fortress of Sigiri many detached rocks have been joined by massive walls of stone, supporting platforms of various sizes and unequal heights, which are now overgrown with forest-trees. Having surmounted these ramparts, we arrived at the foot of the bare and beetling crag; and perceived, at a considerable distance overhead, a gallery clinging to the rock, and connecting two elevated terraces at opposite ends, and about half the height of the main column of rock. These remains were very different from anything I had expected to discover; not merely from their remarkable position and construction, but as being the only extensive fragments of the ancient capitals of Ceylon which are neither shrouded by vegetation nor overshadowed by the forest.

The ascent to the gallery is by a double line of small steps, cut three or four inches into the rock, each step being about six inches in length: four square holes, visible above, have probably contained supports for a platform to project over this hazardous pathway, and from which missiles would descend with such force and certainty as effectually to prevent hostile intrusion by this approach. By means of these partial footsteps, and assisted by the shrubs that grew in the rubbish where the passage had fallen, we scrambled up; and found that the gallery had been formed by cutting grooves in the rock where it was not quite perpendicular, and these served for foundations of the parapet wall and floor. About one hundred yards in length of this gallery remain entire; and its preservation is to be attributed to the excessive heat of the sun, increased by reflection from the rock to such a degree as totally to prevent vegetation on this exposed portion of the ruins. At one place, at which a cascade appears after heavy rains, water was trickling from the overhanging rock: this gives reason to credit the assertions of the natives, founded on tradition, that a tank was formed, and still exists, on the inaccessible summit of this fortress.

We crept along the narrow grooves from whence portions of the building had fallen; and Captain H——, followed by Mr. B——, after clambering up the loose bricks which formed the termination, succeeded in entering the gallery, and proceeded along it for about one hundred yards: in this distance they occasionally ascended a few steps, but were unable to reach the upper terrace, as at an angle of the rock the gallery had slipped from its scanty foundations. I felt so giddy from the heat as to be unable to accompany my friends; and was sincerely glad to see them descend in safety, for some portions of the crumbling building which they displaced might be heard crashing amongst the boughs of the trees at a great depth below. In several of the huge masses of rock included in the ramparts, tanks have been excavated; they are neatly ornamented, and in size vary from twelve to twenty feet in length; their general depth is about three feet.

On the plain towards the north-east, and connected with the elevated terrace at the east end of the rock, stood the royal buildings: that part which was situated on level ground being surrounded with a wet ditch faced with stone; whilst the more elevated portions are not only of difficult access, but are without any more convenient communication from below than the apology for steps such as I have already described as leading to the entrance of the gallery.

By no means certain that this rock would prove to be the capital and fort of Kásyapa the Parricide, and that my antiquarian expectations might not, if disappointed, be a subject of annoyance to my companions, perhaps of ridicule on myself, and quite unprepared for such extensive remains, I had despatched our servants and baggage to Dambool. From this circumstance I was reluctantly compelled to give up any further examination of these interesting ruins on my first visit; but I returned to Sigiri in 1833, and ascertained that the town lay around the palace to the north of the rock, and traced for some distance a stone wall and wet ditch with which it had been surrounded. I then learned that from the highest terrace many small steps leading to the summit of the rock may still be perceived; but in much too dilapidated a state, and in too hazardous a position, for any one to attempt the ascent, and visit a stronghold which for ages has proved beyond the reach of native curiosity.

I was furnished with copies of Nagara inscriptions which appear on the rock of Sigiri, and on the neighbouring hill, by an old and intelligent priest, the incumbent of the rock-temple of Pedurugalla. He also gave me a copy of a long inscription cut on the rock of Haburenne (six miles from Sigiri): this, I presume, must have been handed down to him by predecessors in his sacred office; as, on my visiting the place, I found many of the characters partly obliterated, and that the foundations of the dágoba which once surmounted this tabular rock could with difficulty be traced. These are in the same character as the alphabet lately discovered by the persevering exertions and ability of Mr. Prinsep.

The priest informed me that his cave-temple had been long in a state of ruin and choked up with rubbish; that its length is one hundred and twenty cubits, its breadth twelve cubits, and that two of the statues which it contained were cut from the solid rock. Near this temple are the ruins of a dágoba; and thirty-six stone pillars point out the site of the assembly-hall of the priests.

The natives, terrified lest I should employ them

in exploring the place, or in rendering practicable the ascent to the summit of the rock, had always deceived me as to the nature and extent of the ruins of Sigiri; which they described as merely a hill, at the base of which were some stone walls, and that the neighbourhood was infested by bears and leopards. Besides other proofs of the presence of these animals, Mr. B——, in clambering over some fragments of the fallen gallery, disturbed a leopard, which bounded down the steep and disappeared in the forest.

The leopard of Ceylon is very destructive to cattle, and sometimes grows to eight feet in length; yet it seldom attacks human beings, unless when wounded and in self-defence. The only instance to the contrary that fell under my observation, occurred to a boy about ten years of age, who was seized by one of these animals; but it relinquished its hold on perceiving some people who followed the boy at a short distance. The little fellow had not received any severe injury; and I am inclined to consider this attack as an impulse of self-defence, for the boy, in turning round the corner of a rock, came suddenly on the leopard stretched in its lair. This animal was afterwards shot by a spring-gun, set on the carcase of a bullock which had been killed on the previous night; and, although of a large size, it had evidently been struck down at one blow, as the marks of its struggles were limited to a small space. The leopard was found to be aged, and under the average length of these animals: it had sprung on its prey from an elevated bank which formed one side of the much frequented cart-road from Kandy to Mátalé, at a place within one hundred yards of my house and the Malay guard.

The Kandians destroy leopards not only with spring-guns, but also with cross-bows set with large-bladed arrows; and catch them in enclosures having a falling gate, and formed round some animal which they have recently destroyed. Leopards are also caught in pitfalls; and by a platform (supporting a great weight of stones) suspended over some bullock recently killed, the whole being so constructed as to descend, and secure any animal which passes underneath. To all these various methods there is the same objection, viz. that the trap often catches jackals and inferior beasts of prey, which are unworthy of the trouble, while the tyrant of the forest is warned by their fate.

The best way to destroy leopards is, to employ natives who are accustomed to watch and shoot these destructive animals: only the week before I left Mátalé, I had an opportunity of seeing the successful result of employing two of these hunters to rid the neighbourhood of a leopard which had killed two fine bullocks within my grounds. The wretched fire-arms with which these men ascended the tree that they were to watch in near the carcases of the cattle, did not give great promise of their earning a reward which they were only to receive on producing the body of the feline offender. I also felt inclined to doubt their knowledge of the art they professed, when they assured me that the leopard would not return until nine or ten o'clock A.M. next day. However, on the following morning, at that same hour, I heard two shots with scarce an interval between the sounds; and, on proceeding to the place, found a large leopard lying dead on the carcase of the bullock, and that the two balls (or rather bolts of iron which the hunters had fired) having entered within an inch of each other, and passing right through the heart, had produced instant death.

Amongst the many instances which I have known of leopards when wounded attacking people, one is worthy of notice, for the presence of mind exhibited by a Kandian carpenter, upwards of sixty years of age, who resided in the neighbourhood of Mátalé. While looking for game, this man perceived and fired at a leopard, crouched in the jungle: the animal, although wounded, instantly sprang forward and struck him down, at the same time seizing his left arm in its mouth In this predicament, and notwithstanding the leopard stripped the greatest part of the flesh from his arm, the old man drew his Kandian knife from his girdle and killed the animal by repeated stabs. The carpenter recovered from the severe bruises he had received, and partly regained the use of his arm. While the poor man was bleeding profusely, one of his relations was sent to inform me of the accident: with as little delay as possible I despatched the same messenger in charge of a bandage to tie up the arm. About the time I expected him to have reached the wounded man, he returned to the court-house, and stated that on his way he had discovered something of value fixed in the roll of linen, and to deliver this safely was the cause of his return. Conscious pride in his own honesty had made him forgetful of the danger of his friend. He now exultingly held up the bandage, and pointed to the ornament, the cause of his delay, a common pin! This happened in 1829, and may serve to give some idea of the changes that have occurred since that time in the knowledge and use of manufactured goods by the Kandians, when I state that in 1836 every article of British manufacture, which natives might require or could afford to purchase, was hawked through the most remote native hamlets, was offered for sale at every cabin-door, and might be procured at prices which would barely remunerate the importing merchant and native pedlar.

To return from this digression to the ruins of Sigiri. We found the gallery which wound along the rock had been formed of brick originally coated with a cement, so durable that large portions of it still remain. From the rock, above and overhanging this passage, much stone has been removed by fire, and by wedges, in the same manner as is still practised by the Kandian Galwadouás (masons, literally stone-carpenters,) when they have occasion to rend large blocks from the quarry. On my second visit I remarked that the projecting rock ove the gallery, at least so much of it as is within reach, had been painted in bright colours, fragments of which may still be perceived in those places most sheltered from the heavy rains.

On visiting the embankment of the tank of Sigiri, I found it to be of considerable size, and that the only gap in it might be easily repaired; but the number of inhabitants in that neighbourhood would be insufficient to cultivate the fields which the tank would irrigate, or so many of them as at present to render the repair of the embankment an advisable speculation for individuals: for such a purpose I could not even recommend, as judicious, an advance of money by Government.

The fortress of Sigiri often changed masters, yet never stood a siege: this is a sufficient proof how often in Ceylon timidity and treachery, cold hearts and polluted hands, smoothed the path for foreign invaders and ambitious regicides. It likewise witnesses to the truth of Cingalese history, from which we may learn that, under their despot Kings, self-interest was the only rule of Cingalese conduct: and that the natives readily acknowledged any ruler who could reach the throne; but, unless from fear, gave him no assistance in prosperity, and left him without even sympathy in adversity.

From Sigiri to Dambool, a distance of fifteen miles, the pathway lay through woods and low jungles, which are occasionally cleared, and cultivated with cotton. This crop, at the time I now speak of (1831), was always sold or bartered on the field to the inhabitants of the mountainous districts, who were then ignorant of the value of labour. They prided themselves on their economy (esteemed a great virtue amongst Kandians), when they descended from their hills carrying on their shoulders cocoa-nuts and areka-nuts, which they bartered for cotton: a week was often spent in their journey, and the sudden change of climate and temperature was commonly followed by a severe and lingering illness. On their return, the whole family were employed for weeks in cleaning, picking, spinning, and weaving a piece of coarse cotton cloth; which in two years after they might purchase at their own doors for the value of four days' labour of one individual, who could always get employment on coffee estates or in making Government roads: but, until the freedom of the people was established by an order in council and the charter, there were but two coffee estates formed, and the service on Government roads was not only compulsory, but unpaid.

From Dambool we returned by Nalande, a stage of fifteen miles; in the middle of which lies the Andagalla pass, an abrupt ascent and stony path shaded by magnificent trees and hemmed in on either side by rocky mountains. At Nalande we halted during the night; and, had it not been for the cunning of the post-holder, would have enjoyed an opportunity of shooting elephants from the verandah of the rest-house. Three of them had broken through the fence, and were close to the house (probably attracted by the thatch), when their noise awoke the post-holder, who, aware that our elephant-guns were loaded, lost no time in discharging his own, and frightening away the intruders before we were disturbed. His reason for this trick was obvious; and his protestations in nowise staggered our belief that his gun did not go off by accident, but designedly, to prevent the chance of our killing any of the animals, as the effluvia from such a mass as a dead elephant would have forced him to vacate his quarters for at least six weeks.

CHAPTER II.

TO TRINKOMALEE.

" What, ho!" cried the devil, "go rig out my bark,
Built of the cypress-tree;
O'er the foam-tipt waves of the ocean dark,
Tho' we leave in our track a stormy sea,
We'll sail right merrily.
The vessel that crosses our gloomy way
Right strong and stout may be;
But never again shall the light of day
Behold her dash far, far away,
From her plunging bow the feathery spray!—
A shattered mast alone shall tell
Of the goodly ship that sailed so well;
The greedy shark and the slimy sea-eel
Will thank me, I ween, for a plenteous meal!"

* * * * *

So on he sailed from zone to zone,
Till he came to the Garden of Eden, Ceylon;
And the devil chuckled with might and main,
As he thought how his mischief he there began,
When he first declared war 'gainst the race of man!
Now it chanced to be " upon a day
In the merry, merry month of May:"
He found it so hot he began to roar,
And, what's strange for the devil, he cursed and swore,

And he fled to his boat with hurried pace,
In haste to quit such a roasting place;
And, going, he shriek'd with doleful cry,
"It's high time for me back to hell to fly:
If I've any refractory spirits there,
I'll send them to Trinkomalee;
'T will be pretty warm work for them to bear,
Since it's too hot even for me!"

DIABOLUS.—*Colombo Journal.*

New Carriage-road to Trinkomalee. — High-priest of Dambool. — Kabuk-trees. — Meerisagona-oya. — Commencement of the North-east Monsoon.—Tropical Rains.— Insects.—Floods of November 1835.— *Accident. — Haburenne.— Halting-place. — Graves.— Ancient Canal and Artificial Lakes.— Desolate Hut.— Elephant Flies.— Rest-house of Gantalawe. — Mederigiri.— Minigiri.— Priestesses in Ceylon.— Tame Buffalo Shooting.— Buildings at Trinkomalee.— Cholera in the 78th Highlanders.— Sacred Promontory.— Worship of Eiswara. —Monument to Francina Van Rhede.—Her Fate.—Ancient Temples at Trinkomalee.— Hot Wells of Kanya.— Sailing of the Jupiter.— Menick-denna-nuwara.— Nitre Cave at Nalandé.— Unhealthy Military Posts.*

In August 1833, accompanied by Captain F——, I proceeded by the carriage-road lately opened across the country to Trinkomalee: this work had been commenced, and continued from Colombo as far as Dambool, six years before, and was then given up in consequence of the severe sickness which broke out amongst the labourers. The road from Kandy to Mátale having been previously formed, it was extended in 1832 from the latter place to Dambool, to join the Colombo line; and from thence to Gantalawe, thirty miles from Trinkomalee: this is a distance of seventy miles, and the breadth of the road was sixteen feet; yet the whole was traced and formed under the direction of Captain Atchison (Ceylon Regiment) between the beginning of May and the end of September 1832. The last thirty miles of this line is through an uninhabited forest, of which Captain Atchison remarks, that the existence of tanks, "the ruins of fallen wihares, remains of deserted villages, and other remnants of antiquity, prove that the vast wilderness of beautiful and valuable forest-trees through which the new line of road passes, heretofore supposed a trackless desert, obnoxious to the existence of man, and destitute of water and inhabitants, once contained a considerable population, by whose labours an extensive tract of irrigated lands was regularly cultivated." The tracing of this line was almost entirely directed from the tops of trees; and much difficulty was experienced in procuring a sufficient quantity of water for so large a body of labourers working in an exhausting climate. These difficulties were surmounted; and this most useful work was completed in the healthy portion of one season; thereby preventing the grievous loss of life which must have ensued had workmen been employed during the continuance, or soon after the termination of the periodical rains. These commenced with great severity as the road was finished; and, on the same day that this most desirable object was accomplished, the glorious order in council abolishing compulsory labour in Ceylon reached Colombo.

According to my usual custom when proceeding to the northern parts of the district, I stopped for a night in the house of my old acquaintance, Nikowola, High-priest of Dambool, a shrewd man, who, during the Kandian rebellion, was one of the few of the yellow-robed fraternity that adhered from policy, if not from principle, to the British interest. In later years, his invariable hospitality to Europeans, and zealous endeavours to assist the established authorities, proved that he really identified his interest with the side he had espoused; and his good offices during the formation of the Trinkomalee road were not only acknowledged, but rewarded by Government with a small grant of land at his native village. The acquisition of these fields had been his favourite object, and the gift afforded him the utmost satisfaction; but, before visiting it as proprietor, he was summoned to Kandy to be a witness for some chiefs and priests who were accused of treason: in returning, he was suddenly taken ill, and died on the road within a few miles of his promised land. The erection of his funeral pile, by those friends who squabbled for his inheritance, was the first act of possession exercised after the acquirement of this much coveted property.

Five miles beyond Dambool we crossed the bed of the Meerisagona-oya, at a ford which for nine months of the year is only a space covered with sand; but the banks of this stream, above and below, were about eight feet in height, the perpendicular sides being supported by matted roots of trees, particularly the kabuk, which flourishes on the banks of all streams in the dry level districts, and may even be found at an elevation of three thousand feet. The kabuk-tree grows to a very large size, and is a strong and durable timber of a red colour. By natives it is asserted (and, wherever I have seen the attempt made, the event justified their belief,) that water will always be found by digging near kabuk-trees, and at farthest but little deeper than the lowest of the roots.

Although the Meerisagona-oya was now, and for months had been, without a drop of water in its channel, I have known it impassable even to horses for eight days together: detentions on this road from the swelling of the streams usually occur previous to the setting-in of the north-east monsoon in November. The rains generally commence towards the end of September with heavy showers; after a week of this unsettled weather, rain falls in torrents for half the day, the remainder being bright sunshine. Previous to the fall of these quotidian deluges, the sky in the quarter from whence they approach becomes gradually darkened upward from the horizon, and appears of an inky hue, so dense that the distant hills look less solid than the advancing curtain of clouds. The plains seem lost in dull shadows; and the mountains are lighted with a lurid gleam of dusky red that escapes from the open part of the heavens. Every second, this clear space, with its pale, cold blue sky, is visibly contracted by dark swollen masses of vapour which are gradually subduing the sickly lights that linger on the highest pinnacles. At first, during these symptoms, there is an oppressive calm, under which everything in nature seems to droop: the leaves hang listless on the boughs; the beasts are in the forest; the birds seek shelter in the covert; numerous flocks of white cranes following each other in lines, or forming themselves in angles, alone attract the eye as they seek new ground and prepare for the approaching storm. Before a breath of air is felt, tiny whirlwinds are seen beneath the bushes twirling round a few light withered leaves, or trundling them along the footpath. These fairy hurricanes are succeeded by a rushing sound among the trees overhead, accompanied by the rustling and falling of decayed leaves; then a gentle and refreshing air suddenly gives place to cold breezes, gusts, squalls, until heavy drops of rain crowd into descending sheets of water, transforming steep paths into cataracts, and broad roads into beds of rivers. Before the murky curtain that is closing over the sky, flickers a cold misty veil, and a dull vapour rolls in advance along the ground; these appearances arise from the raindrops splashing on the dusty ground, or jostling and splintering as they descend from the teeming darkness. On a particular occasion, being surprised by one of these avalanches of rain, I returned to my house at Mâtale; but, with my horse, had to swim across a stream that I had passed only two hours before when the water was not three inches deep.

It is after the first heavy showers that the houses in Ceylon are commonly invaded by snakes and venomous insects, dislodged by the water from holes and crevices in which they have been sheltered during the dry season. Centipedes and scorpions are the most numerous of these intruders; the bite of the former and the sting of the latter being equally severe, but neither are dangerous to grown-up persons in good health. The myriads of white ants that acquire wings and take flight at these periods are extremely annoying; attracted by the lights, open or latticed windows afford no obstruction to the irruption of their overwhelming hordes, which soon begin to fill up the glass shades that surround every lamp, to preserve the flame from being overlaid by multitudes of insects, or blown out by the circulation of air. Flying-bugs, beetles, ear-wigs, and eye-flies add to the masses that hover round your person, overspread the tables, or scramble over each other on the floor: these insects are far more disgusting and troublesome than their larger brethren, usually classed as venomous or considered as dangerous.

In the last days of the month of November 1835, the rains exceeded in violence and duration anything of the kind I had hitherto witnessed, and did great damage in the south-western portion of the island. Soon after the commencement of this deluge, the thickness of the clouds, and the closeness of the rain, had contracted the visible horizon to a few yards around the house where I resided; and the darkness rendered it difficult to read at midday. Before the second evening every ravine was filled, and each streamlet had become a river in size, and a torrent in rapidity: down two of these, that passed my quarters, the dead carcases of buffaloes and bullocks were rolling and tumbling; occasionally some one, still alive, and lately swept off, might be seen hurried along while still plunging and struggling in hopeless strife with the raging waters. The soil of the mountain near us, softened and saturated by the continued floods, had no longer tenacity to retain the great stones or loose masses of rock that rested on its steep sides and arched summit: they shifted, then rushed with resistless force, crashing through the forest, or thundering over the bare rocks until they reached the level grounds. So appalling was the continued darkness and the sound of falling rocks, that the villages along the base of the mountain were abandoned until the rain ceased, and the sun appeared, on the fifth day.

On the fourth of these melancholy days, a man, lame and severely bruised, presented himself before me, and, pointing to the Hunusgiri range of mountains, groaned out that the side of a hill had shifted into the valley and entombed his wife and three children: his small property, his house, his garden, and his rice-field were also overwhelmed by the same catastrophe. His account of it was, that, while resting in the verandah of his house, he was awaked by an unusual noise, and could just distinguish, through the gloom, stones rolling past, and felt his cottage shaking from the battering of those that struck against it. He opened the door, alarmed his family, then fled; and had only advanced a few yards, when he perceived an immense mass of earth and trees and rocks pass over the house, which thus became the tomb of his family. The unfortunate man had received severe contusions from the stones that bounded down the hill, preceding the great body of earth borne forward on water that had accumulated in some crevice of the mountain, and produced the calamity. Great damage was done by this flood to roads, bridges, and rice-fields; the destruction of cattle was immense, and the loss of human life considerable, from accidents similar to that which I have just related.

Amongst other changes caused in the face of the country by the rains, I saw a garden (in which stood several full-sized cocoa-trees) that had bidden farewell for ever to its owner's bounds, and now seemed perfectly at rest on his neighbour's property; a glorious opportunity for litigation, of which it is not likely two Kandians would fail to take advantage.

Passing the abrupt rock and empty tank of Innamaloe, in which we saw two elephants, and after frightening several others from our path, we reached Haburenne, sixteen miles from Dambool, and found ready prepared for ourselves and followers leaf-sheds that admitted the little air that crept through the drooping foliage of the close surrounding forest. It was now near the end of the dry season, the weather intensely warm, the neighbourhood noted as being one of the hottest parts of Ceylon, and the water as being of the worst quality; but we had no alternative in halting here, for there was neither water nor village within reach of our loaded coolies on the Trinkomalee direction. The flat bare rock of Haburenne was once the site of a dágoba and Buddhist establishment; no remains of these now exist, although a long and partly obliterated inscription in the Nagara character points to their situation. From this place the rock-fort of Sigiri bears a striking resemblance to a crested helmet resting on a cushion; it is about six miles distant from Haburenne, and half-way between it and the nearest hills of the Mátalé district.

Long before daylight next morning we were proceeding through the forest that extends from Haburenne to Gantalawe, and halted at the first open space, a very small plain near the banks of the Gal-oya. A little water still trickled along the rocky bed of the stream, and to this our Kandian coolies eagerly rushed, for they are in the habit of continually refreshing themselves by small draughts from the springs and rills that abound in the mountainous parts; and although warned by me, they had miscalculated their own powers of resisting thirst in a temperature so much above what they were accustomed to, and in a place where no water could be procured. In this solitary glade, and shadowed by a clump of trees, our breakfast was soon prepared; and here we found ourselves in the immediate neighbourhood of the graves of most of the small party who had been appointed to guard and bring back the tools and stores which were left here, when about twelve hundred people were released from work at the commencement of the rains in the preceding autumn. Even the Caffre soldiers, who acted as pioneers, and who are less liable to suffer from a noxious climate than any other race, were unable to resist the fatal miasma generated by the heat and moisture acting on the accumulated vegetable deposit of this extensive wilderness of wood. Although the Caffres are so strong in body and tough in constitution, it is a remarkable fact that comparatively few of their children grow up; and I understand it is to pulmonary complaints that their rising generation usually fall victims.

After breakfast we resumed our journey, and, three miles from the place of our halt, reached the Alutwewa-oya, a stream of the same size as the one we had left: these two, running in the same direction, once formed the principal supplies of the Kaudella tank, which is now a swampy plain of great extent, situated between Minneria and Gantalawe on the old footpath to Trinkomalee. Before leaving the forest, we crossed the remains of a canal which is said to have connected the tanks of Minneria, Kaudella, and Gantalawe, and to have reached up from the former of these to the Ambanganga at Ellaherra, from whence it was supplied with water. Until this canal shall have been traced through the Konderawe hills, the extent and difficulty of such an undertaking must excite doubts whether it were successfully accomplished : it is declared to have been of sufficient size, and to have been used as a means of conveyance for produce, as well as for the supply of water necessary to fill the tanks, and irrigate the country through which it passed. Its length, including these artificial lakes, could not have been under one hundred miles ; and, if it is found to have been completed, I should then have little doubt that the succession of tanks thus connected and supplied were the waters to which the vanity of a King gave his own name, dignifying them with the appellation of the sea of Prákrama. This monarch reigned in the middle of the twelfth century; and from the commencement of a great excavation at Ellaherra I procured an inscription, stating that this canal had been completed by the King Prákrama Bahoo.

On the bank of the Alutwewa-oya we found the frame and roof of a temporary hut, and within it were a broken chair and table, around which lay portions of books, whose leaves were occasionally turned backwards and forwards by a passing breeze. We ascertained that these, and similar remains, which were battered against the ground, or projected from the mass of decayed foliage amongst the surrounding jungle, were the remnants of the library of a medical sub-assistant. He had been taken dangerously ill at this place, and was able to get himself removed, but, having no transport for his baggage, it had here remained unprotected and exposed to the fury of the stormy season; and now, with the skeleton hut, lonely situation, and dreary forest, presented a perfect picture of desolation. In those flats and jungle-covered districts, subject to long periods of dry weather, fever generally follows the setting-in of the rains; but I believe the ill effects of the malaria generated in such situations might in a great degree be prevented by having the houses, particularly the sleeping apartments, elevated at least six feet above the ground. Permanent Cingalese houses are always raised considerably above the surrounding country, and constructed so as to prevent a current of air passing either through the inner court or any of the surrounding chambers.

After leaving the Alutwewa-oya, our horses suffered much from a large grey fly, about an inch in length, whose fangs are said to be sufficiently powerful even to penetrate the skin of an elephant; and which, in spite of the exertions of the horse-keepers, and the kicking and fidgeting of the harassed animals, contrived to make several severe wounds on our horses, and much increased their fatigues. As it was necessary to protect our coolies from bears and elephants, we could not ride forward, and in consequence did not get ourselves and them out of the forest until ten o'clock at night; at which time we reached a neglected, half-ruined, wretched building near the village of Gantalawe. This filthy and rickety edifice was not thirty miles from Trinkomalee, and appeared in the Ceylon Almanac under the designation of a rest-house, situated where the former jungle-path (by which the mails still proceed) joined the new road from Kandy and Colombo. The interior arrangements of this station were in perfect accordance with the building; we could procure neither chair nor table, and it was only after considerable delay that we obtained possession of an earthenware vessel with which to commence our cooking.

On arriving at any place at which I was to dine and take up my quarters for the night, I was in the habit, if I had been travelling in the sun, of taking a bumper of madeira and an equal quantity of warm water: this was a sufficient restorative;

and prevented my being chilled, while dressing, in the currents of air that find free passage through most rest-houses, and are inseparable from all leaf-huts. If much exhausted by violent exercise or long exposure to the sun, I took brandy and water; but always in small quantities, not more than a wine-glass full at a time: copious draughts, unless persevered in, (this is often impossible, and never advisable,) aggravate the evils of thirst and exhaustion which they are intended to subdue. Generous living is necessary for Europeans in Ceylon, and nothing is more likely to injure a constitution than bad fare and unnecessary abstinence; perhaps needless fear of climate is equally hurtful, for it prevents the timid from indulging in that change of air and scene which has proved so beneficial to health. The water-lapping hypochondriac and the trembling valetudinarian cannot expect to enjoy themselves in Ceylon: the one has not the strength, the other wants the courage, to visit the magnificent and exciting scenery of this lovely island. In rocks, rivers, mountains, forests,—all that is grand and beautiful in nature,—he sees but forms behind which may lurk some demon of disease that has no existence but in his own distempered fancy. To maintain a sound constitution in Ceylon, it is only necessary to live well, avoid excess, eschew indolence, take sufficient exercise for the body, and give constant employment to the mind. I consider the use of Chinese umbrellas to be of material service in preserving health; they are procured at a trifling expense, are easily carried, and, being formed of paper covered with thick black varnish, are an effectual protection against the rays of the sun. Many Europeans despise this precaution; but no native willingly exposes himself to the sun or rain if he can procure an umbrella, or its substitute in the shape of a talapat, palmyra, plantain, or aram leaf.

The tank of Gantalawe is large; and its principal embankment, extending upwards of a mile, and connecting two portions of a rocky ridge, is faced with stones, eight or ten feet in length, placed like steps, and laid in regular lines. Besides the cheering and refreshing appearance which open plains and a large body of water present when met with in a wooded country and warm climate, this place possesses much beauty, particularly in its numerous groups of forest-trees, scattered through the plains which intervene between the lake and the thick jungle that covers the rising ground and hills on the west and north of Gantalawe. From hence I detached people, whom I had been in the habit of employing in such services, to endeavour to find out the ruins of Mederigiri and Minigiri; the former being somewhere about ten miles distant to the eastward, and the latter situated in the forest to the west of the Minneria tank. Those persons sent to Mederigiri brought back copies of numerous inscriptions carved on the remains of the religious buildings at that place; the others despatched to Minigiri returned, declaring they had been unable to find the ruins they were in search of. I attributed their want of success to superstitious fears, for I found they were aware of a tradition setting forth that only priests or women could visit Minigiri without the risk of incurring divine vengeance; and from this legend, I presume, a nunnery or asylum for Buddhist priestesses had formed part of the religious establishment which existed there. Institutions for priestesses in Ceylon were not numerous at any time, and that class has ceased to be mentioned for several generations; so also we may gather from native histories, that religious enthusiasm in Cingalese women seldom superseded domestic ties, or induced them to volunteer for unnecessary mortifications.

The tank of Gantalawe is a work of the King Mahasen, and was undertaken towards the end of his reign, which terminated A.D. 301. An apostate from orthodox Buddhism in his youth, he became a firm believer and a bigot in his latter years, and bestowed all the lands irrigated by this lake on religious establishments: from this circumstance is derived its name of Dantalawe or Gantalawe, (plain gifted to temples,) corrupted by Europeans into Kandelly.

From this place to Trinkomalee is twenty-eight miles; but having passed the pretty little tank of Weneriancolom, and reached the plains of Tamblegam, I there embarked in a boat, and not only escaped twelve miles of close jungle and dusty road, but enjoyed the refreshing sea-breeze and pleasing scenery of the bays of Tamblegam, Kotiar, and various others, which collectively form the great inland basin so well known as the harbour of Trinkomalee. In our morning ride we met a young sportsman with a European complexion and abundance of big guns: he informed us of his success the day before in killing two wild buffaloes; complained of being interrupted by a native, whom he could not understand, and had abruptly dismissed; and ended his frank communication by stating, what I already guessed, that he had but lately joined his regiment at Trinkomalee. Two miles farther on we overtook a native, who soon made known to us, by most obsequious gestures and a grievous clamour, that he was on his way to the district judge to claim compensation for the loss of two buffaloes which had been shot by the gentleman we had so lately passed. He said, his claims and remonstrances had been unheeded by the European gentleman (who probably did not understand a word he said), and that his other buffaloes were in imminent danger (most likely some had already bitten the dust).

Trinkomalee has been so often described, that I shall only now say that its scenery is beautiful, its harbour admirable for safety and invaluable from situation ; while the fortifications and the buildings they contain appeared to me equally uncomfortable, unserviceable, and unhealthy, and that they must contribute to the sacrifice of many valuable lives. Unless the whole of the external works and internal buildings are completely changed, it is to be hoped they may be abandoned as a monument of misapplied labour, reared by ignorance and retained through apathy.

A very eminent medical man, who had examined the military buildings in the fort of Trinkomalee at the time when that awful disease, spasmodic cholera, broke out amongst the troops stationed there in 1832, is said to have given his opinion to the late gallant Admiral Sir John Gore in the following brief and emphatic sentence : "The position and construction of the barracks are admirably adapted for originating, and the hospital for maintaining, disease." The circumstances attending the progress of this dreadful visitation peculiarly mark the capricious and baffling character of that most malignant disease, which for a few days committed such fearful ravages in the 78th Highlanders.

The first case in that regiment (there had for ten or twelve days previously been casualties amongst the natives in the town) occurred on the 12th of October: the man died the same evening. The second case was on the 14th, and the third on the 15th of the same month. Several cases then appeared; and, being all from one barrack, it was vacated, and the men belonging to it were dispersed in the church and other buildings. Cases, however, appeared on the 19th and 20th in the other barracks; and in consequence it was deemed advisable to apply for leave that the men should be removed to the Arrogant hulk, a roomy vessel calculated to contain the crew of a line-of-battle ship. The admiral (whose conduct during the continuance of the disease was beyond all praise) immediately assented; and, at daylight on the morning of the 21st, three officers and one hundred and eighteen non-commissioned officers and privates marched to the dock-yard, three miles from the fort, and embarked in the hulk, which was moored within fifty yards of the shore. In the evening, and during the night of the 22nd, several cases occurred in the hulk; and next day the men were landed near the fort by the boats of the Melville, Sir John Gore's flag-ship. Nine men, too ill to be moved, were left in the hulk with four others to attend them: on the 24th, only two of these were alive. The crisis of the disease, both in the fort and in the hulk, was from the night ot the 22nd to that of the 24th: in these forty-eight hours, twenty-five men (one tenth of the whole force) died. The cases after that day became gradually fewer and less virulent, and by the 2nd of November the disease had ceased in the fort of Trinkomalee.

Only one officer out of thirteen was attacked, and the case was not a severe one. The situation of the officers' quarters (more sheltered, and at a little distance from the men's barracks) may in some measure account for their escape: but it is more difficult to assign any satisfactory cause for the great disproportion of serjeants; no less than ten, out of twenty serjeants, having fallen victims to the disease. Out of twenty-six soldiers' wives, only two died; amongst fifty children, only three were attacked, and two of these recovered; eighteen out of twenty serjeants were seized with the complaint, and ten died; and one hundred and fourteen rank and file, out of two hundred and fifty-two, were attacked, forty-six of whom died: these cases all occurred between the 12th of October and the 2nd of November. It was not perceived that the characters or habits of individuals had any effect in protecting them from this disease, or in provoking its attack; it seized alike on the cheerful and the desponding, the bold and the timid, the temperate man and the confirmed drunkard; but it was observed that men of dissipated habits sank soonest before this fatal malady.

I have elsewhere remarked, that in the same season of the preceding year, in the districts of Mátalé lying nearest to Trinkomalee, a violent epidemic carried off great numbers of elephants and other wild animals, but did not affect the inhabitants. At that time, however, it was remarked to me by several old natives, that sickness amongst wild animals and cattle generally preceded by a year any pestilence amongst the population of the country.

The rocky promontory occupied by the fort of Trinkomalee is by the natives appropriately dedicated to Siva (the destroyer), in his ancient name of Eiswara, and is regarded with great veneration by his votaries. They believe that, in the earliest wars of the gods, three of the peaks of Mahameru were thrown down, and driven to different parts of the world; one of these is Koneiswara-parwatia, or Trinkomalee, which thenceforth became, equally with Kailasa, the abode of Siva.

It is probable that there is no more ancient form

of worship existing than that of Eiswara * upon his sacred promontory, and that it has been connected with the rites of Siva by the votaries of the latter at a more recent period. In Wilson's Sanscrit dictionary, the translation of Eiswara is given as "God," "an universal spirit;" and the whole scene, as well as the religious ceremonies on the precipice of Trinkomalee, possesses a character of romantic wildness and mysterious antiquity. The priest (a Brahmin), having his head encircled by a string of large beads, and a yellow cloth bound round his loins, placed himself a few minutes before sunset on the giddy height of the farthest rock that rises over the dark and fathomless ocean: of the votaries, some were perched amongst the dangerous crags; while the more timid or less devout knelt, prostrated themselves, or reclined in safety, on the short grass which clothes the promontory. The priest, after performing his ablutions, placed himself in various picturesque attitudes; and occasionally, as he dropped some betel-leaves or rice into the sea, bowed himself with great apparent reverence towards a chasm in the rock, which is believed to be the residence of the spirit, the object

* In the Raja Wallia, Kuwạni, of the aboriginal race of Ceylon, mistress and wife of Vijeya their conqueror, is represented as having been warned of her hard fate by Eiswara in a dream.

of his worship. After the sun had gone down, the Brahmin gracefully waved a censer, then held it at the full stretch of his arm above his head, while the incense flamed up, flickered, and disappeared; then, as the perfume spread around, he concluded his incantations by casting a cocoa-nut into the ocean, and receiving the offerings on behalf of Eiswara. The oblations consisted of copper coins of the smallest denominations, cocoa-nuts, rice, and betel-leaves: — assuredly, although he had a numerous congregation, the priest was but poorly remunerated for his ministration on such a dangerous altar.

At the time I saw these ancient rites, the scene was unpolluted in Pagan eyes, and the effect to me rendered more interesting and unique from the absence of the wan visages and formal dresses of the European soldiers; they had seen these ceremonies too often to notice them.

The summit of the promontory is considerably higher, and close above the perilous situation on which the priest had been officiating; it is formed of a huge loose mass of rock; and this primeval altar of Pagan superstition now bears the monument of a Christian suicide; — a pillar, of a form alternately square and octagonal, commemorates the unhappy fate and dreadful death of a young and beautiful woman. The inscription is nearly obliterated;

so far as it could be made out, the following is a copy furnished to me by a friend:—

TOT GEDAGHTENIS
VAN FRANCINA VAN
RHEDE TUEN VAN
MYDREGT DESEN
A°. 1687 : 24 APRIL
OP GEREGT

The lady's name and the date is distinct; and tradition fills up the particulars of the catastrophe of Francina van Rhede. She was the daughter of a gentleman high in the Dutch service, had been betrothed, and at the time of her death was about to be deserted by her affianced husband, a captain in the army. He was on board a vessel that had spread its sails for Europe; but, before getting clear of the coast, the ship had to tack, and pass out parallel to the precipices that form the southern boundary of the fort of Trinkomalee. The motions of the vessel had been watched with intense interest by the forsaken fair one: as it approached the rocks, she rushed from her apartment, and flew along the edge of the cliffs, close under which the vessel was gliding. The point was nearly gained, the swift vessel and false lover were turning from her towards a foreign land; a moment she balanced herself on a projecting crag, then plunged from the dizzy height. Her mangled remains were rescued from the rocky fragments that project through the waves at the base of the precipice, and its summit still bears in her monument the memorial of devoted love inspiring dire revenge.

> "Alas! the love of women! it is known
> To be a lovely and a fearful thing:
> For all of theirs upon that die is thrown;
> And, if 'tis lost, life hath no more to bring
> To them but mockeries of the past——"

An extensive range of temples, dedicated to Siva, once existed at Trinkomalee: these, in 1622, were pulled down by the Portuguese, who employed the materials in building fortifications. The Malabars possess several works in the Tamul language, that profess to describe the extent and wealth of these establishments in the days of their prosperity, as well as the miracles performed in them from the time of their dedication, when the King Kolakotu, having completed its endowment, retired into a sacred secret chamber, and from thence passed body and spirit direct into the bliss of Siva. In these descriptions the authors have copied much (unless the buildings were exactly similar) from the description of the pagodas at Trinkomalee in the Carnatic. In an account of the Trinkomalee temples,* we find it mentioned that the Cingalese King Gaju Bahu, on visiting them, caused nume-

* Translated from the Tamul, and published under the signature of Indiophilus in the Colombo Journal.

rous rice-fields and gardens to be formed, and granted these for the support of the pagoda; thereafter he sent to the Soli country (Tanjore), and procured various tradesmen and labourers, to whom he assigned lands, for which they and their descendants were to perform services to the temples. Gaja Bahu reigned from A.D. 113 to 125, and his munificent gifts are declared to have been an act of expiation for the sin he had committed, by *entertaining the intention* of pulling down the temple of Siva, and erecting one to Buddha in its stead. Cingalese history is so far confirmed by this Tamul record, although their details are conflicting; for the Cingalese account states that Gaja Bahu brought the inhabitants from the Soli country as prisoners, while the Tamul writer notices it as a voluntary migration: still the fact of a Sólian colony being established at Trinkomalee in the reign of that King remains undisputed. As there is considerable mystery in the Cingalese details of the reign of Gaja Bahu, it is probable his famed warrior Neila Yodya was only a successful negotiator, whose arguments were judiciously supported by an army which Gaja Bahu is declared to have marched over the Saitubanda, (Adam's bridge,) to the continent of India. These concurrent statements show that Trinkomalee, and the low country in the north of Ceylon, were then under the control of the Cingalese King; and is an additional reason for considering the embassy from Ceylon to the Romans, in the time of the Emperor Claudius, as wandering mendicants, or at best the representatives of some petty chieftain of the Malabars.

The hot wells of Kanya are situated near a range of wooded hills eight miles from Trinkomalee: they are seven in number, of small size and different degrees of temperature, varying from 100° to 110°. As might be supposed, these springs of warm, pure, clear water have given rise to various legends amongst the natives, who regard them with superstitious reverence, and account for their origin and name in the following fable. To delay the King Rawana, and thus prevent the success of one of his undertakings, Vishnu appeared in the form of an old man, and falsely informed the King that Kanya (the virgin-mother * of Rawana) had died. On hearing this, Rawana determined to remain and perform the usual solemnities for deceased relatives, whenever he could find water for the requisite ablutions. Vishnu, hav-

* It is said, in the Cingalese accounts of Rawana, that he and his brothers, Kumbakarna and Weebeesana, were miraculously brought forth to Vishrawana by Maya; but who then was, and always continued to be, Kanya (the Virgin). Vishrawana was a Brahmin ascetic; Kanya, a daughter of a fugitive King of the Asurs.

ing ascertained his wishes, disappeared at the spot, and caused the hot springs to burst forth. From the solemnities then performed in honour of Kanya, the springs have ever since retained her name.

As none of the Kandian coolies who accompanied me had ever been near the coast, I was anxious to see the effect produced, and hear the impressions made on them, by a view of the ocean. I perceived that the effect was evident disappointment; and ascertained that the sea inspired in them neither ideas of magnitude or extent, nor feelings of awe or admiration. Before leaving Trinkomalee, having ascertained the hour that the Jupiter was to weigh anchor for England, I ordered the coolies to be with me at daylight, and had then an opportunity of showing them a fifty-four-gun ship under sail. When the sails were unfurled, and while the vessel stood across that beautiful piece of water (the inner harbour), with her white canvass sweeping past the wooded islands, they were evidently surprised and delighted. The ship tacked, — they turned to each other in silent admiration; nor was there a word spoken until the Jupiter disappeared in noble style, apparently grazing the dock-yard point beneath the promontory of Fort Ostenburgh.

This exhibition amply recompensed the coolies

for their disappointment on seeing the apparent smallness of the ocean, and was the constant subject of conversation on their homeward journey.

In returning from Trinkomalee, I ascertained the site of an ancient town, called Menik Denna Nuwara, the ruins of which are in a forest eight miles from Dambool, and between the former precipitous path which led to Nalandé through the Andagalla pass, and the new road which winds round the mountain of Lenadorra. At Menik Denna Nuwara are the remains of two tanks, the ruins of a dágoba, a wihare with numerous stone pillars, a stone bed (one end of which rests upon a rock, the other extremity being supported by pillars): there are also stone steps, and foundations of houses, to show that this was at one time a station of some importance.*

The mountain of Nikwoolla, or Heereedewatai Kande, rises behind these ruins; and a plain near its summit has apparently been a place of retreat in times of danger, as it is strewed with fragments of pottery, and various kinds of fruit-trees, not commonly found wild, still flourish on this bleak plateau. A pond, which contains water at all times of the driest seasons, must have been the great

* The three inscriptions I procured from Menik Denna Nuwara appear to be a mixture of the Nagara with the most ancient form of Cingalese letters.

attraction of fugitives to this natural stronghold: such ponds, however remarkable, are not uncommonly to be met with near the top of the highest mountains, and even on the summit of the bare and elevated rocks of Ceylon. The traditions regarding Menik Denna Nuwara assert that it was a residence of the King Sirisangabo, but that it was greatly improved in the beginning of the fourth century by Sri Danta Kumara, the royal importer of Buddha's tooth.

The last stage before reaching my home was Nalandé, distant fifteen miles from Mátalé, and the same distance from Dambool. Nalandé, as a military post, which it was for some years, proved very unhealthy: its small fort occupied the summit of a rocky hillock, and in situation as well as insalubrity too closely resembled many of the military positions which were originally occupied by the British troops in the Kandian country. In the neighbourhood of Nalandé are two caves, from which a small quantity of saltpetre was prepared under the native Government. Now that we have ascertained the amount of the scanty population of the Kandian country, and the pitiful resources of its sovereigns, we cannot give credit to those who directed the British force and ruled our possessions in Ceylon. Previously to our taking possession of the interior of the island, under the government of Sir Robert Brownrig, we had long maintained a hostile yet humiliating position; for the Kandian King, a perfidious and powerless tyrant, often deceived those sent to negotiate with him, and at other times disgraced and defied our military array. The supply of gunpowder which the late King possessed when he recovered his capital of Kandy in 1803, and with which he succeeded in expelling the British forces from the Kandian kingdom, would not have formed more than twenty thousand musket cartridges, or about as much as is usually expended by one regiment on a common review-day. The idea of the general insalubrity of the climate, of which so much was said at the time that so little was effected by the British power, now proves to have been partly the exaggeration of ignorant timidity, and partly the inexcusable want of ordinary information, which led to the selection of stations for troops in places where military strength was unnecessary, but where disease was certain and fatal.

CHAPTER III.

ELEPHANT-CATCHING.

* * * Signs of power and rule
Conferr'd upon us, and dominion given
Over all other creatures that possess
Earth, air, and sea.—MILTON.

Elephant-catching. — Characteristics of Elephants. — Noosing Elephants in open Forests. — Tree-snares. — Elephant Kraal. —Hunting.—Accident and Amputation.—Elephant Charge.— Gay Assembly. — Rhodias. — Securing the Elephants. — Elephants caught in the Square at Kandy. — Native Roads. — Presence of mind in an old Elephant-hunter. — Accident. — Elephant Stables. — Elephants occasionally capricious and treacherous. — Elephant-keeper killed. — Destruction of Elephants.

For some time after my appointment to the Mátalé district, along with other duties I superintended the catching and training of elephants, until, by the abolition of all compulsory services, the inhabitants were relieved from a severe task, dangerous to the people, yet unprofitable to the Government. The various classes of hunters, train-

ers, leaf-cutters, and elephant-doctors in Mátalé were sufficient to furnish nine trained elephants every three months ; so that while the establishment was maintained, and the weather permitted, there was seldom a week in which a party was not employed either in driving or catching. Out of six kraals,* five were formed within four miles of my house; and the elephant stables were erected so near, that I could visit them twice a day, to see the animals properly fed, and prevent unnecessary severity on the part of the persons employed in training them.

Before proceeding to describe the manner in which elephants are captured in Ceylon, I shall offer a few observations (the result of my experience) on the characteristics of these animals. I think their intelligence or sagacity has been much overrated; and that the merit of some of the most wonderful feats for which their intellect has got credit, ought to be set down to the weight of their unwieldy carcases, such as their throwing down and pulling up trees, or removing timber, in which the tame ones are always directed by their keeper, who communicates his ideas upon the subject to them by means of an iron instrument resembling a boat-hook. The cocoa-nut trees,

* Kraal, the term used by Europeans for a strong enclosure for catching elephants.

which are thrown down by wild elephants, are upset by continual shaking, produced by pressing their heads against those plants which are least able to resist; but a goat will show more ingenuity, and contrive to reach leaves, or the top of such plants as he may covet, in (comparatively speaking) more difficult positions than can be done by an elephant. Their sparing the lives of human beings, which from previous impressions I was at first inclined to consider as magnanimity, I soon learned to class as stupidity, with ignorance of their own power, and how to apply it; for I have oftener seen them fail than succeed in their fierce but awkward attempts to kill persons completely in their power. Another circumstance which assisted in convincing me that the instinct of the elephant is not of that superior order which is usually assigned to it, was the facility with which two half-trained elephants were re-captured after they had escaped into the jungle; and I was then assured by the hunters, that, so far from becoming more wary, such elephants as, after being partially or entirely trained, had broken loose in the jungle, were easily retaken. They are fond of clambering on steep hills, and do not shun slippery rocks, on which so clumsy an animal is necessarily insecure. I have known three instances in the Mátalé district of elephants being killed by falling down precipices.

Elephants, although not pre-eminently sagacious, are in general peculiarly docile; yet there is amongst them an endless variety in temper as well as in appearance, and some few are found so sulky and untractable as to be entirely useless. In all, the sense of smell is acute, and their hearing on a par with that of other animals; but their sight is not quick, particularly in a bright light, which they generally avoid. On plain ground, their long step or shuffling trot does not exceed the speed of an active man; and I have known two instances of European gentlemen who, in an open path, owed their escape to their speed exceeding that of a pursuing elephant; but, in jungle, the pace of an elephant is but little retarded by forcing through brushwood so thick as to be impervious to man.

There are several different ways of catching elephants in Ceylon; but that requiring least preparation and most dexterity is noosing them in an open forest. For this purpose, having ascertained the position of one, the hunters steal up against the wind, carrying their atmaddoos (strong ropes made of bullock's hide, with a noose at one end). Having got close to the animal's flank, they watch an opportunity, either when he starts off or attempts to turn round, of slipping the noose under a hind-foot, at the same time taking a turn round a tree with the other end of the rope. Checked and tripped, the animal stumbles; and, before recovering, additional hide-ropes are fixed to his other legs, which are afterwards entangled by cords made from the keetul (sugar-palm) tree, and twisted from one foot to another, in the form of a figure of eight. The elephant is then fixed to the nearest tree and a shed erected over him, unless tame ones can be procured to escort him to the stable.

Another method by which elephants are caught, with less danger to the people but greater injury to the animal, is by laying a large noose of gasmaddoo, a thicker kind of hide-rope,* in a path, covering it slightly with earth, and fixing the other end to a shady tree in which a man is concealed, who holds a leading rope attached to the noose. The elephants being driven towards the snare, if any of them put a foot within the noose, it is raised around his leg by the man who is on watch: by the animal's exertions to escape, the noose is tightened; and, the hunters coming up, the capture is completed. Elephants caught in this way so often overstrained themselves before the hunters came up, that I discontinued catching with gasmaddoos.

* This kind is called gasmaddoo (tree-snares), to distinguish it from the smaller, called atmaddoo (hand-snares).

In the maritime provinces it was the practice to catch elephants in very large kraals; and a multitude of people driven to these hunts were placed in a semicircular chain, sometimes embracing a great extent of country, until, gradually advancing as the elephants removed, the extremities of the line of assailants were brought round so as to reach the enclosure. By noise during the day and fires at night, the encompassed animals were gradually pressed forward towards the fence; then, unable to proceed except by the passage left on purpose, they rushed into the toils, and the entrance was immediately secured before the enraged captives had time to discover their dilemma. From the great kraal the elephants were forced or enticed into a narrow funnel-shaped passage, in which, being unable to turn, they were easily secured, and, as they came out, were attached to two tame elephants to be conducted to the stables.

As the Kandians combined the different systems of catching elephants by driving them into kraals, and then securing them by both gasmaddoos and atmaddoos, I shall give a few details of that interesting sight, an elephant-hunt, as it was conducted prior to the abolition of compulsory labour. In the Dombara district near Kandy, there does, or lately did, exist a herd of half-tame elephants that were kept for the purpose of inducing passing herds to continue in the vicinity of a kraal, formed at a short distance from the villages of the elephant-hunters of that province. Two or three good tusk-elephants of a large size, two female decoys, a sufficient body of people, a due proportion of pipes, tom-toms, hide-ropes, and hunters' spears, formed what was the requisite array and all the necessary instruments for driving in and securing a herd not exceeding in number twenty elephants.

The enclosure for catching elephants, commonly called a kraal, is composed of trees about a foot in diameter; these are sunk three or four feet into the ground, and rise twelve feet above it: on the outside of these upright timbers, trees are placed lengthways, and tied to each post by jungle-ropes (tough creeping-plants); these longitudinal pieces are farther supported by trees with forked ends sloping from them, and resting in the ground at some distance from the fence. The space between the upright timbers is left of sufficient size to admit of a man passing through; and in choosing the situation and arranging the plan of the enclosure, it is absolutely necessary that the entrance should be at a spot where the elephants are in the habit of passing, and that at all times the kraal should have an abundant supply of running water. As elephants cannot be driven far without great expenditure of human labour, and risk of accidents to the people employed, I seldom used the large kraal at Mátalé, but constructed several smaller ones in situations where the sides of a ravine, ledges of rock, or other natural barriers could be made available. I have sometimes been successful in securing a herd in an enclosure of very frail construction, by making it the interest of the hunters, and giving sufficient encouragement to those amongst them who were distinguished by energy and courage.

The kraal having been completed, and the people being arranged so as to surround the herd, driving is commenced by firing a few blank shots, followed by the rolling pattering sound of tom-toms and shouts from the beaters. On the large trees persons are stationed to give information of the elephants' movements, and prevent their resting under the shade; for if the day be clear, and the brushwood of a low size, it is difficult to dislodge them from the protection of a forest-tree with thick foliage. On two occasions I witnessed men, thus stationed, lower themselves down from a branch (but of which they still kept hold) upon the backs of wild elephants, and regain their position in the tree, whilst the animals were effectually and speedily dislodged by the loud shout, sharp goad, and unexpected descent of these watchers. When the herd approaches near to the kraal, the decoys, which are without any trappings whatever, are taken in front; and they following the keepers, who are on foot, become leaders to the wild ones, who thus seduced enter into the snare, while the hunting tusk-elephants, being close on their track, move up, and the gate is fastened under their protection and by their assistance. At the same time the hunters spread themselves around the fence, ready to resist the first efforts of the animals, for, frightened by the tumult and enraged at their entrapment, they sometimes charge furiously at the barricades, but are soon repelled by sharp sticks, blunt spears, and smoking brands.

On one occasion, however, a large female elephant whose young one had accidentally been shot, disregarding all obstacles, rushed with such violence against the enclosure, that a portion gave way before her weight, and, falling on those people who were watching outside, injured several of them: one man had his arm nearly severed immediately above the elbow. When I saw this person some time after, the stump was healed; and I learned that the necessary amputation had been performed by the Vedarall (native doctor), whose whole surgical apparatus consisted of a knife a pair of scissors, and a searing-iron.

In general, the violent excitement of the leaders of a herd on their entrapment is soon over, and the whole draw up with their heads in a line, in the thickest brushwood that is within their prison. Occasionally some one more valiant than the rest, after various scrapes of his feet, having duly elevated his trunk and sounded a charge, rushes forward as if irresistible; but a few pricks from spears directed against his feet and proboscis are sufficient to send the single champion discomfited and sulky back to his ranks. It is impossible to conceive a more awkward figure than an elephant charging, with his great triangular ears set out like studding-sails from a huge head, in front of which ascends the trunk like the funnel of a steam-carriage, while the main body comes lumbering after, terminated by a half-cocked, scanty, scrubby tail. The tails of those elephants that inhabit thick jungles are usually found denuded of hair, or with but a few broken stumps near the extremity: when the hairs are thick, and seven or eight inches in length, they are used for forming bracelets and other ornaments; and, being difficult to procure, are proportionably esteemed.

Amidst the confusion of tongues, and straining of voices, by those employed about an elephant-kraal, the few notes of a Kandian pipe may be distinguished: this instrument is played for the purpose of soothing the captives, and seems to have some effect in rendering them tranquil. Nothing appears to excite their anger so much as the barking of a dog, for I have known a whole herd made furious by the yelping of a cur that had intruded into a kraal.

At night, fires are kept burning around the enclosure; and against its supporting beams the hunters and watchers establish their bivouacks: next day the wives and families of the men, dressed in their gayest and best attire, bring their husbands provisions, and display their own ornaments to the numerous assembly. The Rhodias* might be seen in some corner, and were easily recognised; not from any inferiority in personal appearance, or deficiency of ornaments on their females, but from saluting any one who passed, by raising their joined hands above their heads, and then making a most submissive obeisance. It was they who furnished the hide-ropes for catching elephants, as any one, even of the lowest caste, would have been degraded by cutting up a dead bullock; yet, when made, all classes would use these ropes, and, if not strictly watched, would not be ashamed to steal what they were too proud to buy.

The elephant-catchers having completed their preparations, the entrance is unfastened, the hunt-

* A race of outcasts who were formerly exposed to great cruelties from the ignorance and intolerance of the native despotism.

ing elephants introduced, and with their protection the people fix their gasmaddoos and arrange their hand-snares. A tame elephant is brought up close to the wild one that is to be secured, who is assailed from under cover of his civilized brother: one of the hunters pricks the animal's foot; if he lifts it, another whips a noose under, and, raising it up, pulls the cord tight; if successful, a shout announces the feat, as a prize is given to each of those who fix the two first ropes. These prizes were generally dress-clothes; and I have seen one-half of them earned by a little elderly man, who might constantly be perceived in the most dangerous situations, from which he always contrived to extricate himself, apparently without difficulty, and always without injury. He was not only elephant-hunter, but was also headman of his village as well as its astrologer; and from these situations derived his appellation of Naket Gammachy.* It is the duty of the two riders that are placed on each trained elephant to prevent as much as possible any annoyance to the hunters; and it is a very remarkable fact, that the wild elephants seldom offer to molest a tame one or his riders, under any circumstances of provocation. After having secured one of the herd, and tied him so that he

* Naket, an asterism or planet; and Gammachy, head of a section or village.

can barely put one foot before another, a tame elephant is brought up on each side, and to these he is fastened in such a manner that he can neither resist nor lie down: the trio then move off in solemn procession; and, according to ancient custom, if the captive be a tusk-elephant, the pipes and tom-toms play before him until he reaches the stable.

Under the native sovereigns in the Kandian country, elephants without tusks were seldom captured, as they were not used in state processions; nor had any been trained for agricultural purposes, and but few as a means of conveying baggage, until the British set the example of employing the strength of elephants to clear forests and move heavy bodies. By the assistance of female decoys, and the inhabitants surrounding and driving the herd, elephants were sometimes brought into the town, and their capture completed under the eye of the King, in the square before the palace at Kandy. This was by no means so difficult an undertaking as it might appear to those unacquainted with the state of the Kandian country before it came into possession of the British in 1815; for, under the native Government, keeping the roads nearly impassable, so that the interior might be inaccessible, was that part of the policy of the later Kings in which they were eminently successful. The approaches to their capital, even the paths in the immediate vicinity of the palace, were more likely to deter travellers, than to excite suspicion in an elephant following his dalilah; and now, although the roads around Kandy are excellent, and its streets broad, still the jungle is barely a stone's-throw distant from the old palace or new Government-house. Under the sovereigns of the Mahawanso, from B.C. 543 until A.D. 302, and even in much later periods, the Cingalese roads must have been very different from what they had become under the native sovereigns who had to maintain themselves against European powers. In Cingalese history frequent mention is made of the long journeys performed in carriages by Kings and Queens of the olden time: in the level country, and at the dry season, (even without a regular road,) this would not be difficult; but in the neighbourhood of Anurádhapoora, Polannarrua, and even in some of the mountainous passes,* the remains of roads sufficient for a carriage may still be traced. In the reign of the last Kandian King the highways were sufficiently difficult for a man on foot, generally impracticable for a horse; and several of the paths that led through easy passes in the moun-

* From Dambool to the Andagalla pass, and through the valley of Gantony in Mátalé, the ancient road from Anurádhapoora to Adam's Peak is well defined.

tains around Kandy were shut up, and the more difficult and circuitous were alone permitted to be kept open.

If it is intended to use the tree-snares in catching elephants, they are driven towards the place where the noose is concealed under a slight covering of earth or leaves: they, however, carefully avoid the spot where the earth appears disturbed, and may be seen with their huge snouts pointed up and smelling at the man who watches in the tree above, holding a line (formed of some creeping-plant) communicating with the noose. Whilst thus engaged, a push from a tame elephant sends some of them staggering into the snare, which is immediately (by pulling the leading rope) raised up round one of their legs; the first step the animal makes tightens the noose, and, the rest of the herd being driven away, the farther securing of the captive is easily accomplished.

So accustomed were the natives of the interior to elephants, that those persons who were unconnected with the hunting establishment might be seen crossing through the kraal rather than go a few yards further by the outside of the enclosure; and on their way, if charged by any of the captives, the people seemed to calculate to a nicety the pace necessary to insure a safe retreat, and slipped through between the barricades, while the pursuer's head was met by a sufficient number of spear-points to prevent his rushing against the timbers. On one occasion, a fierce and very large elephant charged towards the entrance before it could be closed; the hunting-elephant (who should have defended the post) fled; the people followed, with the exception of the old man who was chief of the Mátalé hunters; he remained unmoved, supporting a great beam poised on its end, which his party had been in the act of placing when the charge commenced. Confident in his own resources, the old man looked round in triumph, then gradually lowered the piece of timber; and so well did he judge both time and distance, that the furious animal was brought up by her forehead being dashed right against the end of the descending beam. The shock actually shook the ground for some distance, and the half-stunned animal recoiled for several paces; while the headman re-assembled his runaway gang, who, in terror lest they should receive the punishment which their timidity deserved, were in haste to display zeal where personal safety was no longer compromised.

This gallant old man had been but lately appointed to the charge of the elephant-hunters, when his predecessor was disabled by being caught, thrown down, and shuffled, first between the forefeet, and then through the hind ones, of a wild elephant.

This headman eventually recovered, although several of his ribs were broken; and not only his clothes, but a great part of his skin, had been grated off in the rough operation above described.

Spears used in elephant-hunting should have thin handles, of a tough light wood, ten feet in length; and for heads have iron balls, from which a small point projects, but not so far as to permit it to pierce entirely through the thick skin of an elephant. With common spears dangerous wounds were sometimes given, and sores formed which were aggravated by the discipline of the stable. Spears were no efficient protection to the hunters, and were apt to induce fool-hardiness in those to whom they were issued; yet all were most anxious to have them. I have witnessed a man, when run at by an elephant, place his spear against the animal's forehead, and allow himself to be pushed back until he made his exit between two trees of the enclosure.

On another occasion, some of the less experienced hunters, seized with a panic, having overthrown Mr. T—— and myself, while an old hunter was gradually retreating before an elephant, the man came in contact with my prostrate friend: the spear was instantly shivered, and the unlucky hunter seized in the elephant's trunk. Fortunately I soon regained my feet and retained my gun; and still more fortunately, considering the hurry in which I fired, the ball passed through the animal's head without injuring the man, who was released from a gripe so severe that it had already forced blood from his mouth and ears. This took place at a slight temporary kraal, hurriedly formed, and therefore without any place for myself or friends, such as was usually prepared, in some large tree overhanging the enclosure. Mr. T—— and I, however, by the active civility of a neighbouring village headman, had been furnished with a native couch; and this, covered with a white cloth, gave our position an air of dignity which was quickly and ludicrously reversed by the rush of the runaway spearmen from the untoward charge of the elephant.

Elephant stables, when filled with animals recently caught, present a most unpleasant sight: in front, the appearance is that of a parcel of malefactors in the stocks, the animals being so fixed as to be unable to move their heads or legs; the latter are bound to four separate posts, and their heads project from between two large beams that reach to the top of the building. The cords with which they are bound produce numerous sores; and, to prevent flies from irritating these and annoying the animals, fires of green wood are kept smouldering in every part of the building. In such a miserable position few would survive if they were not taken to water, and allowed to lie in it for several hours every day; and, as this cannot be done without the assistance of tame elephants, it is useless and cruel to catch too many at one time: the number must, therefore, depend on the numerical strength of those already trained, and attached to the hunting department.

Elephants from the time they are caught, until tame enough to be fastened to one post only, are not permitted to lie down in the stable; and the time required to make them sufficiently tractable for this indulgence varies from one to three months, according to the disposition of the animal and skill of the keepers. When removed from the stables to the water, it is the duty of the keepers daily to scrub their elephants with rubbers formed by cutting across the fibrous covering of the cocoa-nut; sometimes a rough stone is used in place of this instrument of luxury, and appears to give as much delight to the patient as shampooing in a warm bath would afford to a wearied traveller.

When any of the tame male elephants become furious (which they do periodically), they are bound to a tree with a strong iron chain, and supplied with food and water, but cannot be unloosed until the symptoms abate: the time this infirmity continues, varies from four days to four weeks, and is said to be longer in those with tusks than in other elephants. When this season is approaching, they become dangerous even to their keepers; and I believe there are few, if any, of the old hunting elephants that have not killed persons employed about them, often with circumstances of peculiar cunning and treachery. In 1829, one of the hunting elephants at Mátalé, having shown symptoms of a capricious irritable temper, was in consequence secured to a tree near the stables; next day, as the keeper was standing barely within reach, the brute suddenly seized him at the moment another elephant was passing, and pressed the unfortunate man against this animal until one of the thick blunt tusks came through the keeper's body. About the same time another tusk elephant, when introduced into a kraal in which twenty-two wild elephants were enclosed, contrived by the most violent exertions to unseat his two riders in the midst of the herd, through which the men crawled, and escaped without any very serious injuries.

I will conclude these remarks on elephants by expressing my satisfaction at the permission, even encouragement, given since 1831, (when Sir R. Wilmot Horton assumed the government of Ceylon,) to the destruction of these animals, who had so long lorded it over the agriculturist. Their rapid decrease in numbers since then is undoubtedly one of the great causes (perhaps next to the abolition of compulsory services the greatest) of the extraordinary prosperity which is now enjoyed by many districts, where, prior to that period, great loss of human life and diminished cultivation were occasioned by these comparatively useless animals.

CHAPTER IV.

THE VEDDAHS, ABORIGINAL INHABITANTS OF CEYLON.

* * * * * Foreign laws despis'd,
And kept unconquer'd and unciviliz'd.—POPE.

The Veddahs, the aboriginal Inhabitants of Ceylon.— Village and Forest Veddahs:—their method of killing Elephants.— Kuwani—her Death.— Yakkas.

THE Veddahs are an uncivilized race, thinly scattered over an extensive, unhealthy tract of country, lying between the maritime province of Batticaloe on the eastern coast, and the Kandian hills. They are the descendants of Yakkas, the aboriginal inhabitants, who were in possession of the eastern part of Ceylon when Vigeya and his followers landed B.C. 543; and, having then escaped from the fury of these invaders into the depths of the forest of Bintenne and Veddaratta, have there preserved the purity of their race, and the superstitions of their ancestors. All Veddahs are considered to be of the Goyawanzae (the highest caste now existing in Ceylon); and such of them as I have seen do not in any respect differ from what other natives would become, if compelled to use the same exertions, to endure the same privations, and, like them, to live as wanderers in a forest-wilderness. The village Veddahs have permanent places of residence, cultivate small portions of land, and communicate, although they do not mix, with the other natives of the island. The forest Veddahs subsist by hunting, or on such fruit as the earth yields spontaneously; and they obtain arrow-blades, the only article of manufacture which they covet, through the intervention of their own headmen and their brethren of the villages. Their headmen (Kandians of the neighbouring districts), in talking to Europeans, generally exaggerated the wild nature of the Veddahs; and never endeavoured to amend the habits, extend the comforts, or improve the appearance of these poor people. This is easily accounted for; the less civilized the Veddahs were, and the less they were known, the more easy it was for those in authority over them to impose on their credulity, and thus obtain for a trifle ivory and dried deer-flesh, the produce of their bows. This race has, perhaps, the scantiest measure of covering of any people who know the use of cloth and pretend to wear it; their whole dress consisting of a small piece of cotton cloth depending in front from a string tied round the loins. The Veddahs* "have a curious way by themselves of preserving flesh: they cut a hollow tree, and put honey in it, and then fill it with flesh, and stop it up with clay, which lies for a reserve to eat in time of want."

The Veddahs may more properly be termed rude than savage, being as free from ferocity as from any trace of civilization. Their present state is an inheritance from their ancestors, who, driven by oppression and treachery into solitudes, had to suffer hardships, under which they retrograded to the condition in which we now find them, and in which they have continued for more than twenty centuries. I cannot in any other manner account for the extraordinary fact of a people declining into the lowest state of mental debasement, accompanied by the endurance of bodily hardship, and thus continuing for so many ages, although acknowledged to be equal in rank with the best of a comparatively civilized nation, in the midst of whom they lived, and with whom they possessed a common language. The cruel and perfidious conduct of the Singha race of conquerors naturally

* Quoted from Knox's account of his captivity in Ceylon in the seventeenth century.

inspired the Yakkas with feelings of terror and distrust, which in after-times were maintained in their descendants by continued acts of violence of the Cingalese towards the Veddahs.

The different families of the forest Veddahs are said to preserve boundaries in the woods, and only within their respective limits to kill the game which is their principal food. Without any regular religion, the Veddahs (like every other untutored race) feel the force of an invisible and superior power, which evinces its influence by undefined terrors, and the consequent belief and worship of evil spirits: they also make offerings to the shades of departed ancestors, and to figures temporarily prepared to represent the controlling spirit of some planet which they believe to exercise an influence over their fate.

During the Kandian dynasty, the Veddahs paid tribute in wax and elephants' tusks, and obeyed headmen from the adjacent districts; afterwards, by the influence of these persons, they were led, in 1817, to join the rebellion raised against the British Government. The weapons they use are clubs, and bows with arrows, the blades of which vary in length from four to fifteen inches: it is with these long-bladed arrows and wretched bows that Veddahs kill elephants, not by striking in the foot as was commonly believed, but by creeping close up to the animal and shooting to the heart. Should the elephant have escaped receiving a mortal wound, the hunters follow his track and persevere until he falls exhausted, or by a fresh attack, when, in addition to the ivory, they recover their arrows. Activity saves them from danger in this pursuit; and so cautious and stealthy is their pace, that they seldom startle any game which it is their object to approach: from this cause the Cingalese have obtained the belief that no wild animal will fly from a forest Veddah.

The following are some of the most remarkable events, connected with the aboriginal inhabitants, which are to be found in Cingalese history or have been preserved by tradition. Vijeya, a prince of the royal family of Singhapoora,* an exile and adventurer, driven from that country by command of his father, the King Singhabahu, landed in Ceylon, then called Lanka, at Tammenatotta,† B.C. 543, accompanied by seven hundred followers. Having advanced into the forests of that district, Vijeya formed a connexion with a beautiful female of the country, called Kuwani (of the Yakka race);

* Probably Singhea, on the banks of the Gunduck, province of Bahar.

† Contrary to the opinion of the natives, I imagine this place to be Tamblegam in the Tamenkada district: there are several villages called Tammena, but none of them on the sea-coast.

and soon after, by her means, discovered that Pusamitta, daughter of the chief of Logalla,* had been given in marriage to the chief of Lagalla;† and that under the direction of the bride's mother, Kondanámika, the town of Sri-Wasta-Poora ‡ was for seven days to be a continued scene of festivity. Vijeya determined on attacking the inhabitants while engaged in these rejoicings; and the Yakkini, Kuwani, mixing in the crowd, gave the signal of massacre. Vijeya and his followers rushed from their ambush, surprised the unsuspicious revellers, killed their chief Kalaseno, and so great was the slaughter of the Yakkas, that (says the Cingalese account) their blood flowed through the streets like streams of water in the rainy season. Before Kuwani betrayed her kindred and countrymen, Vijeya ratified former promises to make her his Queen by the most solemn oaths: the performance of these he afterwards evaded; and, having despatched an embassy to the continent of India, procured from thence a Princess of the royal race of Pandi, whom he married and made Queen. The discarded

* Logalla, in the Ouwa district.

† Lagalla, in the Mátalé district.

‡ I suppose this place to have been near Myungana in Beentenne; and that its name of Sri-Watta, or Wasta-Poora, was derived from the garden Mahanaga at Mahawelligam, the first spot in Lanka sanctified by the presence of Gautama Buddha.

Yakkini, with her children by Vijeya, viz. a son Jiwahahatto, and a daughter Disala, having wandered towards her former residence, entered into the town of Lankapoora, after leaving her children in the neighbourhood. One of the Yakkas, who recognised her, making use of this expression, "Is it for the purpose of again and again spying out the peace we enjoy, that she is come?" accompanied his exclamation by a blow that killed the unfortunate Kuwani. Kumara, her uncle, enabled the children to escape to the mountains near Samantakuta, where they were brought up, and their numerous descendants retained the attributes of the Yakkas.*

The spirit of Kuwani is still supposed to haunt the country, and inflict misfortune on the race of the conqueror by whom she was betrayed. Kuwanigalla is a bare mountain of rock on which are two stones, one slightly resembling a human figure in a standing attitude, the other looking like a seat. It is on this that traditions assert the Yakkini sometimes appears, and casts the withering glance of malignant power over the fair fields and fertile valley of Asgiri.†

* The details of Vijeya's treachery, and the fate of Kuwani, are principally taken from Turnour's translation of the Mahawanso.

† A sequestered and most romantic spot in the Mátalé district.

From the account of Gautama Buddha's visits to Kellania on the western coast (a short time prior to the invasion of Lanka by the Singha adventurers), we perceive that it was then the capital of the surrounding country, occupied by the Naga * race, who probably submitted when the Yakkas † were subdued, and the massacre of Sri-Wasta-Poora had terminated all opposition to the unscrupulous victor.

Vijeya died in the thirty-eighth year of his reign, from a disease (a species of leprosy) which he is supposed to have received as a punishment from those gods whom he had called to witness the oath he swore to Kuwani and afterwards violated. The body of Vijeya was deposited in a cave called Saega Lenna, near Sri-Wasta-Poora.

Perjury, and the massacre of a hospitable and unoffending people, were not events with which Buddhist historians would willingly commence their history in Ceylon: they have, therefore, slightly encumbered with fable these passages in the life of Vijeya; but their flimsy allegories do not materially interfere with the detail of events recorded of this kinsman of Buddha, the founder of the

* Nága (hooded snake). The Nagas were probably snake-worshipers before they were converted by Gautama Buddha.

† Yakka (a devil). The Yakkas were, previous to the arrival of Gautama, demon-worshipers; neither was their conversion general.

great dynasty of Ceylon. To brighten the fame or palliate the aggressions of a conqueror whose race gave a new name to Lanka, the Cingalese historians have denounced the Yakkas whom he attacked as identical with the demons which they worshipped. These writers, however, do not conceal the fact, that, in the contentions for sovereign power that arose amongst the immediate successors of Vijeya, the assistance of the Yakkas was eagerly sought for and duly rewarded.

Panduwasa, the nephew and successor of Vijeya, being attacked by the disease that had proved fatal to his predecessor, and imagining that he had inherited the curse of the Yakkas with crown of their conqueror, sent for the demon-worshipers: their rites were performed, the monarch was cured, and future protection promised to the race of the successful exorcists. After this, we find them taking an active part on the victor's side, when Pandukabhaya succeeded in defeating his uncles and seizing the throne, B.C. 437;* and he even permitted his confederates, the Yakka chiefs Kalawelo and Chitto, to exercise great authority, and the latter on days of public festivity sat on a throne of equal height with the monarch's. This fact is sufficient evidence that it was necessary to conciliate the Yakka chiefs; that they were still

* Turnour's translation of the Mahawanso.

powerful, their followers numerous; and that the race then retained its separate character, although it appears to have merged soon after in a general appellation derived from their Singha conquerors. The account* of an attack made on a settlement at the rocky mountain of Rittigalla (within thirty miles of the capital of the island), B.C. 382, by one of the chiefs of Dootoogaimoonoo is the latest mention which I have met with of these aborigines under their ancient name of Yakkas.

* In the Cingalese work Saddhamma Lankara.

CHAPTER V.

TO THE MOUNTAIN OF LAKAGALLA.

* * * Pale grey crags that frown above us;
Which seem like records pointing us to read
Of desolation past.—*The Deluge.* READE.

When Nature smiled, and o'er the landscape threw
Her richest fragrance and her brightest hue.—ROGERS.

Set out for Lakagalla. — Cingalese Carriage-road. — Ambulam. — Uses of a Theodolite. — Native Impostor. — Priest of the Abudha Deiyo. — Elephants caught by Torch-light. — Accident in Fishing. — Inquest. — Fishing in the Fields. — Opalgalla. —Ancient Canal.—Man seized by a Crocodile. — Ruins on the Ambanganga. — Infanticide. — Elephant and Buffalo Paths. — View of the Lagalla Mountains. — Narrangamma.— Lakagalla. — Nelu Plants. — Elk-hunt. — Legends. — River Prince. — Last Funeral Rites of Cingalese Kings. — Rich Grazing Country. — Cinnamon-trees. — Sacred Trees of Buddha. — The Champaka. — Beautiful Scene. —Ascent of the Batandua Pass. — Venomous Reptiles. —Mungoose attacking a Hooded Snake. — Elephant killed by falling down a Precipice.

TRADITIONS connected with the history of Rawana, and the positions of the places mentioned in the account of the Veddahs, having been communicated to me by a rebel who had long been skulking in Lagalla and Beentenne, I determined on visiting the mountain of Lakagalla. In April 1832 I started for that purpose, accompanied by Mr. S——. After proceeding a mile along the Trinkomalee road, we struck into a jungle-path on the right; and crossing a large stream, which, rising near Dombara peak, flows by the base of the Hunusgiri range of mountains, we entered the valley of Gantony. We then turned down the valley to the left by another path, which evidently at a remote period had been a broad road; and its formation showed that it must have been intended for carriages, although no ingenuity had been exerted in avoiding the steep ascents that occasionally occurred in its line of direction. When a native King of the olden time made a progress towards Adam's Peak, his carriage must have been impelled up these eminences by the force of people, who were always at hand, as the inhabitants of every district through which the royal procession passed were compelled to attend to provide its supplies and carry the baggage. Wherever a path crossed or diverged from this road, an ambulam existed, or its foundation might be perceived. An ambulam is generally a strong shed of a small size, raised on a stone foundation eight or ten feet in height: under its shade travellers rested during the heat of the day; or, if benighted, its elevated position offered them security against elephants. Near these huts is often seen the far-extending peepul with its ever rustling leaves and ample shade, or the light-green lively foliage and solid trunk of the tamarind, the rise of which may be referred to the repast of wanderers, who, hundreds of years before, had rested at the ambulam. At one of these shady spots, where a tributary rivulet rushed from its rocky channel and joined the larger but scarcely less impetuous stream, we found our breakfast prepared, and the people of the neighbourhood ready to gratify their quiet unobtrusive curiosity by a sight of white men, horses, and a theodolite. This instrument had acquired a most extraordinary character in the district; viz. that by it Europeans had the power of discovering level passages through the highest mountains, in the same way as a watch could tell them what o'clock it was, although there was no sun shining at the time: the ticking of the watch, and the turning of the compass in the theodolite, seemed to the Kandians to be direct vitality. Having seen a gentleman continually using the latter instrument in tracing the road in the Ballakadawe pass, (which, although formerly an exceedingly steep jungle-path, was afterwards made an easy cart-road with a slope in most places of one foot in twenty,) the natives, from the comparative ease with which they ascended by the new line, believed that Mr. Hamilton,* by means of his three-legged watch (as the natives called the theodolite), had discovered a level way, although the ascent in three miles was actually seven hundred feet.

Amongst those persons who came to pay their respects to me at this place, were two remarkable impostors residing in this neighbourhood, and acting in different departments of knavery: one of them had lately abandoned his claims to supernatural power, to save himself from present injury; and the reputation of the other I had completely ruined by convicting thieves to whom his god had promised concealment and security on receiving part of their plunder. The former of these knaves, an old man, had, unluckily for himself, inspired his neighbours with a belief that he had the power of bringing rain by performing certain ceremonies; and they had spread his fame over the whole district. From this, and his knowledge of the appearance of the sky, and the various signs of coming showers or approaching heavy rains, he had long imposed on the people, and reaped considerable profit; until at last their eagerness of belief outrunning his powers of imposition, not only destroyed

* Lieutenant Hamilton, 78th Regiment, who traced the road from Mátalé into Kandy through the Ballakadawe pass.

his occupation, but nearly cost him his life. It was urged by some one, and acquiesced in by all, that, as there was no doubt of his ability to call down rain when necessary, it ought not to be left to his caprice when this talent should be exercised; and that, when required by a whole village, he should be obliged to furnish rain in sufficient quantities: that, if he did so, he was to be liberally rewarded; but on the contrary, if he were contumacious, and refused to give the necessary supply, that he should be tormented with thorns, or beat into compliance Having suffered severe punishments on various occasions, he at last made up his mind no longer to be a responsible agent for the weather, and loudly and constantly denied having any authority in the matter. This, although deemed to be a false excuse, proved a sufficient protection to him during several seasons in which there was no deficiency of moisture; but, this season the people, losing all patience from a long-continued drought which was destroying their crops, dragged the recusant cloud-compeller to various villages, in which he suffered severely for his supposed neglect. Even the chief of the district had determined on having rain by force, if fair means proved insufficient, and had sent some of his followers to bring the conjurer to the village where water was most required: it was while on his way there that he was fortunate enough to see me, and, making his escape, threw himself on my protection. In the court-house the old man stated that he was in terror of his life, for at present there was every appearance of continuance of the same dry weather that had already done so much mischief; and then gravely proceeded to prove to me by many oaths that it was no fault of his that no rain was forthcoming. I had some difficulty in protecting this old impostor, particularly as a few slight showers fell near his village, which was situated on one of the highest inhabited parts of the district; and I have no doubt the people thought, not that they had been the infatuated dupes of a rogue, but that I was imposed upon by a churlish wizard.

The other knave to whom I have already alluded as one of those who presented themselves before me, was a priest of the Abudha-deiyo, the unknown god, more properly the god of secrecy, probably the same as Mercury. His temple in the division of Bogambera is the only one I know, and of it I only lately heard; but, soon after its existence was brought to my knowledge, I had the satisfaction of detecting a gang of robbers, by identifying stolen property in a portion of their offerings, and thereby disparaging their spiritual ally, the god of thieves.

Resuming our journey, about a mile farther on we passed an elephant-kraal situated on a bend of the river at Gigirinné: at this place I once witnessed, from an overhanging tree, the extraordinary scene of a herd of elephants driven into the enclosure by torch-light. Surrounded on every side by blazing chules, confused by the noise of tom-toms and the screeching of Kandians, the bewildered animals rushed into the snare, at the same time that the hunting-elephants came up and occupied the gate by which the herd had entered, until the beams could be secured. The hunters and beaters, who had been out six days in vain attempting to drive the same animals into the enclosure by daylight, immediately closed around the barricade, intimidating the enraged captives by waving lighted brands in whatever direction the animals rushed. After a few violent efforts, the whole herd drew up, closely pressed together in a small spot of thick brushwood, from which their eyes might be seen glaring at the blaze of torches which lighted up the forest and was reflected in the river. The morning after the herd had been driven into the kraal, on returning to have them secured, I perceived that a very young elephant was drowned in the deep corner of the stream, and that its carcase was equally an object of aversion and irritation to the others, who occasionally vented their rage by striking and butting at the floating body.

From the stream along which our way had

hitherto lain, (and which in this part of its course changes its name with that of the villages through which it runs,) I have often been supplied with mullet of a large size, caught by the Mohammedan inhabitants who reside in its vicinity. They are always the most successful and keenest of native sportsmen; and about this time one of them lost his life in the eager pursuit of a mullet, which he had driven into a small cavern in the rocky bank of the river. In his exertions to secure the fish, his head and shoulders became wedged in the narrow entrance, with his mouth under water; and thus he was suffocated in the presence of his companions, who were pursuing their sport, unaware, until too late, of the fatal accident. These circumstances were clearly proved on the inquest; but in place of "accidental death," which I suggested as a proper verdict to the Mohammedan jury, they considered it more applicable to their view of the case to return a verdict "that the time of the deceased was come, and his fate accomplished." They afterwards added, that, in the death of the deceased, no blame was attributable to those who were present at the time of the catastrophe.

An inquest, in every violent, sudden, or suspicious case of death, was an ancient Kandian institution, and these inquests, like most of their customs or laws, only required the superintendence of those who had no private ends in view, to render them in practice, as they were in theory, well adapted for the protection of life and property.

During heavy rains I have often been amused, and was at first much surprised, to observe Moormen establishing small weirs, and arranging bamboo fishing-baskets, in the paths through the garden and fields surrounding my house at Mátalé. The reason of their selecting these grounds for the scene of operations, was their being free from low jungle, and therefore but little infested with land-leeches; yet the situation was apparently inaccessible to any other than flying-fish, being situated between two broad ravines, the banks of which were fifteen or twenty feet in height. Except in the rainy season, no water ran in these dells; and even then, unless when the rains descended heavily for several hours, only insignificant streamlets trickled through a bed of shrubs and grass: but, after half a day of tropical rain, these ravines were filled with roaring torrents, and every foot-path became the course of a tributary rill, up which rushed thousands of small silvery fish into the toils of the exulting Moormen. When these heavy showers were falling, they remained without shelter, evidently enjoying the sport; and their shaved heads, oiled skins, and scanty raiment presented little that could suffer, even from the pelting of a tropical shower during the change of monsoons.

From Gigirinné we proceeded along the base of Opalgalla, a hill on which the foundations of a small fort can be traced: vague tradition assigns its construction to Yakkas, the alleged architects of every ruin in Ceylon the origin of which is unknown, and of every work too difficult to be imitated, or too clumsy to be acknowledged by Cingalese.

At Ambona, the stream, near the banks of which we had been travelling for ten miles, was joined by the Nalandé-oya (which rises in the rocky mountains that surround the romantic vale of Asgiri), and here changed its course from north to east. From this place, until its junction with the Mahawelliganga at Kotawelle in Tamankada, a distance of forty miles, it retains the name of Ambanganga; and the spot where these two rivers join is nearly opposite to Dimbulugalla, a solitary mountain rising from the plains of Beentenne.

At the entrance of a large canal near Ellaherra, a wall of immense strength had been formed across the river; yet, notwithstanding the great size of the stones employed in the construction of this work, and although the remains of the dam are now at a considerable distance from the usual course of the river, still part of it is occasionally displaced by floods in the rainy season. From the description given to me by an old and intelligent headman of that village, who explained the extent and position of the work as it appeared in his youth, this embankment had served for a bridge, as well as a dam to turn water into the canal. From a stone pillar, in that part of the work that remains, I procured an inscription in the ancient Cingalese character, signifying that the canal was completed by the happy, victorious, and illustrious monarch of Ceylon, Prakrama Bahoo.* This canal is said to have been formed, not only for conveying part of the water of this river into tanks, and thus increasing the extent of irrigated lands, but also for purposes of inland navigation, so that loaded boats might pass from here to Gantalawe, near Trinkomalee, and also by another branch of the same canal to the ancient capital of Polannarrua.

In the upper part of the course of the Ambanganga crocodiles are very rarely seen; but, as two men were wading across the river near Ellaherra, (a short time previously to my visit,) while the water was discoloured from a recent fall of rain, one of them was carried off. The eldest of the two was in front, and hearing a scream, in which he fancied the word kimbula (crocodile) was ex-

* Prakrama Bahoo reigned from A.D. 1153 to 1186.

pressed, he turned round, and witnessed, at the spot he had passed but one instant before, the troubled water closing over the turban of his unfortunate companion. A slight eddy, then a gentle ridge in the water, marked the course of the loathsome reptile as it ploughed along the bed of the river to deposit its prey, and repose beside it in some dark and caverned channel, beneath the tangled roots of the forest which everywhere overshadows the banks of the Ambanganga.

The description of the ruins farther down the river was furnished to me by the native whom I sent to copy inscriptions; and his account was afterwards confirmed by inhabitants from that district. Near the junction of the Heerattee-oya with the Ambanganga are situated the dilapidated rock-temple and dágoba of Gaetyagamma. Farther down, the river, for a distance of three miles, winds so as nearly to surround extensive ruins, now known by the name of Maluwaya: this place is overgrown with jungle, and the principal remains are described as three buildings situated at some distance from each other. One of these, founded on a rock in which there is an excavated chamber, is called the Patrippooa; at each of the others there is a stone trough, one of them formed in the rock, the other having been removed to its present situation: a long inscription, in an old form of Cingalese, was discovered in the vicinity of these buildings.

The river, previously to being joined by a considerable stream, the Kaluganga, rushes through a narrow chasm called Námalkumara-ella, and forms a large and very deep basin beneath the fall.

Turning to the northern extremity of the Hunusgiri range of mountains by a path in some places overhanging the river, we entered the district of Gangalla, and proceeded through unbroken jungle to the flourishing village of Kamberawe.

Not long after I passed this way, I had to investigate an alleged case of child-murder, which was supposed to have taken place in the desolate path which winds through the forest on the bank of the Ambanganga. It appeared, however, that the accused, a woman, while travelling from Ellaherra, became so fatigued as to be unable to carry the youngest of two children who accompanied her; and the child, not quite four years old, could not walk farther: the mother, rolling up the infant, placed it in a small spot clear of brushwood, and then proceeded with the other child to the nearest village. The forest abounding with elephants, and the people being unarmed, search was deferred until morning: when they reached the spot, no trace of the child could be found, neither could any marks of wild animals be discovered near the place. In this unsatisfactory state the case remained, and no farther information was obtained regarding the fate of the infant. The only cause of suspicion against the mother was her having left her husband's house after a quarrel, and the journey being contrary to his wish.

The Cingalese have been accused of infanticide; and the charge was not at one time altogether without foundation, although I believe the instances were rare. With abundance of food, and the ease with which a family may now be subsisted, I cannot doubt the crime will soon cease; probably even at this time it does not exist. I only knew one instance — it happened in 1830 — of two people, the parents, being suspected of perpetrating this crime: the accused persons were extremely poor and uncommonly ignorant, belonged to the lowest class, and were in bad repute with their neighbours. The crime, if the child was born alive, had been perpetrated, not by open violence, but by neglect and exposure: the cause was said to have been the prediction of an astrologer, that if the child lived it would injure its parents. In this case the proofs, though strong, were insufficient to warrant a conviction of the accused parties; and, as regards the general conduct of the Cingalese to their children, I have invariably seen that they treat them with the utmost kindness, and too often spoil them by over-indulgence.

After halting a night in the Buddhist preaching-house of Kamberawe, we started next morning for Pallegamma, and on our way crossed a precipitous and elevated range of wooded hills which separates Gangalla from Lagalla. Along the summit of the ridge extended an elephant-path; and the same may be found on nearly every range in the thickly wooded parts of the interior. A buffalo-path is easily known from an elephant's, as buffaloes make as few abrupt ascents as possible, and they show considerable sagacity in the manner they evade the precipitous places which an elephant would slip down or scramble over. If the elephant-path is also frequented by buffaloes, on arriving at any place where a horse would be unable to get up, you may be sure to find that a buffalo-track diverges, and by a zig-zag or circuitous route avoids the obstacle, but rejoins the road.

An opening caused by the falling of some decayed trees on the top of this rocky range of hills enabled us at last to extend our view beyond the surrounding jungle to the forest-encumbered valleys of Lagalla, over which grassy slopes and wooded summits of mountains rose to a height of six thousand feet. Advanced from these the rocky pinnacles of Lakagalla attracted our attention, and we perceived its precipices beetling over the artificial-looking crags called the Brahmin Rocks. Having descended to the village of Pallegamma on the banks of the Kaluganga, we there rested during the heat of the forenoon, and then proceeded by a rocky path, through several small but prettily situated villages, to Narrangamma. This is a large village; and from its proximity to the mountains, as well as its elevation above the sea, combines the advantages of a pleasant climate and picturesque situation. Amidst its bright green rice-fields several masses of rock were surmounted by watch-huts; around the margin of the cultivated lands a few of the houses might be distinguished; and the presence of the cocoa-nut trees showed the position of the remainder of the village scattered near the base of Lakagalla. In the morning we commenced ascending the mountain, and, after passing the cool clear stream which flows from it, entered a small level plain covered with rich black mould. This place preserves the name of Uyangamma-tenna-wewa (lake of the garden-flat): and here the growth of underwood is prevented by the thick shade of forest-trees, and by the circumstance of the ground being occasionally inundated. Into this rock-encircled basin huge masses of stone, which occasionally detach themselves from the Mátalé peak, plunge with a tremendous crash; and the natives believe such occurrences are the forerunners of domestic troubles in the country. Under this impression, the descent of one of these crags, and even the distance to which the sound of its fall extended, were officially communicated to me by the principal native in the district. From various names of neighbouring places, and for other reasons, I believe the Yakka town of Lankapoora* was situated around this mountain; and this circumstance, conjoined with still more ancient traditions, has obtained from native superstition a belief that its formation was miraculous, and that the sounds of its falling rocks are mysterious prognostics of public misfortune. If the narrow gap through which we entered into the Uyangammatenna were filled up, even to the height of four feet, the peaks of Lakagalla might again be reflected in its embosomed lake.

In ascending, we found several springs of the purest water; and breakfasted, at an elevation of three thousand three hundred feet above the sea, on a spot from which we saw into the valley of Meemoorra on one side, and on the other our view extended over the districts through which we had passed to the plains on the north and east of the Kandian territory. Through these levels

* Although in the Pali account of the Yakkas it is called Lankapoora, the Elu (Cingalese) history mentions Lagalla.

we could discern the course and occasionally saw the silver light of the Mahawelli-ganga, where it flowed near the isolated mountain of Dimbulu-galla in the direction of Trinkomalee. The upper part of Lakagalla is covered with coarse grass, which spreads in patches over the moist mass of solid rock that forms the summits of the mountain; trees and thickets occupy the sheltered ravines; and, near its base, the nelu forms a dark disagreeable jungle. The nelu is a brittle jointed plant, of which there are several varieties in Ceylon; and at this time it chanced to be in flower, which, with this species, happens (according to the natives) every eighth year, and they assert that after blossoming the plant decays: its flowers smelt strongly of honey, and attracted so many bees as to render our passage through it by no means pleasant. On the joints of the nelu roots were clusters of large, deep, bell-shaped flowers with yellow hearts and scarlet edges: these had no separate leaves, and appeared so general, and so completely united to the nelu roots, as to induce the native belief that they were two different flowers proceeding from the same plant.

In the forenoon, having made preparations for an elk-hunt, I took my station to watch a gap which, according to one legend, was caused by Rama's arrow when he slew a giant of the Rakshas, whose cumbrous form, rolling upon the plain, was transformed into the mountain of Laka, and remains a monument of the power and wrath of the conquering god. The high, narrow, angular peak overhanging the gap; the armed natives watching on crags which projected over the ravine; with the shouts, shots, and echoes from those who were beating up the game, combined to render this the perfection of wild sport and savage scenery.

My guide this day was an old Kapua, who said he was a priest and worshiper of the Ganga Bandera (river prince): from his recitation I obtained some verses, which he repeated to prove that the very spot where I stood was hallowed by legends of the olden time.

(*Translation.*)

Through the vale of Meemoorra* while sweeps the wild storm,
The red thunderbolt's gleam shows Lak'galla's rude form.
Hallow'd region of spirits! † when tempests rush by,
Frowning o'er their dark course, thy scathed peaks ‡ shoot on high.

---

* Meemoorra is a deep narrow valley beyond Lakagalla; and in the mountains which form the opposite side is a nitre cave, the most productive in the Kandian country, although the quantity it yielded was so trifling that it is not now worth working.

† Some legends say it was the birth-place, at least a chosen haunt, of Kartikeya (Mars).

‡ From one side Lakagalla shows three peaks: one of them is so sharp, pointed, and narrow, as to resemble a steeple of surpassing height; all of them are of solid rock.

Here stern Rawan was vanquish'd, and in that dread hour
Lakagalla was rent by the conqueror's power;
It was Rama's keen shaft cleft the mountain in twain,
And Lak'galla's bright lake made a desolate plain.

The malignant spirit called Ganga Bandera, Oya Bandera, Oya Yakka,* &c. is properly an object of terror, not of worship; and under very many different appellations the identity is easily perceived: he is the representative or personification of those severe fevers to which, from some occult causes, the banks of all Ceylon rivers are peculiarly liable. The manner of making offerings to the Ganga Bandera is by forming a miniature double canoe, ornamented with cocoa-nut leaves so as to form a canopy: under this are placed betel, rice, flowers, and such like articles of small value to the donor, as he flatters himself may be acceptable to the fiend, and induce him to spare those who acknowledge his power. After performing certain ceremonies, this propitiatory float is launched upon the nearest river: in a sickly season I have seen many of these delicate arks whirling down the streams, or aground on the sandbanks and fords of the Ambanganga.

The ceremony with which the ashes of Cingalese

* The river king, prince, or devil, the washerman's fiend, the water-fiend, are some of the names given to the visible signs of sickness that sometimes follow the course of running water in Ceylon.

Kings were consigned to supposed annihilation in the waters of the Mahawelli-ganga seems to have been derived from these rites; and was admirably adapted to perpetuate the feelings of mystery and awe which it was the policy of Ceylon monarchs to maintain when alive, and after death to transmit to their successors. The body of a Cingalese King was burnt with many ceremonies; and the fire, kept up until the tenth day, was then extinguished. The fragments of bones were next collected, and buried (together with certain offerings made during the ceremony) at the spot where the monumental dágoba was to be raised. The ashes, enclosed in an earthen urn, were consigned to a man dressed in black, wearing a mask, and mounted on an elephant: he then headed the procession, and was followed by all the chiefs and people in funeral array to the Mahawelli-ganga. On arriving at the river, the mask descended from his elephant; and bearing in one hand the urn, in the other a drawn sword, embarked in a double canoe ornamented with plantain-trees and cocoanut flowers. The vessel having been towed into the middle of the river, the mask held up the urn, cut it in two with the sword, then dived into the river, and disappeared. The royal dust of the "race of the sun" vanished in the waters; the frail and gaudy vessel drifted to destruction; the elephant, removed across the river, was never again to be used; and the people (who had collected the ashes), conveyed to the opposite side, had the penalty of death attached to their return.

Part of these extraordinary funeral rites are alluded to in an inscription cut on a rock at Polannarrua, of the date A.D. 1200, thus: "After the demise of Nissankha-malla, who formerly reigned in Ceylon, and subsequent to the immersion (of the ashes) of a number of Kings who succeeded him, and had, like so many diminutive stars, twinkled after the sun had gone down," &c.

In the legends regarding Lakagalla, we pass from the era of Ramachandra, and the wars of Rawana, to the time of Vijeya, a Hindu conqueror, who landed B.C. 543, and afterwards established his power over the various tribes which then occupied the country. It was at the marriage festivities of a chief of Lakagalla that Vijeya surprised and massacred a multitude of Yakkas, and thus secured that ascendency in Lanka which enabled him to found a dynasty whose patronymic became the name of the island, and, after enduring through twenty-three centuries, only fell before the British power in A.D. 1815, when the last of one hundred and sixty-five Cingalese Kings passed from the Kandian throne to a British prison.

From Mátalé to Narrangamma, by the way we

had come, was nearly double the distance of a jungle-path leading over the range of mountains which we had doubled by passing round its extremity at the Ambanganga. I had directed a large body of people to make this short line passable for a horse, and to clear the jungle on each side; as afterwards, by this route, the inhabitants of Lagalla might reach the court-house in half the time that the journey now occupied. Departing for Puackpitia, we passed at a considerable elevation across successive ridges of hills, in most places free of jungle: the higher parts of these open grounds were covered with illuk and common lemon-grass, herbage too coarse for the pasture of any animals except buffaloes, but useful for thatching houses or forming temporary huts.

The lower slopes produced, in immense quantities, the finest grass I had seen in the island; this it is which has rendered proverbial amongst Kandians the milk of Lagalla and the fatness of its cattle. The people of the neighbouring districts profit by its rich grazing grounds, and drive bullocks and buffaloes in thousands (when their services in cultivation, or as beasts of burthen, can be spared) to fatten in these luxuriant pastures: neither can the proprietors prevent this intrusion, as by Kandian custom all pasturage is common, unless fenced in by the proprietor; that is to say, he has the right of property, but, when left unenclosed, cannot obtain compensation for a trespass.

In the wooded valleys that intervene between the successive ridges over which we crossed, cinnamon-bushes were abundant; and a few trees of this spice were pointed out with stems about eighteen inches in diameter, and of height proportioned to their size. The barks of these large trees had a strong flavour, but when chewed felt coarse and gritty.

We halted during the heat of the day on the brow of a hill, beneath a clump formed of a shady peepul and fragrant champaka, from whence we looked back to the pointed peaks of Lakagalla and the country beneath it, now fast fading in distance; all the lower landscape being rendered more indistinct by our elevated position, and the quivering of the heated air that played on the sunny space around us.

The trees of Buddha form one of the most beautiful characteristics, and one most commonly met with in travelling through the Kandian country; they are generally of great age, and guarded from injury by superstition: their huge trunks, caverned by time, seem appropriate emblems of an ancient worship. Two or three terraces, built up with stone and filled with earth, surround the sacred bo-tree; contiguous to which, and often coetaneous, the sapu (champaka) entwines its branches amongst the boughs of the peepul. On every side of these terraces are raised rough miniature temples of stone, about two feet in height, including the little cupolas with which they are surmounted. It is scarcely possible to imagine a more pleasing or innocent picture of simple religion, than pilgrims, passengers, and particularly family groups of all ages, even little children, offering their handfuls of flowers. Neither is there any difficulty in procuring these, the purest material offerings by which man attempts to propitiate superior power; for here the champaka sheds its scented flowers, bunches of gay marigold or glittering chrysanthemum gild the terraces, and delicate jessamines and delicious white roses twine around or straggle through the stiff awaria,* completing the appropriate decorations of these rude altars and sylvan memorials of a religion of peace.

The blue haze, that in a cold climate softens the distant landscape only, in the noon of a tropical country spreads over every part of the scene, blending its beauties with a dreamy and enchanting softness. In the present instance these beauties were enhanced by the "ethereal mildness" arising from the elevated situation of the place, and ample shade of the trees under which we rested; whilst the blue hills, and smell of rich meadow-grass,

* Plumeria.

served to recall impressions and views, certainly less beautiful, but still distinct to memory, although in a country long since left, and then far distant.

We stopped for the night at Puackpitia, a village built on both sides of a rapid stream that dashes through a narrow cultivated valley overshadowed by the steep Batandua mountain and its sombre forests. Through these, next morning we ascended to the top of the pass, our horses scrambling after us without much difficulty, on a good foot-path which was afterwards much more generally used than the previous buffalo-track in the same direction. Several times on our way we passed polongas and other poisonous snakes dangling by the neck from a branch near the road; these reptiles had been killed by the labourers employed in widening the path: and, in descending on the Matale side, I narrowly escaped running against a most disgusting insect that had been gibbeted in the narrow path. It was a tarantula of most uncommon size, with feet almost as large and not unlike fingers, which, as well as the whole of its body, were covered with long, straight, brown hair. This custom amongst Kandians, of hanging up venomous reptiles after they are killed, (a fate and indignity never practised on the hooded snake,) is general, and may perhaps be a remnant of the nága (hooded snake) worship. The natives imagine the naga to be of an amiable disposition as regards mankind, and consequently to be at enmity with polongas and other venomous serpents that war against the heels of unwary men. Whatever may have been the origin of the custom, when a Kandian kills a venomous reptile (a hooded snake they will not in any way destroy), he either hangs it up to the bough of a tree, or, if there is a fire at hand, consigns it to the flames; thus making sure that the creature will not revive, and preventing the possibility of passengers trampling on the fangs while the poison is still active.

A few days before starting from Mátalé, I had an opportunity of seeing a mungoose (ichneumon) attacking a large hooded snake; it occurred in my garden: and, when I reached the spot, the little animal was fiercely assailing a large snake, that, with distended hood and elevated head, seemed anxious to escape, yet was obliged to face its active enemy. I did not see the conclusion of the feud, as the combatants disappeared amongst rank grass near which they were fighting. These encounters are not uncommon; but I could not ascertain if the mungoose was equally inveterate against polongas, and the other poisonous snakes, as it is against the nága: all the instances mentioned to me by natives, of mungoose and serpents fighting, related to the hooded snake, which, it appears, is never the assailant. Neither could I ascertain satisfactorily whether the little animal had an antidote (as by natives is generally believed), against the poison of its antagonist, in the mimosa octandra, the Cingalese name of which is nakulishta (desired of ichneumons).

Near the Batandua pass, an elephant, in attempting to reach the leaves of a bo-tree, a food of which they are remarkably fond, had tumbled headlong from a precipice; and, falling on his thick, straight, short tusks, had shivered them to the extremity of their sockets. The animal was killed by the shock; and a Kandian, who passed soon after, secured the shattered ivory, which he produced to me, and pointed out the rock from which the animal had fallen.

Nearly clear of the forests of Dankande, and already looking down on the Mátalé valley, we were congratulating ourselves that the horses had passed without accident: when we came to a narrow platform, supported along the face of a sloping rock, my pony passed without hesitation; but, in the middle, Mr. S——'s horse, feeling the spars bending, got frightened, started, and fell. Hearing the clattering of his hoofs as he rolled over and over, we expected to find the animal killed or disabled; but, on clearing a path obliquely down to the bottom of the rock, we perceived the horse quietly grazing and perfectly unhurt; so effectually had the thick brushwood, matted with creeping-plants, which spread over the lower part of the rock, broken the force of his rolling fall.

CHAPTER VI.

COLD PLAINS.—NUWARA ELLIA.

'Tis sweet to wander 'midst thy solitudes
Where the bright lamp of day hath early shone,
And hearken to the wild note that obtrudes
Upon the listening ear its plaintive tone.

W. GRANVILLE, ESQ.

Kondasála Road. — Taking of the last King of Kandy. — His Appearance. — Kondasála. — Captain Johnson. — View from the Dhiatalawa Mountain. — Hanguranketa. — Maturatta. — Halgaran-oya Plains. — Alut-nuwara. — Gigantic Balsam.— Terraced Rice-fields. — Murder of Mr. Kennedy. — Kewlygeddra. — Kandian Houses. — Badoolla. — Temples. —Himbleatwelle. — Primitive Method of Ladies' Travelling.— Oomaoya. — Fort M'Donald. —Accident, and extraordinary Wound. —Legends. — European Vegetables. — Seeta Talawa.—Seeta Koonda.—Nuwara-ellia Convalescent Station.—Cool Climate. —Pedrotalla-galla.—Lightning. —Donna Catherina, Queen of Kandy. — Gampola.

IN the beginning of January 1833 I proceeded to visit the elevated portion of the island, famous in the Ramayana and the most ancient Hindu legends by the appellation of the Asoka Aramiya.

Part of this land of romance had lately excited a more lively interest in the European population, from the establishment of a Convalescent Station, where, close to the equator, the temperate climate of extra-tropical countries might in all seasons be enjoyed.

In leaving Kandy by the Kondasála road, the varied scenery affords many beautiful views of the course of the Mahawelli-ganga, and over the green hills, to the mountain ranges of Dombara and Mátalé: these, sweeping round, confine the view down the river, and form a lofty barrier to the heated plains of Beentenne. It was to these mountains the last King of Kandy fled, on the invasion of his country and the occupation of his capital by the British forces in 1815: deserted by his followers, he could offer no resistance to advancing enemies; and, as he was universally detested, his retreat was soon betrayed, and his person secured, near the village of Meddamahanuwara.

The party that seized the King was composed of natives from Saffragam, under the orders of Eknellegodda, a friend of Eheylapola: nor were the unheard-of cruelties practised on that chief's family the only incentive to perseverance on the part of the people of the Saffragam district; they had their own sufferings to revenge, and their leader had ventured too far to indulge any hopes of safety, unless the downfall or death of the tyrant should be accomplished. If the King should regain authority and secure his person, Eknellegodda must have felt certain that he would have been added to the list of forty-seven headmen, many of them friends of his own, who in the previous year had been brought from Saffragam, and were impaled at Kandy by the tyrant's order. Driven by torrents of rain from a hut prepared for him in the forest on the face of the mountain, the King had descended to a native house in which he was discovered by the party in search of him. Their abrupt and unceremonious entry—the first time for fifteen years, since he became King, that he had been approached without awe and servile humility—for a moment seemed to confound him; but, as the party pressed forward, he suddenly assumed a dignified demeanour, waved them off, and dared them to touch "their King!" There was a check for an instant; but the chief urged on his followers, and the order to "seize him" was obeyed by a low-caste man, afterwards a servant in the Saman temple of Saffragam.

The following is the description of this King, Wikreme-raja Singha, given to me by a Malay officer who had been taken prisoner when Major Davie surrendered, and was afterwards compelled to accompany the King in the following year, 1804, when he proceeded towards Colombo and attacked Hangwellé.

The King had a light copper-coloured complexion, regular features, a handsome beard, broad shoulders, and a very full chest; he walked very slowly, carried himself particularly erect, and caused even the principal chiefs who approached, or had occasion to pass at whatever distance before him, to assume a crouching attitude. My informant, however, vouched for the King's cowardice in the affair at Hangwellé, and his subsequent cruelty during a rapid flight. I believe I have given the ideas, although not the words, of my informant faithfully, as I find in my memorandum of his conversation the concluding paragraph to be, "When he walk, he go slow slow, and stoop-e backward: the Adikars he make go so (stooping until his hands touched the ground), most like the cat."

Four miles from Kandy, on the opposite bank of the river, are the remains of the palace of Kondasála, the residence of Sree Weera Prákrama Narendra Singha, the last King of the Cingalese royal race. Dying without issue in 1739, the family became extinct; and a brother-in-law of the deceased monarch, a Prince of Madura, was chosen as his successor, and ascended the throne by the name of Sree Wijeya Raja Singha.

The buildings at Kondasála were burnt by the

detachment of troops under the command of Captain Johnson, when, in 1804, that officer by his gallantry and conduct relieved himself from the imminent perils in which he had become involved by the neglect or mismanagement of others. Deprived of that co-operation and assistance which he had been led to expect, and without which no rational hopes of his success, or even of his safety, could then have been entertained, he marched a small and unsupported detachment from Batticaloe, traversed the Kandian country, took possession of its capital, crossed the Mahawelli-ganga twice, recrossed it at the place where Major Davie had surrendered his troops to be massacred after abandoning an ally to be murdered, then fought his way down the Aetgalla pass through the forests of Mátalé, and finally, after encountering and overcoming every species of hardship, conducted his victorious party to Trinkomalee.

Beyond Kondasála, the path continues near the bank of the Mahawelli-ganga, whose waters may be heard dashing amongst the rocks, and echoed by the woods through which the road passes for several miles before reaching the Maha-oya. After passing this stream, there is an ascent of three miles to the rest-house of Gonagamma, fifteen miles from Kandy. At this place I left the main road to Badulla, and struck off towards Hanguranketa, over a ridge of the Dhiatalawa mountain, from whence there is an extensive view over Walapané and Dombara, districts only separated by the Mahawelli-ganga, which is seen for a considerable distance, foaming and rushing through forests, in a succession of rapids, down to the plains of Beentenne.

Hanguranketa possesses two temples; one dedicated to Vishnu, the other to the goddess Patine: they are of mean construction and in bad repair, but serve to remind the passenger that this place was a royal residence in the eighteenth century. The palace was accidentally destroyed in the rebellion of 1818; even its foundations cannot now be traced. It was a paltry building; but the following inscription, copied from a stone in the vicinity, shows that its royal architect had no deficiency of lofty epithets.*

"Be it known that this is the patent whereby the victorious King (who kept his court in the city of) Sangaruanketa, of illustrious and royal lineage, and effulgent with prosperity, did, whilst abiding at this place, dedicate lands in the Wanny district unto the sacred bo-tree, on this day, being Thursday the 10th day of the increasing moon, in the month Wesack, of the 1646th † year of the glorious era of Saka."

* The King was Sree Weera Prákrama Narendra Singha.

† A.D. 1724.

From Hanguranketa the rugged track, miscalled a road, winds over stones, along watercourses, and through swamps; then crosses a mountain torrent, the Bilhool-oya; after which for two miles there is a steep ascent to Maturatta, a military post, the commandant of which had civil jurisdiction over the surrounding districts. Untenable as a military position against an intelligent enemy, this station appeared to be only commendable for its cool climate. Next morning, leaving Maturatta, I ascended to the Halgaran-oya plains, about four thousand feet above the level of the sea. When I reached them, the mist prevented me from seeing to advantage the famed beauty of the scenery; and the cold wind and heavy rain determined my speedy departure from this uninhabited region: so I turned to the left through the Bingulan Taláwe,* and descended by a precipitous path to the valley and village of Alut-nuwara.

In a forest through which I passed, my attention was particularly attracted by a gigantic balsam with flowers of pure white streaked with scarlet: this plant was called by the natives maha puddaloo-mal.

Alut-nuwara derives its appellation of nuwara (city) from having been the place of refuge of a fugitive King: when pressed by powerful enemies,

* Taláwe, an elevated and open space.

Cingalese monarchs were accustomed to seek shelter on the mountains, or in the secluded valleys of this district; and the places where they resided have in many instances retained the addition of nuwara to their names, although they may never have had a royal residence more permanent than a leaf-hut. Kolagalla-nuwara, on the banks of the Bilhool-oya below Maturatta, is one of these stations; and on the other side, in a deep valley beneath the lofty Pedratalla mountain, a small hamlet bears the poetic yet correctly descriptive name of Mandara-nuwara, the city of shadow.

Near Alut-nuwara the Halgaran-oya descends in cascades; and, with several smaller mountain streams, supplies water to the numerous rice-fields into which the valleys, small hills, and declivities of the mountains have been formed. The gorge of the Halgaran-oya valley, facing the Dombara mountains, opens from Alut-nuwara between the Yakkagalla (devil's rock) and a wooded precipice, on the verge and summit of which stands the Buddhist temple of Waterangodda; beneath, the entire slope is niched into rice-fields laid out in terraces, many of them not more than three feet in breadth, and looking like the seats of this mountain amphitheatre.

From Alut-nuwara, where I stopped a night, my way lay over a mountain ridge covered with grass; and, before reaching Madoolla, the spot was pointed out to me, near a large bo-tree, where Mr. Kennedy was murdered by a party of Kandians in the rebellion of 1817. This officer, who belonged to the medical staff, and the small military party (Caffres I believe) that accompanied him, found themselves beset at this place by a host of rebels, who kept up a fire of match-locks from behind trees and stone walls. While their enemies were still at a distance and concealed, the military party were lavish of their ammunition, without producing any effect; but, as their fire slackened, the Kandians gradually approached, and when the last of the cartridges of the unfortunate party were expended, and several lay dead or disabled, the rebels closed upon the remainder and completed their destruction. To one of the leaders, Kewlygeddra Mohattal, Mr. Kennedy surrendered his sword; and the savage, seizing it by the handle, stabbed him to the heart. Kewlygeddra was an inferior headman, lame, and of a ferocious disposition, who had escaped from the gaol of Kandy, in which he was confined, charged with the murder of a native: he was one of the first who rushed into open acts of treason; and having considerable influence over the people, from the terror inspired by his vindictive character, he continued to be one of the most persevering of the rebel leaders.

When he was at last secured and placed upon his trial, he pleaded, in mitigation of the crimes charged against him, that he had complied with the British officer's, Mr. Kennedy's, last request, (which he seemed to think somewhat capricious and inexplicable,) viz. that of being put to death by his own sword. Kewlygeddra said he discovered the wish of the officer by his delivering the handle of the sword, while he held the point turned towards himself. This defence did not avail, for sentence of death and immediate execution were the reward of crimes which had rendered this miscreant equally obnoxious to the British Government and his own fellow-countrymen.

I ascertained the site of the ancient station of Madoolla by straight fields still retaining the name of streets; as tomtom-beater's street, potter's street, &c. From this place, passing over a ridge of hills, I entered Gampaha, a small district which forms part of the romantic valley of the Ooma-oya, and there was comfortably lodged in the house of Dimbulané Dessauve. Kandian chiefs' houses of the Cingalese time were all built on the same plan; and consisted of one or more squares of houses, with doors from each chamber opening into the inner courts. There was but one exterior door; and, until natives began to follow European models, the windows were too small to admit a person's head. Without the King's permission a chief could not have windows, use whitewash, nor tile his house.

From Gampaha to Badoolla the path lies through an open grazing country, crosses by a bad ford the rapid stream of the Ooma-oya near Toopetty, then ascends for several miles, and, passing along the side of the Narrangalla mountain, offers, before commencing an abrupt descent, a view over the whole valley of Badoolla. It appears, except at one narrow outlet, entirely surrounded by hills; and the mountain of Namina Koole rises from its farthest limit at least four thousand feet above the plain, and six thousand seven hundred above the sea. The valley of Badoolla, intersected by numerous canals from the mountain streams, is formed into rice-fields, with the exception of a few elevated spots, which, tufted with cocoa-nut trees, looked like islands of palms in a sea of verdure: the largest of these is occupied by the fort and village. The fort is insignificant both in extent and strength; and was originally a royal residence when Ouva, for a short period in the early part of the seventeenth century, existed as a separate kingdom under Kumara Singha. At Badoolla there is a temple of Katragamma-deyo; also a wihare and dágoba, built by Makalan-Detoo-Tissa in the third century of the Christian era: this dágoba undergoing a thorough repair, is the only instance I recollect in Ceylon of effectual measures taken to prevent the decay of an ancient religious monument of Buddha.

The road from Badoolla to Upper Ouva is carried over steep hills, and leads past the military post of Himbleatwellé, situated on the summit of a bleak hill four thousand feet above the level of the sea. The view from this station is very extensive; the nearest features of the scenery being the innumerable green hills of Ouva, with here and there a copse in the sheltered recesses, extensive plains dotted with stunted trees, the bottom of steep and very narrow valleys terraced into rice-grounds; and, except in the direction of Veddaratte, over which the eye wandered until the outline of objects faded in distance, the scene had a continued boundary of mountains.

In this district, where the face of the country is so uneven, and the paths in general extremely steep, native ladies of rank, while travelling on visits of ceremony, formerly rode *à la fourchette* on the neck of a slave. Whether the progress of "reform," and the improvement of roads, have caused this primitive method of conveyance to fall into disuse I cannot take upon me to say.

The extent of pasture land in Ouva is very great, and the number of cattle by no means proportioned to the extent; this is partly owing to the great number destroyed during the rebellion: but bleak winds and a scorching sun causing a scarcity of pasture in dry seasons, is probably the principal objection to Ouva as a grazing district. Between Himbleatwellé and Fort M'Donald I re-crossed the Ooma-oya, and perceived that the stream had the same impetuous character, and that its banks preserved the same wild and rugged scenery as had attracted my attention in its downward course through Gampaha.

Fort M'Donald, the military post at the village of Parnagamma, was named after Major M'Donald of the 19th Regiment, who performed arduous services in this part of the country during the rebellion of 1817 and 1818, with much credit both for decision when courage was required, and for humanity to the deluded natives when resistance was at an end. One of the officers who was with Major M'Donald, when with a small party he maintained his position (on the hillock where the fort now is) against seven or eight thousand Kandians, was Lieutenant Fretz, who was afterwards commandant of the place, and there met with an accident, which (although at the time I speak of, 1833, five years after the occurrence, it had not injured his health) eventually caused his death in 1836. Whilst shooting at an elephant, the gun burst; and the end of the barrel, with a long screw-nail across, was driven into his forehead: notwithstanding the complete destruction of the musket, the elephant was severely wounded. This lump of metal could not be (at least was not) removed; and Mr. Fretz continued, after a partial recovery, to do his duty, although a large place, over which he wore a patch, always remained open between his eyebrows. After his death it was ascertained that the upper part of this lump of metal (which weighed two ounces and three quarters) had destroyed part of the skull behind the left eye, and that the place was filled up by a strong membrane: the lower end of the iron projected through the palate, and rested on the tongue; the screw-nail was across the bone of the nose. Notwithstanding these severe injuries, and the warm climate, his health seemed little impaired; his eye-sight was not affected; and his last illness, inflammation of the brain, lasted but three days.

One of the plains of Upper Ouva that extends towards the base of the higher mountains is Nuga Talawa (banyan-tree plain), and a portion of it retains the name of Malegawa-tenne (the palace-flat): here a peepul, known by the name of the Deewuran-gaha (tree of the oath), grows from a corner in the lowest of three terraces which are surrounded with stone walls. This position, as well as the age of the present tree, shows that it only marks the spot of some sylvan memorial that existed in the olden time; probably a nuga (banyan) which gave the name to this plain. On a broken pillar lying beneath the tree there is carved an inscription in the ancient Cingalese character, but so much defaced that I was unable in my short visit to transcribe any part of it. The palace-flat is now a rice-field watered by a stream, which, after being conducted for several miles along the summit of a projecting ridge of hills, is allowed to rush down the rocky side of Balella Kanda, and then meanders round the green knolls towards the Malegawa-tenne. Tradition states that the formation of this watercourse was directed by Rawana; that on this plain he had a palace, to which Seeta was conducted after his death and her release; and the tree is said to mark the spot where the goddess offered a solemn oath, that during her captivity she had preserved inviolate her fidelity to Rama (Vishnu).

The tract of open ground in this vicinity is now generally known as the Wilson plains, from the name of the present commander of the forces, Sir John Wilson, K.C.B., which was given to a subscription bungaloe built on the verge of the plain, near where Rawana's canal dashes from the rocks of Balella Kanda.

It was at Fort M'Donald, and in this neighbourhood, that potatoes were first successfully cultivated to any extent in Ceylon, so as to supply the market, as is now done (since 1830), at a moderate price; and, although at Nuwara-ellia they grow still larger and finer, it is from Upper Ouva that the general supply is obtained. They will grow at a much lower elevation, but are then inferior in size and flavour. Not only potatoes, but most European vegetables, are now general in every good garden in the interior of the Kandian country; but the seed requires to be continually renewed from England, or the Cape of Good Hope. By attending to this point, a resident European might with little trouble raise peas, many kinds of beans, lettuce, radishes, cress, (the common kind grows wild,) beetroot, parsley, celery, carrots, turnips, onions, and cabbages.

Having ascended the wooded range, and skirted the rocks of Hakgalla, we were within the precincts of the pleasure-grounds of Rawana:* this is a region varying from five to seven thousand feet above the level of the sea, and is included within the steep ranges of mountains, in ancient

* Nandanodiyana (pleasure-grounds), and Asoka-aramaya (asoka-groves), are the Hindu names of this elevated region; and sanctified to Hindu pilgrims by the events of the Ramayan, and the traditions of Rama and Seeta, which are still preserved by the Brahmins of Katragamma.

legends called the walls of Rawana's garden; these extend from Adam's Peak to Hakgalla, and from Pedro-talla-galla to Gallegamma Kandé. After passing through a swampy jungle, in which I remarked fern-trees of thirty feet in height, and turning round the northern end of Hakgalla mountain, we reached an open valley fringed with barberry-bushes, and diversified by groups and single trees of the superb rhododendron arboreum: the dell was surrounded by hoary forests, whose rich but sombre colouring was unable to counteract that sullen gloom which shade and silence threw over the scene between Hakgalla and the massive Pedro. This is the Seeta Talawa (plain of Seeta), where it is believed the goddess was concealed together with Trisida, the niece of Rawana, who was her sole companion. Hanuman, eluding the vigilance of the guards, contrived to penetrate to their bower; and having delivered to Seeta the ring of Rama, with assurances that her release would be accomplished, he proceeded to set fire to the neighbouring forests. It was this conflagration which cleared Nuwara-ellia, and other plains in this region of genii; and as they now are,—that is, barren of useful productions,—Vishnu has doomed them for ever to remain. Thus speak the legends, Hindu and Cingalese; and it is probable their credit may long remain unrefuted by extensive cultivation. A stubborn soil, deficient of limestone,* covered with grass so coarse as to be unfit for pasture, would render these lands more difficult to improve, and less likely to yield a fair return to European agriculturists, than hundreds of thousands of acres still lying waste in Great Britain. The cold climate and requisite exertions would alike deter natives from attempting improvements here, even if they possessed the requisite capital and agricultural instruments.

A basin where the Seeta-ella bursts from under the rock, after an underground course of fifty yards, is called the Seeta Koonda: here, round holes formed by the eddying stream are pointed out as the marks of the feet of the elephant ridden by Rawana, when Seeta† vanished and re-appeared,

* Limestone is found about fifteen hundred feet below the level of Nuwara-ellia, at no great distance, in a straight line.

† Cingalese traditions mention the route by which Seeta, accompanied by the young Trisida, was removed from Rawana's fort of Sri Lankapoora (which existed far to the westward of the present island, and was afterwards submerged) to the forests where it was intended to detain her in concealment. The places mentioned in her journey still retain nearly the same names; yet, as her route passed twice near Anurádhapoora without its being mentioned, we may conjecture that the tradition is of a prior date to the foundation of that ancient city, B.C. 500.

Route of Seeta:—from Lankapoora, Manar, Trinkomalee, Parawaha forest (in Nuwarakalawia), Naya-coombura, Nalandé, Wahakotta, Gongawelle, Yattawarra-ella, Malgamadennia, Kat-

where the stream now does, in her exertions to escape from the persecution of the demon King.

Ascending from the Seeta Talawa, and passing through a broad belt of jungle, I reached the plain of Nuwara-ellia; a clear space, about eight miles in circumference, covered with coarse grass, having an uneven surface bounded by forests, and overshadowed by Pedro-talla-galla. Many small rills, and the water from numberless springs, trickle through the tufted vegetation that covers the soft, black, mossy soil of this place; and a large stream, after descending in cataracts from the mountain, winds and doubles along the level bottom of the largest plain, its tortuous course being marked by scattered rhododendron trees.

Nuwara-ellia, established by Sir Edward Barnes in 1829 as a military convalescent station, has fully justified the sanguine expectations formed of its cool and salubrious climate, when first visited by Dr. Davy in 1819. The following account is extracted from the Colombo Journal:*

"Perhaps there is in no country a climate more congenial to the natives of Great Britain, both as

tugastotte, Hallolua, Payangomua, Udelagundennia, Kattu-Keetule-kaely, Atbagé-oya, Kattudahinna, Nidankotu-ella, Pusellawe, Aggahakaely, Rawanidala-ella, Máwéla, Garinde-ella, Punawa-ella, Dimbula, Seeta Koonda.

* An extract from a letter signed M.D., written and published in 1832.

regards salubrity and comfort, than Nuwara-ellia; the temperature of the air never approaching to what is called tropical heat: and though the cold is so great as to produce ice, still that piercing wind so frequently complained of in England, and so productive of pulmonary complaints, is never felt. The utmost range of the thermometer for the last year (1831) did not exceed 73°, and this acme occurred only once; it has been thirty-three times between this and 69°: 38°, 40°, and 42° are common temperatures at night in the months of January, February, and March; perhaps 65° might be stated as nearly the mean temperature by day, and 55° by night, for the entire year."

Besides a large and substantial country-house built by Sir Edward Barnes, and the military and other public buildings, many whitewashed cottages and smoking chimneys enlivened the scene, and interrupted the heavy outline of continuous jungles. Numerous pretty rides and paths have been formed around the plain, branching into different valleys; and one is conducted to the summit of the highest mountain in Ceylon, Pedro-talla-galla, which rises two thousand and seventy feet above the plain, and eight thousand two hundred and eighty feet above the sea.

Previous to a change of monsoon, scenes of fiery conflict in the sky are commonly perceived in all parts of Ceylon; but here, elevated amidst clouds, and mountains wooded to the summit, the effect, always sublime, is occasionally astounding, when lightnings crash through the aged forest, gleaming beneath your path in some deep valley, and quivering in its rippling stream. Within the tropics, lightning, if not more vivid, is far more varied than it appears in colder climes: it is not uncommon in the Kandian country, after a clear sultry day, to see the approach of evening heralded by "dark rolling clouds" piling themselves aloft, then spreading along the sky until the advancing masses flash their electric fires; sometimes, like fluttering pennants or heraldic scrolls, they waver before the dazzled sight; and frequently, as if escaping from a grasp, blaze for an instant, then scatter through the heavens, like the thunderbolts of Jove as depicted by the ancients.

Nuwara-ellia was a temporary residence of the Queen Donna Catherina, when, amongst the varied scenes of an eventful life, she was driven from her capital by the Portuguese after her second marriage, A.D. 1628. Donna Catherina was the daughter of the Cingalese Prince Weera Bahu, who for a short time had maintained independent authority at Kandy, but from which he was driven by a more powerful competitor. His daughter was educated as a Christian by the Portuguese at Manar;

afterwards they proclaimed her Queen of Kandy, and proceeded to enforce her asserted rights, with the intention of promoting their own interest, and revenging themselves on Wimala Dharma. He had been their ally, but was far too able and ambitious to continue as the instrument or become the dupe of their crooked policy; he therefore proclaimed himself King, and maintained his independence despite the secret intrigues and open hostilities of his enemies. He defeated the adherents of Donna Catherina, although supported by the Portuguese army; and married his rival (then twelve years of age), who remained a prisoner in his hands. By her he had two sons, who survived, but did not succeed to the crown of their father; for, on his death, Donna Catherina married his brother Senaratna, who quietly ascended the throne, and, dying several years after, left the country divided between his own son by Donna Catherina, and her two sons by his brother Wimala Dharma.* Her first husband had been educated as a Christian; her second was a Buddhist priest, until he saw that the yellow robe was the only impediment to his becoming a King. The Portuguese assert that Donna Catherina died a Christian (which may be true), and repented

* More particulars of Wimala Dharma will be found under the head of Portuguese history.

of her heathen alliance: this may be doubted, as the conduct of the Portuguese rulers was certainly less honest, and their policy less successful, than that of her royal husbands, who are believed to have owed much of their prosperity to her abilities and advice. She was beloved by her husbands; and the Portuguese have nothing to allege against her character, unless it be apostacy from their religion, which, to judge from their conduct, had little of Christianity except the name.

In 1827, a road being traced from Nuwara-ellia to Kandy, it was soon afterwards made passable for horses: by it I descended a stage of fifteen miles, through an unbroken forest, and with a descent of three thousand feet to Ramboda. This village and rest-house are beautifully situated on the steep slope of a mountain between the two waterfalls of the Puna-ella and Garindé-ella, two streams whose waters unite at a short distance off in the valley below the village: there are also several cascades which descend from the surrounding mountains, and add to the beauty of the scenery around Ramboda. From thence to Gampola is twenty-two miles, with an intermediate stage at Pusellawe; here the rest-house is situated near a forest, but in a country generally free of wood, and possessing a delightful climate. Gampola is a large village, near a well-watered and highly cultivated plain on the banks of the Mahawelli-ganga, which is navigable for boats from this place to Peradennia, a distance of nine miles, and only three from Kandy. Gampola is mentioned in Cingalese history as early as B.C. 502, when Suddhódana, a brother or cousin of the Queen who then reigned, and who had accompanied her from Kimbulwatte-nuwara,* settled at this place. About two hundred years later, Uttiya, the brother of Kellania-Tissa fled to Gampola, when his intercourse with the Queen was detected at Kellania. In A.D. 1347, it became the capital of the island under Bhuwaneka-Bahoo the Fourth, and continued so for fifty years; it was then dignified with the state name of Gangasripoora (the royal city on the river). A few carved stones are the only remains of a royal residence whose very foundations are now obliterated. Crossing the Mahawelli-ganga by a ferry at Gampola, and re-crossing it at Peradennia, seemed an unnecessary and inexplicable arrangement: altogether the distance from Nuwara-ellia to Kandy is fifty-two miles by this path.

* Kapila-wasta-poora in Maghada.

CHAPTER VII.

HORTON PLAINS.

Ay, this is solitude! no life is here!
The black woods frown on me, as if I were
The first who dared disturb their solemn stillness.
READE. *The Deluge.*

* * * The unwieldy elephant,
To make them mirth, used all his might, and wreathed
His lithe proboscis.—MILTON.

Elephants at Gampola. — Burning Lemon-grass on the Mountains. — Nuwara-ellia Road. — Leopards. — A Tawalan alarmed. — Gems. — Iron. — Native Steel. — Man shot for a Monkey. — Path to Totapela. — Horton Plains. — Solitude. — An Echo. — The Governor visits Horton Plains — is received there by the principal Native Chief. — Cold Night. — Morning at the Horton Plains.—Elk-hunting.—Sources of the Mahawelli-ganga and Walawe Rivers.— Elephants bear great change of Climate. — Bilhool-oya. — Descent towards Gallegamma.— Scenery. — Gallegamma. — Ornamented Bungaloe. — Wallawe River. — First Adikar's House. — Mahawellitenne Adikar. — Return to Gallegamma. — Ascent of the Gallegamma Pass. — Horse killed. — Natives at the Cold Plains. — The Gaura.

ON one occasion, whilst proceeding to Nuwara-ellia, which I visited almost every year after it was established, I was accompanying a lady on horseback, and following a palanquin in which were two children, when we entered Gampola, thirteen miles from Kandy. I was surprised at seeing so few people in the village, and those evidently moving in great haste; but the cause of the unusual calls which we heard on approaching the place, and various unwonted signs of energy amongst the people, were explained before we had reached the middle of the village, when a shot, fired from a tree in a garden near us, was followed by a continued shouting in the same direction. Amidst the tumult I could understand that "the elephants" were moving off towards the hill of Ambulawe; a piece of information I was particularly glad to hear, not having any guns with me at the time, and being equally ignorant of the number and position of these intruders. The coolies carrying the palanquin, being Kandians of Mátalé, were but little alarmed, although they soon perceived the cause of excitement amongst the Gampola community, and merely quickened their pace to the rest-house. On reaching this place, we found that a herd of elephants had come into the gardens of the village; and after maintaining their position for a great part of the day, until one of their number was killed, and all of them wounded, they had only been finally dislodged at the time we were passing through the village.

At night, the mountain of Ambulawe, over Gampola, presented a brilliant and interesting sight; dotted lines of ruddy flame were raging along its whole extent, consuming the coarse vegetation with which it was overgrown, and casting back a lurid light on the blackened and smouldering surface over which the fire had passed. Lemon-grass is the general covering of such parts of the hills (in this division of the country) as are not overgrown with jungle: although apparently with an even surface about seven or eight feet in height, this grass grows in tufts; and it is this peculiarity that gives to the conflagrations here that dotted appearance which is their remarkable characteristic. The burning proceeds rapidly against the wind, as it bends the long grass over the flames, in which it is immediately withered and scorched; then bursts forth in a blaze, succeeded by showers of sparks and clouds of half-illumined smoke. In this manner the fire extends itself, a loud crackling noise being distinguished by any one who is near, and a hollow roaring sound being heard by those at a greater distance, until the progress of the conflagration is arrested by dark woods that occupy every deep ravine. The roots of the grass are not destroyed by the raging flames that pass over the land; and, after two or three days' rain, the blackened bushes and calcined earth are hid by herbage of the most brilliant green; and in that state, young and tender, even lemon-grass affords good pasture to buffaloes. The strong flavour of lemon given out by this plant when bruised, although pleasant for a short time, becomes, if one is long exposed to its effects, particularly tiresome and oppressive.

In the last visit I made to Nuwara-ellia, in 1836, I found the cart-road nearly completed and already passable: this was a great undertaking if we consider the distance, fifty miles, and the elevation above Kandy of full four thousand five hundred feet; also the precipitous and rocky nature of the country, where the bridges were so liable to accidents from the sudden floods of mountain-torrents, and the roads to damage from avalanches of earth and stones displaced in the rainy season.

The country around Nuwara-ellia is much infested with leopards; and so fond are these animals of preying on dogs, that they have been known (although in general afraid of man) to seize a dog running on the road immediately before his master, and then dash back into the jungle. It is a remarkable fact, that a panic is produced amongst cattle by merely the smell of a leopard. I first perceived an instance of this near my own house, when one morning the cattle-keeper was driving out the cows to a pasture-field: on coming to a bush that grew on the road-side, they suddenly began to snort, then turned round, and rushed past the keeper back to their pin-fold, around which they assembled in evident alarm. The Kandians immediately pointed to the marks of a leopard which had rested at the back of the bush; and, as it was near the house, had removed when daylight had aroused the people. Returning from the plains on the Ouva side of Nuwara-ellia, I was witness to a ludicrous scene arising from the same cause, when the whole cattle of a large tawalan (drove of baggage-bullocks) took fright at the place where a leopard had been lying. Round they all turned, as if by signal; and off they all started, kicking and plunging, down a steep slope: the confused jingling of bullock-bells, shouting of drivers, and jostling of animals, continued until some of the bullocks and all the rice-bags were cast upon the ground. The loads, however, were so attached to the animals, that, although easily dislodged from the back, a rope connected them with the horns of the bullock; so, in less than two minutes, the sloping glade was covered with cattle riding at anchor, with their heads fast to the rice-bags, and their heels flourishing in the air. I have heard it asserted, that the kotia (Ceylon leopard), although generally agreeing with the description of the leopard more than that of the panther, has some peculiarities not found in either of these quadrupeds; amongst others, that it cannot entirely retract its claws into their sheath.

In many of the swampy bottoms about Nuwara-ellia are numerous pits which were dug by those people who were searching for gems: an unprofitable pursuit, that was eagerly engaged in so long as it was a monopoly in the hands of a Government renter, but which has been nearly abandoned since the search for precious stones was unrestricted. In 1819, Dr. Davy anticipated this result: he says, "There is good reason to believe that the individuals engaged in this pursuit, who are not very numerous and chiefly Moormen, would be better employed in cultivating the ground that they ransack."

Iron is found of good quality in the plain of Nuwara-ellia, and is smelted by the natives in temporary furnaces, with a general simplicity of apparatus that is quite astonishing. A pair of double bellows formed of bullocks' hides, with wooden pipes, blowing into a clay furnace about the size of an ordinary boiler, seemed all that was necessary. In Oodegodde of Mátalé, the natives prepare steel by enclosing a small piece of iron, surrounded by wedges of the wood of a particular shrub, in a cylinder of clay, which is then placed in a furnace for a sufficient length of time: the case, when removed from the fire, appears vitrified, is about a foot in length, and an inch and a half in diàmeter; the bit of steel is little larger than a man's finger.

At Nuwara-ellia, and scattered over the colder parts of the island, but not in great numbers, is a species of very large monkey of a dark colour: some of those I saw were much bigger than the wandura; and one that passed some distance before me, when resting on all four feet, looked so like a Ceylon bear, that I was preparing my gun, when Jacko's agility in ascending a tree, and dashing through the jungle, saved him by undeceiving me. A short time before leaving Mátalé, I had to investigate a case (the second within my own knowledge) of a native killed by mistake for a monkey: the unfortunate young man had gone up a tree and was plucking its fruit, when a Moorman, who was shooting in the same jungle, seeing him, (but not distinctly, from the thickness of the foliage,) fired, and, on running up to secure the game, found his neighbour lying mortally wounded. After rendering every assistance to the dying man, the Moorman came and surrendered himself: the aged parents, whose only son it was that had been killed, admitted the absence of all malice on the part of the Moorman, but demanded compensation for their loss; and thus, according to common sense and ancient custom, was the matter arranged, so far as the parties were concerned.

From Nuwara-ellia I proceeded, in company with a friend, to examine the most elevated table-land in Ceylon, viz. the open plains extending between the Totapela range and the mountains which overhang Saffragam. This elevated region had received the name of Horton Plains, in honour of Sir R. Wilmot Horton the Governor, from Mr. Watson, 58th regiment, and Mr. Fisher, 78th regiment, who were the first Europeans that visited this tract of country. For the first seven miles our path lay through a close forest of low-sized trees with thick-set gnarled branches, the whole space between their stems being occupied by the ugly and unvarying nelu-plant: the next six miles we passed over an open undulating country with a soil like peat-moss, and covered with coarse grass; crossing in our way numerous small streams which are the sources of the Mahawelli-ganga. We then entered a damp hoary forest, where such was the dense shade of the trees, that the few rays of light that penetrated through the close foliage and moss-clad branches appeared unnaturally bright, and to descend with an intensity that, falling upon "the sear, the yellow leaf" of the broad fern, occasionally produced a gleam so brilliant as to make the surrounding jungle seem doubly gloomy. After a steep ascent for two miles, we emerged from the wood upon the Horton Plains. They appeared to extend for eight or ten miles; and were covered with coarse yellow grass, except in those places where the bright green of dwarf bamboos showed the course of the rills winding through the open space, which appeared radiant with light as contrasted with the sombre woods that encompassed the plain, or the dark thickets which are scattered on its surface and extend through its valleys. The mountains of Lunugalla and Suduhugalla, seven thousand eight hundred feet in height above the level of the sea, rise from this table-land, and serve to relieve the monotony of a forest-bound horizon. This tract was only visited by natives on hunting excursions, and was known to them as the Maha-ellia (the great common or clear space); a portion of it also went by the name of the Wilmantalawa. In these vast jungle solitudes, on every twig, round every tree, the "stilly" damp of ages has twined a mossy vesture: from its slender filaments on the young shoots, slight texture on the smaller branches, and heavy folds enveloping the parent-stem of forest patriarchs, we learn how time, undisturbed by tempest, has woven the solemn drapery of this silent region. In following up the green banks of a rill on the slope of the Totapela mountain, I called to my companion and proposed a change of direction:

he answered, "Very well." Instantly, as if these words had burst a magic spell, and broke "the cold chain of silence" which bound the demon spirits of the waste, the joyous sounds, "very well!" "very well!" "very well!" came hurrying forth from every copse and winding glade in these, the farthest bounds of Rawana's forest labyrinth. Its mouldering rocks, moss-clad forests, and solitary plains offered so few signs of animated nature, that the notes of a small bird were a relief from universal stillness; and the occasional rise of snipe was absolutely startling. The principal inhabitant of this wilderness is the elk, a shy and solitary animal, which soon detects the approach of an intruder, and shrinks from his presence into the thickest cover.

There are vestiges of man's exertions in the faint traces of the residence of fugitive princes, and a feeling of companionship in the name of Nuwara-ellia (city of the open plain); but here the very shadows of the clouds seemed to steal after each other slowly, silently, — I could almost fancy, at measured distances. As evening approached, the mists crept up the glens, spread noiselessly through the glades, then expanded over the forests, until darkness closed a day of universal stillness in this, the last domain of primeval nature in Ceylon. Solitude is insufficient to convey an idea of the feeling of loneliness inspired by this place during a solitary ramble which I commenced, but which I terminated abruptly on seeing the fog rolling up from the low country and obscuring the features of the scenery. I could almost have fancied myself the first or the last of created beings.

How different was the scene which I witnessed on the same ground a fortnight after, when I made one of the party that accompanied the Governor and Lady Horton, who were proceeding by this route to honour with a visit the first Adikar, the principal Kandian chief, Mahawellatenné-Dessauve. We had passed through the thick wood, and were still seven miles from the Horton Plains, when a storm of rain commenced, somewhat heavier as falling from somewhere higher than a shower-bath. The great drops, splintering against each other, formed that combination of Scotch-mist, English thunder-shower, and tropical water-spout, which, taken all together, more resembled a general waterfall than anything understood as rain, or which might be expected, as it did, to clear away and leave the surface of the earth unscathed and unscarred. The open ground was a succession of knolls; and the footpaths being of a slippery peat-mould, was the cause of some of the party falling, and shooting down this novel sort of *montagnes Russes*, assisted by cascades of muddy water, until they landed in the swampy bottoms of black moss that intervened between these abrupt hillocks. However, if the path was slippery, the ground was soft; and, as neither man nor horse suffered from their falls, the open ground was passed and the hill ascended without material interruption, although elephants' footmarks were visible in the forest footpath.

At the commencement of the plain, on the summit of a rising ground nearly as elevated as Adam's Peak (which is visible from thence through an opening in the mountains), stood a picturesque group, the followers bearing the numerous flags and other insignia of the first Adikar. The salutations of the headmen to the Governor being over, the plain resounded with the din of barbarous music and the loud cracks of the Adikar-whips; a weapon of distinction, and a right honourable noise, that were never allowed to herald chiefs of less degree.

Wet, cold, and weary, the whole party remounted, and, scampering over the plain, soon assembled round a blazing fire, which occupied a large space in the temporary bungaloe prepared by the Adikar for the Governor's reception. As might be supposed, at an elevation of seven thousand feet, the fire was not only agreeable, but absolutely necessary; for the slight materials of which the buildings were composed, viz. dry grass laid between upright branches, gave free ingress to the cool air; and those who had brought the largest supply of warm clothing might best congratulate themselves on their foresight.

In the morning, a shot, fired by one of the party near the bungaloe, was followed by a call for people to carry in an elk which had fallen. Now every one was on foot, and formed in various parties diverged across the plains; the air felt cool and exhilarating; the dew-drops sparkled on the leaves; the rays of a level sun glanced from the rock of Keereegalla; the smoke from the bivouacks curled above the thickets; the natives moved briskly; the birds sang blithely; "even the deep blue heavens looked glad;" and the same place, which a few days before appeared so still and melancholy, was now a scene of busy life and noisy merriment.

The snipe-shooting here, although the birds were not numerous, from their being spread over the plain, resembled that sport amongst Scotch or Irish moors; and the climate felt so cool, and the air so light, that walking was no exertion. The ferns, the buttercups, and many water-plants common to temperate climates, grew on the banks of the burns that wandered through the black peat-mosses; and gave a similarity of appearance, as well as identity of climate, that recalled visions of "mine own, my native land," to be interrupted by encountering a group of rhododendrons, or a party of half-clad Kandians.

A pack of dogs, stag-hounds and greyhounds, was kept at Nuwara-ellia for the purpose of hunting the elk, an animal which in appearance closely resembles the Scottish red-deer; but the music of the dogs and the bugle-horn, with the wildness of the scenery in many of the hunting-grounds, appeared to me to constitute the sole charms of the sport, for the chase was easily tired, soon took to water, and there remained at bay, making a feeble resistance, or putting "his last weak refuge in despair."

In front of the building on the Horton Plains, ran the several streams that form the Bilhool-oya, which, in a later part of its course through Saffragam, and along the flats of the Tangalle district, receives the name of the Walawé river; and, after a course of sixty miles, reaches but does not run into the sea at the south of the island, its mouth being completely stopped up by a sandbank. In rear of the bungaloe, the spring from which we were supplied with water flowed in a rill due north; and is probably the farthest source of the Mahawelli-ganga; which, from this spring until it enters the bay of Kotiar opposite to Trinkomalee, has a course of about two hundred miles, the last eighty of which may be again rendered navigable for boats, if the present appearance of improvement in the country should continue, so as to justify the necessary expense of the undertaking. At Beentenne, one hundred miles from the sea, the Mahawelli-ganga is five hundred and forty feet from bank to bank, with an average depth of five feet of water;* but below this there are considerable obstructions from rocky ridges and rapid channels near a village called Kalinga, and for the last thirty miles the river has nearly abandoned its ancient bed, and the great body of water now flows down a narrow channel called the Virgel, into the sea on the east coast.†

Over the whole of this elevated region of Mahaellia, the marks of elephants are as abundant as in other parts of the country; thus disproving the general impression that these animals are unfitted to endure any great vicissitudes of climate: for here we find them ranging over every part of the island, voluntarily clambering to the summits of the highest mountains, and undergoing a change of temperature which, from the plains of Beentenne to the top of the Pedro-talla-galla, is sometimes not less

* Dr. Davy's Travels in Ceylon.

† Mr. Brooke's report on the course of the Mahawelli-ganga, from an inspection made by him in 1833.

than 50°, and with a difference of elevation of full eight thousand feet.* I have elsewhere had occasion to remark on the size of elephants, and to refute an erroneous idea still more prevalent, viz. that in Ceylon they "are generally from ten to eleven feet in height."† I should say the general height of full-grown Ceylon elephants is from eight to nine feet.

In proceeding on the third day to Gallegamma from the Horton bungaloe, the first part of our way lay through the plain: beside our path, as if in unison with the party, the Bilhool-oya held on its merry course, and was occasionally enlivened by the sparkling rills which leaped from rocky banks and gloomy copse into its smiling current. As we approached the extremity of the plain, we could not discern any outlet by which our attendant stream might escape from its happy valley, seven thousand feet above the level of the sea; until the mystery was explained by the river disappearing in a chasm, from which it had to plunge for five thousand feet through tangled brakes and murky jungles which cover the mountain walls of Rawana's garden. As we descended towards Gallegamma,

* A young elephant, brought home by the 78th Highlanders, has withstood the severity of the winters of 1838 and 1839, with less clothing than is required for a cart-horse, and in a house colder than any ordinary stable—a common straw-shed.

† Malte Brun's Universal Geography, 1822.

we perceived the stream after its furious descent emerging from a caverned glen; and, a little farther on, approached its fretted current hurrying through various rocky channels: but "once again we met," and crossed its separated waters peacefully gliding in many a miniature canal through the levelled terraces and bright green rice-fields of Gallegamma.

The views we saw in descending from the plains were magnificent, particularly at one spot, from which the eye is directed between two ranges of projecting mountains, to rest on the lower hills of Saffragam, the dreary forest-flats of the Magampattoo, the distant hills of Katragam, and the white salt-encrusted lakes which were conspicuous at a distance of forty miles, and served to separate the misty outline of the coast from the clearer blue of the ocean. The horizon appeared on a line with mountains which we knew to be six thousand feet in height; clouds rolled in the valley beneath our feet; others floated high in air; some rested on the mountains; and a long chain of vapour appeared to hang suspended across the lowlands, which were darkened by its shadow: the whole completing a beautiful scene of earth, air, and ocean, displaced from the relative position in which we are accustomed to view these elements. While I was still on the pass of Gallegamma, and observing the bungaloe at a great distance below, the clouds suddenly lowered, and a storm burst over the opposite range of Hagalla, which was for some time obscured by the spray of a thunder-shower that dashed against the rocky surface of this bleak mountain. The storm swept by, and left us to admire the white skeleton tracery of gigantic trees gleaming on the huge dark mass of Hágalla: this appearance was produced by rills and streamlets rushing down and uniting in channels graved by the slow unceasing hand of time, and now suddenly filled by lines of sparkling foam. The clefts and watercourses of Hágalla are assigned by tradition to the time of Rawana, and are said to be the furrows of Rama's arrows; the mountain itself, in the same spirit of fiction, is believed to be the transformed body of one of his giant adversaries the ancient inhabitants of Lanka, the enemies of the gods.

At Gallegamma, the large temporary building prepared by the Adikar for the reception of the Governor and his party, was ornamented on the outside with arches tastefully arranged, and decorated in the Kandian manner with young cocoanut leaves, plantain-trees, and fruit. The inside was hung with cloth, in front of which wreaths of beautiful mosses and flowers divided the roof into compartments, and in the centre of each was a sunflower. It is hardly possible to see the close resemblance that roofs thus decorated bear to those of rooms in many modern houses, (although these are copies of older models,) without perceiving or fancying that such natural embellishments first suggested the idea, afterwards perfected in more durable materials.

From Gallegamma we started early next morning; and after passing the decaying but not ancient temples of Alut-nuwara, and crossing the Wallawe river, near which the Adikar's elephants were stationed, and ornamental arches prepared, we reached the house of Mahawella-tenné (first Adikar), situated near the village of Ballingodda, eighteen hundred feet above the level of the sea. His large and commodious house, built nearly on the plan of the European houses in Colombo, was approached by an avenue of orange and lime trees. In front of these, and on every approach, were ornamental arches embellished with various kinds of rustic tracery, and profusely decorated with leaves and flowers. On the outside of the buildings was all the splendour of native pageantry, and in the interior we found that European luxuries had been liberally provided by this loyal chief; whose anxiety to receive a visit from the Governor had induced him to exert his influence in opening a horse-path from the Horton Plains to Gallegamma, including a pass of five thousand feet descent.

Mahawella-tenné had been appointed to the highest native situation in the Kandian country in 1835, as a reward for his exertions and fidelity in bringing to the notice of Government a most extensive conspiracy of chiefs and priests, who contemplated (by means equally wicked as they would have proved contemptible for the end proposed) the subversion of the British power.

During our stay, in the evenings dancing-girls performed what appeared to me an inelegant and tedious dance; and others maintained a monotonous, tiresome recitation and chaunt, which they dignified with the name of singing. In the forenoon, the Adikar's elephants were more amusing, and performed various feats, at the same time evincing great docility in the midst of a noisy crowd.

After spending two days in this hospitable abode, the party returned to sleep at Gallegamma, and to be ready at an early hour on the following morning to scale the steep mountains that rose abruptly from the bungaloe. We had commenced the ascent before clear daylight, when the earliest effects of the sun appeared in first tinging, then lighting up the clouds that reflected a dubious gleam on the gigantic ridge over which they were suspended; but, in a few minutes, the direct rays of the sun were kindling bright lights on the summits of mountains whose base still rested in "shadows, clouds, and darkness." In the mornings, particularly during the north-east monsoon, the level grounds and Kandian valleys are commonly overspread by a dense white fog, above which the mountains rise in clear relief and peculiar beauty. The path being too steep to ride, all the party proceeded on foot, and had turned round a sharp angle formed by a succession of rocky fragments that extended above and also down the side of the mountain; but only a few of the horses had been led past this corner, when a heavy sound, succeeded by a noisy clamour, announced an accident. A horse had fallen over, and lay upon a ledge of rock that overhung the wooded ravine: there were some hopes of saving the animal, and by considerable exertions he was raised on his feet; but, apparently from some injury already sustained, he was unable to stand, and, sinking backwards, fell over the precipice. Soon after, a shot echoing up the narrow dell announced the termination of the animal's sufferings.

The cool air of Horton Plains, and the blazing fire and good cheer of the bungaloe, were again enjoyed with even a keener relish than before, from the agreeable but sudden change of climate we had made by our day's ascent. The natives, on the contrary, appeared to feel most uncomfortable, and remained turning themselves round like so many roasts before the numerous fires that blazed during the whole night, to the imminent danger of the dry-grass edifice in which we were lodged. It was once on fire, but the wakeful attendants put it out before it could spread; and it was not till the party had returned to Nuwara-ellia, but before the furniture was removed, that the whole became a prey to the flames.

One of the range of plains that extend amongst the hills lying between Nuwara-ellia and Adam's Peak is called Gaura-ellia; this name it is said to have obtained in consequence of a large and fierce animal, called a gaura, which was caught there about fifty years ago. This creature is probably, we may say certainly, extinct in Ceylon, as none have been seen by Europeans; but in several parts of the country, particularly in Lagalla, its former existence is vouched for by the names of places, as "the Gaura-field," "the Gaura-flat," &c. But, except that it was an animal, they have no tradition concerning it, either as regards its shape or size. Knox, writing in the latter part of the seventeenth century, says, "They have a beast called a gauvera, which much resembles a bull; his back stands up with a sharp ridge, and his legs are white halfway." I presume it must be the same species of animal described by Mr. Hodgson, in the 66th number of the Journal of the Asiatic Society of Bengal (1837), from specimens which he had procured with great difficulty from the Nipal forests, where it is called gauri-gaw.* He gives the size as ten feet from snout to rump, and the height five and a half feet at the shoulder.

* The gour, a species of bull, which, by its description (as taken from a young one), must be the noblest in appearance of all known animals, ranges the hilly portions of the jungles (of Borabhum and Dholbhum), defying pursuit.—From a paper by Lieutenant Tickell; *Journal Asiatic Society*, 1833.

CHAPTER VIII.

TO THE ANCIENT CITY OF MÁGAM.

The lingering bee, by night surprised in Lanka's sacred flower,*
Less hopeless durance finds than man entwined in Beauty's bower
By chains unseen, whose mystic power can captive bind the soul,
While lightning thrills impel the will o'er reason's due control.
The sweetest flower in Nature's realm, and Beauty's softest
bloom,—
This tempts the insect, that the sage, to rapture and a tomb!
'Twas night that closed, and morning's light the mánel's *
flower shall see
Its hundred rosy petals ope, and set the insect free;
But wanton Beauty's fearful deed shall cause o'er Lanka's isle
A mournful gloom, and its loved King shall light his funeral pile.
To sacred friendship more than true, to wisdom more than just,
With that of India's murdered sage unites the royal dust:
Their kindred spirits whispering roam, where sacred bo-trees
wave
Their ceaseless, rustling shade † above the King and poet's
grave.‡—*Suggested by Cingalese traditions, vide page* 174.

---

* The manel, a pink water-lily of delicious perfume, commonly offered before the figures of Buddha. Its flower closes at sunset.

† Sasaladala (the shaking leaf); one of the names of the bo-tree,—Ficus religiosa.

‡ Near Matura, on the banks of the Neela-ganga.

Return to Colombo. — Native Complexions. — Harbour and Fort of Colombo. — Cinnamon Gardens; — their Formation. — Cinnamon. — Galle Road. — Arrack. — Galle. — Cogel. — Kustia Raja. — Belligamma. — House Lizards. — Musk-rats. — Matura. — Murder of Kálidás. — Tragedy. — Dondera. — Temple of Vishnu. — Ruins. — Great Elephant-kraal. — Wallawe. — Mágampattoo. — Colonel H——'s Encounter with a Bear. — Hambantotte. — Salt Lakes. — Elephants. — City of Mágam. — Ruins. — Kerindé. — Ranné. — Night Scene with Elephants. — Rock and Temples of Mulgiri. — Sea-fish. — Kandy Road. — Bridges. — Botanical Garden. — Captain Dawson.

In January 1834, after a continued residence of nearly six years in the Kandian country, I revisited Colombo, on my way to examine the ruins of Mágam, and other remains of antiquity in the maritime provinces of the south and south-west parts of the island. On again entering the fort, the first impressions excited by its appearance on my landing from Europe were vividly recalled, particularly the delight I felt on seeing its lines of Suriya trees. Ever green, and always in flower, they produce a cheering effect and pleasing shade, with which I was the more charmed, as I had suffered several months of sea-sickness; and the only other tropical country I had seen was that glowing heap of sand and cinders, St. Jago, in the Cape de Verd Islands.

From long residence amongst the Kandians, and from being accustomed to their complexions, I was led to contrast their uniformity of colour, features, and dress, with the endless variety of hue, countenance, and clothing of the people of the maritime provinces near Colombo. They are seen of every shade, from deadly white to burnished black: those who are of Cingalese blood, free from exotic mixture, have the most pleasing colour; while the slightest mixture of native blood with European can never be eradicated, and in some cases seems to go on darkening in each succeeding generation, until, as in many of the Portuguese descendants, we find European features with jet-black complexions. The Dutch descendants, with native blood, are now undergoing the blackening process, although in general they have only reached as far as a dark and dingy yellow. At the same time, it may be doubtful whether the sickly white of long-resident Europeans is not more disagreeable to the eye than any of the various shades of black or brown. To avoid the inroads of white ants, chests, cabinets, every kind of furniture which in cold climates have their station on the floor, are here seen mounted upon stilts: these, being formed of yellow jackwood, occasionally produce a ludicrous resemblance between the inanimate articles and the easily-discomposed, thoroughly-unsettled, thin-legged, long-bodied, dingy-coloured, climate-worn European.

The harbour of Colombo is only capable of receiving very small vessels; and the road where the large ships cast anchor, at upwards of a mile from the shore, is exposed to the south-west monsoon. The fort of Colombo was commenced in 1518 by the Portuguese; but its present extent and strength have been gradually accomplished by them and their successors the Dutch, whose predilection for fortifications causes the principal towns on the sea-coast of Ceylon to be uncomfortable places of residence, from their being surrounded with walls that exclude the sea-breeze. While carrying on some repairs near the Battenburgh bastion,* the labourers discovered a large stone, on which was an inscription signifying that beneath it were deposited the mortal remains of Juaz Monteiro, of Setwelo, the first confirmed vicar and primate of Ceylon, who died A.D. 1536.

Those persons, particularly Europeans of temperate habits, who reside in the maritime provinces of the south-west of the island, the towns of Colombo and Galle inclusive, are probably less liable to sickness than in any other part of the world: but it has too high a temperature and too moist a climate for longevity; and I believe there are many more instances of extreme old age to be found in the vicissitudes of the Kandian climate, than in the monotonous languor of the maritime provinces.

*In 1836.

The cinnamon gardens near Colombo are merely plantations of that valuable shrub extending over several thousand acres of sandy soil, resting in some places on black moss. Although the roads by which these plantations are intersected afford pleasant and retired drives, from which in some places there are distant views of Adam's Peak and the Kandian mountains, yet the grounds have no great pretensions to beauty; and neither from the manner in which they are laid out, nor the condition in which they are kept, is the appellation of gardens applicable to these plantations. Their general appearance is that of a copse with laurel leaves and stems about the thickness of hazel; occasionally a plant may be seen, which, having been allowed to grow for seed, has attained a height of forty or fifty feet, with a trunk of eighteen inches in diameter. There are also jambu, cashew-nut, bread-fruit, and other trees interspersed; and these, with the cocoa-nut trees that rise beyond the limits, in some measure relieve the sameness of an extended copse-wood.

Falck, who governed Ceylon for the Dutch from A.D. 1765 until 1785, was the first person who attempted the formation of cinnamon plantations; and disproved the native belief, whether inspired by prejudice or interest, that the flavour of the spice was destroyed by cultivation. A circumstance, which is generally credited, shows that these valuable gardens were not formed without great perseverance in the face of general opposition. It is said that the first plantations, in spite of every care taken with the young plants, soon and suddenly withered; and it was discovered that boiling water had been poured on them during the night by persons instigated by the headmen, who benefited by the former mode of collecting the bark. Although this anecdote is generally believed, I should imagine that an experiment that could have failed through such means must have been of very limited extent; for steadiness of purpose (such as this system of destruction of the young plants would have required), either in good or evil, was no characteristic of Cingalese character. It is understood that, from the time of Falck until the cultivation of cinnamon was generally permitted, viz. in 1833, but little change had been made in the method of cultivation; but that lately it had been much improved by the exertions of individuals.

The flower of the cinnamon is not larger, neither is it unlike that of a none-so-pretty, only that it is of a yellow hue: the fruit resembles a small acorn, which, when ripe, is soft and of a dark purple colour. Cinnamon may be propagated by seeds, plants, or layers; roots also, if carefully transplanted, will thrive in those portions of the island which are favourable to the culture of this spice: a sandy soil over moss or black vegetable mould is generally considered the most favourable ground for cinnamon-planting.

The finest quality of cinnamon is that taken from twigs or shoots of the proper size and of the exact age: if the bark is too young, it has a green taste; if too old, it is rough and gritty. The rods cut for peeling are therefore of various sizes and lengths, depending on the texture of the bark: these are first peeled, then scraped on the outside, and, while drying, curl up into long narrow rolls (commonly called quills); these are stuck into one another so as to form pipes about three feet long, which are then made up in round bundles. Taking the bark at the proper age, seems to be the point that most materially affects the quality of the spice. Such of the hills in the Kandian country as have a moist temperate climate, and the maritime provinces from Tangalle on the south to Chilaw on the west, are the only portions of the island favourable to the growth of cinnamon; and over that extent it is commonly met with in the jungles.

From Colombo I proceeded to Galle, a distance of seventy miles, by a road which seldom digressed far from the sea-shore, and was in general level; although at Caltura, Bentotte, and Barbareen, there is a considerable variety of ground and scenery.

From the few open fields which lie on this road, the view extends to the Kandian mountains; and the eye escapes from the wearisome identity of straight stems and star-shaped tops, which with the occasional combination of Gothic arches, formed by the bending leaves of plants of various ages, is all that a cocoa-nut tree forest offers to the notice of a traveller.

From the produce of the cocoa-nut trees, besides oil from the nuts, cordage from its fibres, and numberless other uses, such quantities of arrack are produced (from the liquor which escapes when the sheath of the unopened flower is cut), that it might be prepared for sixpence a gallon; and is sold by retail, after payment of duty, for sixpence a bottle. This low price may be necessary to prevent smuggling; but it is unfortunate that the natives should have such facility and temptation for acquiring habits of drunkenness as the numerous taverns afford. These are now generally established, and too well frequented, in districts where five years before, the manufacture or sale of spirits was prohibited, and its consumption almost unknown. However, this is the only serious evil amongst the numerous blessings which British dominion has lately conferred on the inhabitants of Ceylon.

To save themselves from the fatigue of continually ascending and descending each tree, the persons who fix the vessels into which the juice of the tree pours itself, fasten jungle-ropes or coir cordage from the top of the stems, connecting every tree in a garden. Over these they may be seen passing with little care; accidents are in consequence numerous, and, from the height of the trees, generally prove fatal.

The whole of the south-west coast of Ceylon is covered with cocoa-nut plantations, varied in some places by a few bread-fruit trees, whose rich foliage however is unable to break the general monotony of the scene. At Galle the hills approach the coast, and a promontory of considerable height projects on one side of the harbour; the other side is terminated by a rocky point, on which the fortified town of Galle is situated. This place has the gloomy unprosperous appearance which seems so common a characteristic of fortified towns; it is surrounded by walls so high as effectually to exclude the delightful sea-breeze, and so well built as to give little hopes that the present generation will witness their decay.

Proceeding on my way, at the sands close to the sea, and eight miles from Galle, we had to cross the stream that flows from the lake of Cogel; a piece of water about three miles long, which is surrounded on the inland banks by richly wooded scenery, and on the other side is only separated from the sea by a narrow sandy ridge covered with cocoa-nut trees. Before entering Belligamma, (which is seventeen miles from Galle,) I stopped to examine a figure called the Kustia Raja: it stands on the road-side, is twelve feet in height, and forms part of a great mass of rock in which it is sculptured. One tradition affirms that the statue represents a Prince from the continent of India, who introduced the cocoa-nut tree, and taught the Cingalese its many uses: another and more probable account states, that a King afflicted with leprosy* established himself at this place for the convenience of worshiping at the neighbouring wihare of Agra Bodi, as by the power of the relic there, and the merits of his offerings, he expected to be relieved from a loathsome disease. A remote antiquity is assigned to this statue, which is not warranted by its perfect state of preservation, nor by the details of the dress and decorations on the figure: small figures of Buddha are cut as ornaments on the high conical tiara with which the statue is surmounted, and which formed the head-dress of Cingalese Kings at least as late as the twelfth century† of the Christian era.

* Kustia, Cingalese for scurvy or leprosy.

† The statue of the King Kirti Nisangha, in the great cave-temple of Dambool, is in this dress: it was erected between A.D. 1187 and 1196.

It was dark when I entered Belligamma; and I left it next morning just as the rays of a level sun had struggled through the mist, and disclosed numbers of fishing-boats grouped amidst the rocky islands of its beautiful bay. The numbers of lizards running on the walls and roof are a disgusting and never-failing attraction to the eyes of new-comers, and are much more numerous in the maritime than in the Kandian provinces. They are, I believe, the largest animal that can walk in an inverted position; that is, that can adhere by the feet to a plain surface with their bodies downward, and at first I was by no means inclined to give them full credit for being able to maintain their footing on the roof, and could not help stealing a look upwards, and earnestly wishing their fly-hunts to be discontinued over my head. When any of these creatures, in the anxious pursuit of fly or moth, gets on a loose scale of white-wash, down they come; and very commonly the tail breaks off, and remains wriggling, while the animal runs away with those members over which it still exercises authority.

The musk-rat is also much more common near the sea-coast than in the interior; and, from their strong smell, they are a greater nuisance than the house-lizard. In appearance the musk-rat is more like a small-sized light-coloured mole; and may be heard uttering a most particularly shrill but not loud squeal as it goes along the edge of the wall, and behind the furniture, searching for crickets. It is generally believed that the odour of these animals is so subtle as to affect the wine in those bottles over which they have passed; but I should be inclined to suppose that the taint arises from contact with the cork before the wine is bottled, or, if the mouth of the bottle has been contaminated, it would communicate an odour to the liquor in pouring out.

Matura, eleven miles from Belligamma, is situated near the mouth of the Neela-ganga, in a fertile and populous district, the climate of which is much lauded by the natives of the maritime provinces. In this village, and situated on the right bank of the river, the Hat-bodin (seven bo-trees), although now a cocoa-nut plantation, retains its ancient name, and serves to point out the spot where the funeral pile of the murdered poet Káli-dás was prepared; and here the tragedy, which commenced with his death, was consummated by the self-sacrifice of the King Kumara Daas and five of his Queens.

The name of this spot is derived from the seven bo-trees that shadowed the tombs of these victims of avarice, vanity, and superstition. From the many minute particulars of the event preserved by tradition, as well as those recorded in Cingalese history, the following account is compiled.

The King Dásen Kelliya, after having overcome and expelled the Malabars, who had conquered and governed Ceylon for upwards of twenty years, fell, A.D. 477, by the hand of his son and successor Sigiri Kasoomboo. On the death of Dásen Kelliya, his second son Moogallana fled to the continent of India, and remained there for eighteen years; then returned, and, by the assistance of a foreign army, overcame his parricidal brother, and reigned in his stead. Moogallana reigned eighteen years, and was succeeded by his son Kumara Dás. This monarch, having invited his friend the poet Kálidás from the court of Bhója Raja of Oujein,* was himself residing at Dewinuwara (four miles

* In a Cingalese epigram of this Kálidás, he refers to his own and his father's residence at the court of Bhója Raja; and, from the following data, I should infer that Kálidás was murdered A.D. 522, and in the thirty-eighth year of Bhója's reign. The death of the Cingalese King Kumara Dás, as appears by Turnour's Epitome, happened in A.D. 522.

"In the Ayin-Acberi, Bhója is said to have ascended the throne in the year 541 of Vicramaditya's era."

"Major M'Kenzie, in his extracts communicated to the society, says, that in the Dehkin it is recorded of Bhója, that he reigned fifty years, five months, and three days; and that the famous Kálidasa lived at his court."—Essay on Vicramaditya and Salivahana.—*Asiatic Researches*, vol. ix. p. 117.

The year of Vicramaditya's era 541 is A.D. 484, the commencement of Bhója's reign.

from Matura), and superintending the formation of the rice-fields at Makawita: he had also commenced a temple of Vishnu, which was afterwards completed by King Dapooloo Sen, A.D. 548, and now forms part of the ruins at Dondera-head. One evening, while Kumara Dás was in the house of a courtesan, he observed a bee to alight in the flower of a water-lily, which closed and imprisoned the insect: the King, who was an accomplished poet, wrote the two first lines of the following verse, evidently intending to compare his own situation, entangled in the toils of a courtesan, to that of the bee secured within a lotus-flower.

The King.—Siyatambará siyatamberá siyasaewanée
Siyasapurá nidinolabá unsaewanée.

Kálidás.—Wanabambará malanotalá ronatawanee
Maladederá panagalawa giyasaewanee.

I have here given the nearest resemblance to the sound; but, in the Cingalese, the position of the letters and their number being the same in each line, is considered to add much to the merit of the performance, which is in fact a riddle written by the King, and explained by Kálidás in the same metre.

The King.—Inthrall'd by blushing sweets, their power shall keep
The anxious mind from rest, and eyes from sleep.

Kálidás.—Tho' closed at eve, the glowing lotus see,
Unhurt, at dawn release the captive bee.

The flower referred to is either the mánel, or another great water-lily, commonly called by Europeans the pink lotus: but, in the original, the words are tortured to suit the sound, and fit their place in the line; and, as they also have double meanings, the whole verse is involved and obscure.

Underneath the two lines which he wrote, Kumara Dás recorded a promise that he would grant any reward that might be asked by whoever could complete the stanza. Kálidás, visiting at the house, perceived the writing, and completed the verse: but the courtesan, to obtain the reward for herself, murdered the poet, buried the body beneath the floor, and, declaring she alone had composed the two last lines, claimed a right to prefer a request, with which the King was bound to comply. No sooner, however, had he seen these lines, than he recognised in them the work of Kálidás; and the consequence was, the discovery of the murder, the disinterment of the corpse, and the preparation of a magnificent funeral pile where the obsequies of the poet were to be solemnized on the banks of the Neela-ganga. The splendid preparations and previous ceremonies being completed, the remains of Kálidás were placed on the pile. When the fire burst forth, the King rushed into the flames, and united his ashes with those of his friend and kindred spirit. The same place witnessed the voluntary immolation of the five Queens * of Kumara Dás. It was then, A.D. 522, that the seven tombs were built and seven bo-trees planted: the tombs had fallen into decay, but the sacred trees continued to wave their restless foliage over the ruins, amidst which the spirits of the King and poet were still supposed to wander. Processions, accompanied by music, occasionally repaired to the scene of this catastrophe; and offerings of flowers were presented as late as the year A.D. 1783, at which time a Dutch gentleman made use of the materials of which the tombs were built, and cut the venerable bo-trees.

Dondera, or Dewinuwara (city of the god), is situated four miles from Matura, on a narrow peninsula, the most southerly point of Ceylon, latitude 5° 50″ N. and longitude 80° 40′ E. Here, interspersed amongst native huts, gardens, and cocoa-nut plantations, several hundred upright stone pillars still remain: they are cut into various shapes, and exhibit different sculptures; amongst others, Rama, with his bow and arrows, may be discerned in various forms. A square gateway, formed of

* I am not aware of any other instances of the widowed Queens of Ceylon offering themselves as victims at the tombs of their royal husbands; and Kumara Dás had been educated on the continent during the time his father was an exile, and probably married at that time.

three stones elaborately carved, leads to a wretched "mud edifice," in which four stone windows of superior workmanship are evidences that a very different style of building had formerly occupied the site of this hovel. It is now, however, the only temple of Vishnu at Dewinuwara; a station reckoned particularly sacred by his votaries, as being the utmost limit which now remains of his conquests when incarnate in that perfect prince and peerless warrior, Ramachandra. Although his temple is so mean, the place still retains much of its sanctity; and an annual festival, which takes place at the full moon in the month of July, continues to attract many thousands of the worshipers of Vishnu. From the temple, a broad road, overshadowed by cocoa-nut trees, leads to a group of plain stone pillars near the sea-shore; but from these my attention was attracted by a single pillar, situated on a low rocky point, over which the sea breaks amidst hewn stones, the remains of some ancient building.

If Rama's expedition and conquest of Lanka existed in any form, or had any foundation more material than a poet's fancy, this lone pillar may be considered as an index which has resisted the waste of ages, and now battles with the waves of ocean to maintain its position, and mark the utmost limit which remains of Vishnu's conquests and religion. The pillar is of a form alternately octagonal and square, and exactly resembles columns that are to be seen on the sacred promontory of Trinkomalee.

Near the temple of Vishnu stand a Buddhist wihare and dágoba: and a quarter of a mile farther inland is situated a stone building called Galgana, consisting of two rooms; the roof as well as the walls are of hewn stone, and exhibit excellent specimens of masonry. On the top there appears formerly to have been a dágoba; but the ruin is now covered with shrubs and creeping plants that find root in the interstices of the building. These remains of Buddhism were completed or restored in the reign of Dapuloo the Second, A.D. 686. A stone, which had been rescued from the rubbish near one of the ruins, was pointed out to me at the house of my friend, Mr. B——, the collector of the district, with whom I was residing. It owes its preservation and present place of safety to Mrs. B——, to whom I am indebted for much information regarding the antiquities in this part of the island. In the inscription on this slab I recognised the name and sounding titles of the King Prákrama Bahoo, a zealous restorer of religious buildings, and a most persevering recorder of his own virtues and power: he reigned from A.D. 1153 to 1186.

On an upright stone, near the temple of Vishnu,

is cut an inscription in the ancient Cingalese character; although considerably decayed, by perseverance it might probably be deciphered.

From Matura to Dikwelle, Tangalle, Ranne, and Wallawé, the country is a succession of rich rice-fields in the valleys, and of low jungle on the intermediate heights. It was principally in this part of the country, that under the Dutch, and even under the British Government, the great elephant-hunts were usually carried on, and immense numbers of these animals were secured or destroyed. Cordiner describes one of these gatherings, when the Honourable F. North was Governor, where two thousand men were employed for three months in driving three hundred elephants into a kraal: the sight was no doubt curious and interesting, but is one of the many proofs how wantonly forced labour will be employed wherever it is suffered to exist. In later times I have heard this system of elephant-hunting approved and defended; but I am convinced it was most oppressive and harassing to the people, cruel to the animals, and advantageous to none, with the exception of those who, without incurring any of the dangers, were gratified by the spectacle, or those who directed the proceedings and profited by the hardships of the multitude so long detained in unhealthy jungles.

Wallawé village is situated on the bank of a

river of the same name, which is here of some size, being dammed up at its mouth, less than a mile distant, by a sand-bank through which its waters percolate to the sea. From Colombo to Matura, as I was travelling in a palanquin, there being good moonlight, I allowed the coolies to move on or halt where it suited themselves; but at Tangalle, Ranné, and Wallawé I stopped during the night, as there were elephants in the neighbourhood. In the morning I crossed the Wallawé in a boat to the village of Wanderoope, and found that a herd of elephants had committed ravages in several of the gardens, and had only retired to the jungle at daylight, a few minutes before our arrival. I was now in the Mágampattoo, an extensive and fertile, but unhealthy and thinly peopled district; oppressed by incredible numbers of elephants, bears, wild hogs, and leopards, and abounding in deer, pea-fowl, and game of every sort. At this time, measures are in progress which may do much towards restoring this district to its ancient state of prosperity; I particularly allude to the encouragement held out to labourers, and the facilitating the destruction of wild animals by permitting the sale of gunpowder, even allowing it to be sold from Government stores.

The Ceylon bear, although of small size, is fierce, and much dreaded by the natives; some of whom

I have known terribly disfigured, when they were fortunate enough to escape with life, from the strong arms and sharp teeth of these animals. The rencounter of an active and gallant officer, Colonel H——, with two bears in the Mágampattoo, is a story well known in Ceylon. He had embarked in a native boat, which was driven far past Hambantotte, the post at which he intended to land: having got on shore, although without attendants, and at a considerable distance from any inhabited place, he determined on attempting to reach a rest-house before night-fall. In this determination he proceeded, carrying a small portmanteau and a bottle of brandy; the last article a gift most fortunately pressed upon him by the friend from whose house he started. While proceeding with all possible expedition it became dusk, and Colonel H—— found the path beset with elephants: by them he was chased, but escaped after throwing away his portmanteau. Much exhausted by his exertions, he had proceeded but a short way, when, by the indistinct light, he perceived two bears occupying the path and advancing upon him. As soon as the animals came within reach, Colonel H—— struck the foremost bruin so severe a blow, that the bottle was broken on the animal's head, and the brandy dashed over its countenance: on this the bear made a precipitate retreat, followed by his unanointed companion, and Colonel H—— arrived in safety at the rest-house of Yallé.

At Wanderoope, in the vicinity of the wihare, are the remains of a Cingalese inscription cut in stone, but much defaced; and on an adjoining pillar are coarse outlines of the sun and moon,—emblems of royalty and duration,—signs commonly attached to gifts of crown-land made by the Kings of Ceylon. Hambantotte, eight miles from Wallawé, is situated on a rocky promontory joined to a steep ridge of sand: here a fortified tower commands an anchorage where vessels lie that come to ship the salt which is formed in vast quantities on the shallow salt-water lakes, called Leways, that are scattered along the coast of the Mágampattoo. In the dry season these lakes become covered with a crust of salt, varying in depth from the thinnest sheet of paper to the thickness of ten inches.

When the salt has formed, the country, viewed from the round tower of Hambantotte, presents most peculiar scenery. In the foreground, irregular plains, covered with salt of dazzling whiteness, are everywhere surrounded by forests, to which the prevalence of daluk-trees (Euphorbia antiquorum) gives a peculiarly dark shade and sombre hue. Beyond these, at a distance of forty miles, the blue mountains of the Kandian country rise to a height of eight thousand feet; and where they cease, to the north-east, the low rugged hills of Katragamma continue the ridge almost to the sea-coast.

From Hambantotte I turned inland on my way to the village of Wirawellé, situated fifteen miles from Hambantotte, and within two miles of the ruins of Mágam; but, never calculating on any interruption in the immediate neighbourhood of so large and populous a village, I started before daylight. However, I had only just got clear of the last houses, when I suddenly found myself in the midst of a herd of elephants that we could hear breaking and twisting off branches of trees in every direction around us. Having disengaged myself from the palanquin, I proceeded to the front with my large guns; and the whole party, in most compact order, with speed and silence passed through the herd without interruption: this was fortunate, for there was not sufficient light to have enabled me to take an accurate aim if any of the elephants had attempted to dispute our passage along the road.

The city of Mágam, or, as it is sometimes called, Roohoonoo Mágam, from having been the capital of the Roohoonoo division of the island, is first mentioned in Cingalese history B.C. 285, when Mahanága retired thither, after escaping the death by poison which was intended for him by his royal and devout sister-in-law, the Queen of Dewenipeatissa.

She, afraid that Máhanága might interfere with the succession to the throne, had sent him a present of poisoned mangoes: the gift arrived at a time when her only son was in company with his uncle; the young prince ate the first mangoe, and died, the victim of his mother's treachery. Magamma remained as a principality, but tributary to the Kings who reigned in Anurádhapoora for a period of one hundred and twenty-four years; first, under Máhanága, already mentioned, who was succeeded by his son Yatálatissa, who was succeeded by his son Gotábhya, who was succeeded by his son Kawantissa, who was succeeded by his son Dootoogaimoonoo, who restored the Cingalese dynasty to its former supreme power and ancient capital of Anurádhapoora.

Dootoogaimoonoo had at an early age determined, contrary to the injunctions and threats of his father, the King Kawantissa, to attempt the liberation of the country from the dominion of the Malabars, who, under their King Elála, had conquered and ruled over Ceylon. He held undivided sway over the northern districts, and received tribute from the Kings of the western and southern divisions, the capitals of which were at Kellania and Mágam. The pacific commands of Kawantissa to his son were imperative, the replics of Dootoogaimoonoo insulting and disobedient; and it is from this cause he is said to have acquired the prefix of Dootoo, "the disobedient," to his name of Gaimoonoo: after which he left Mágam, and remained concealed in the district of Udapalata. Whilst residing in the mountains, he heard of his father's death, and that his brother intended to seize on the principality: on receiving this intelligence, he suddenly appeared in the Roohoonoo district, raised an army, defeated the forces of his brother Saidatissa; and finally, having gained his attachment by forbearance and kindness, left him to rule over Mágam. Dootoogaimoonoo proceeded in a course of continued warfare against the Malabars, until, having fought a decisive battle in which their King fell, Dootoogaimoonoo, as it is expressed in Cingalese history, again united the people of Lanka under one canopy of dominion, B.C. 161. The wars of Dootoogaimoonoo, and the prowess of his ten principal chiefs and warriors, are detailed at great length in several historical works, and with a minuteness that approaches to biography, although not unmixed with exaggeration.

Dootoogaimoonoo was succeeded on the throne of Ceylon by his brother Saidatissa, who had previously ruled over Mágam and Ruhunu; and had erected there numerous religious edifices, as well as formed many considerable tanks. Saidatissa died B.C. 122; therefore the principal ruins in this part of the island are of buildings which existed prior to that date. At that time the surplus produce of the south and south-east districts of Ceylon supplied the army of Dootoogaimoonoo with provisions during his long-continued wars with the Malabars. Of the great population that had assembled round their native princes at Mágam in the second century B.C., many followed their fortunes, some fell in the wars; others profited by the conquests of Dootoogaimoonoo, obtaining the spoil of his enemies, and the possession of lands in more enviable situations than in the Mágampattoo. I am not aware of any remains of consequence, religious buildings, or tanks for extensive cultivation, except of these very olden times; although it is probable that this district may have received a temporary check in its progress towards desolation, at the time when Dondera was the occasional residence of several Kings, and for a short time became the capital of the island in the seventh century.

From Wirawelle, a very small village in which I passed the night, I started early next morning; and commenced my route towards the ruins by wading through deep water and mud for two miles, in what had formerly been the bed of a tank. I then crossed to the left bank of the Kerindé-oya, which is here a clear stream, about forty yards broad and eighteen inches deep, with steep banks shaded by very large kabuk-trees. From the river I proceeded for three miles along a ridge slightly elevated above the surrounding marsh, and on which is situated the principal ruins of Mágam: to this ridge is joined the embankment of the Tissa tank; a reservoir that, like others in the vicinity, has burst, and now in the rainy season forms noxious swamps, infested with crocodiles and frequented by immense herds of elephants. The guides directed me in succession to the ruins of Menik dágoba and wihare; ruins of the Poega (assembly-hall for priests), which consists of forty-eight plain, square, stone pillars, one foot on each side, and thirteen and a half above ground; ruins of the palace,—here are eighty-five pillars, two feet square and fifteen feet high. Near these stands an octagonal pillar, nine feet high and eight feet in circumference, to which the state elephant was chained; and the marks of the chain, deeply worn, have nearly obliterated an inscription, of which I could only distinguish clearly the expression Sri (royal). It is called the pillar of Kadol, whose history is minutely detailed in the same works that describe the prowess of the ten chieftains of Dootoogaimoonoo. Kadol was his favourite elephant, that bore him in all his battles, and on which he was mounted when he encountered and slew his rival.

Yátálatissa dágoba is a mass of brick about seventy feet high; it is split near the centre, and overgrown with trees and brushwood: the guide informed us that its great dilapidation was occasioned by the Portuguese, who had attempted to destroy it with gunpowder. It was built by Mahanáma, B.C. 280. About a hundred stone pillars seven feet in height are scattered in groups around this temple, and are the remains of separate wihares,—Tissa-maha wihare and dágoba. The latter is even now upwards of one hundred feet in height, although no part of the spire or its base exists; it has a small opening at a considerable height, and fragments of steps leading towards the aperture are perceptible on the east side of the ruin. Two broken statues, which I suppose from their dress to be Kawantissa, the King who built this temple about B.C. 180, and his Queen, Wiharé Dewi, were lying near the ruins. The small dágoba of Sandagiri is of the same date as Tissa wihare, and built in the usual Buddhist monumental form: like the others, it is covered with shrubs and plants; even forest-trees find a hold for their roots in the ruins of its masonry, and draw nourishment sufficient to resist the withering blasts of the north-east monsoon.

Mágam is situated eight miles from the mouth of the Kerindé oya, and the fields watered by its tanks are said to have extended the whole of this distance. Kerindé is a rocky point on the sea-shore, remarkable for the artificial appearance of its masses of stone, amongst which there is a spring of fresh water, also some remains of masonry; and the outline figures of the sun and moon render probable the tradition that the Kings of Mágam occasionally retired to this place to enjoy the cooling breeze and sea-bathing.

The utter desolation of the great cities, the ancient capitals of Ceylon, only adds to the already numerous evidences that change always accompanies, and decay finally seizes, the most ponderous works of mortal power, as surely as the most fragile scion of the human race.

> "Rome decay'd, and Athens strew'd the plain,
> And Tyre's proud piers lie shatter'd in the main."

Anurádhapoora and Mágam are mentioned by Ptolemy;* but, long before the geographer had recorded their positions, the latter had ceased to be of consequence, and was sinking to obscurity.

The country being in many places under water from heavy rains which had recently fallen, and my leave being limited, I was unable to visit Ke-

* As Anuro-grammum and Mágrammum: "grammum" was used in the same way as "poora," for a "town."

rindé or the Muda wihare, built by Kawantissa to commemorate the miraculous escape of his Queen, Wiharé Dewi, from her marine prison, at the place where it was brought to land.*

In returning from Mágam, I reached Ranné rest-house as the sun was setting behind the rock and temple of Kahandáwia: beneath it spread a great extent of luxuriant rice-fields, watered by the small river of Ranné, the course of which might be traced by gigantic reeds that rose above its banks. As night closed, the jungles were spangled with innumerable fire-flies; and an unusual number of chules (lighted brands) flamed in the watch-huts, betokening an expected attack from elephants. The event proved the correctness of their anticipations, and the necessity of their preparations; for, during the whole night, two herds were making repeated and persevering attempts to break through the slight fence of the rice-field. Whenever any of the elephants endeavoured to force through the enclosure, the scene became particularly animated, from the rush of watchers towards the spot, waving their brands and uttering loud and long-continued shouts: this tumult suddenly ceased, and was succeeded by dead silence for a sufficient length of time to enable the people to listen whether the animals were moving off, or if

* As mentioned in the account of Kellania.

a fresh attack might be anticipated. If the enemy had retreated from the fence, then might be heard the loud abuse of the lazy or timid, who only arrived when their services were no longer required; or the clamorous self-praises of the foremost and foolhardy.

From Tangalle I turned inland for twelve miles, to visit the Buddhist temples of Mulgiri. This rock is about three hundred and fifty feet in height, perpendicular on three sides, but attached on the north to a low, rocky range, of which it forms the abrupt termination. The small level spot on the summit, from which there is an extensive view over the southern maritime provinces, is surmounted by a dágoba: the ascent is not difficult, stone steps being placed wherever the rock was too steep to be easily surmounted. The dwellings of the priests of the establishment are situated near the base of the rock; and behind them, where there is an overhanging ledge, the remains of the oldest temples, now in ruins, may be distinguished. The new temples, as they are called, are excavated under a ledge within a little distance of the summit, and are in good repair. The rock-temples of Mulgiri, although similar in design, are every way inferior to those at Dambool: the old temples were formed by Saidatissa in the second century before Christ; Kaluna Detootissa completed the new temples in the seventh century of the Christian era.*

In returning along the coast I frequently was present when the fishermen returned from their day's labour, and generally with a good supply. Seer-fish always appeared to me superior to any other of the finny race in Ceylon; it has a good deal of the flavour of salmon, lives entirely in salt-water, and is white in the colour. Mullet, pomfret, sole, and whiting are met with generally, but are less esteemed than the seer-fish.

From Colombo I returned to Kandy by the mail-coach, and remarked the immense improvement that had taken place in the face of the country near the great road which was opened under the government of Sir Edward Barnes. When I first visited Kandy in 1828, this line was unfinished; and the numerous obstacles which had been overcome, or were in progress of removal, could not be overlooked: the rock which had been blasted, the embankments that had been raised, were then bare; and the forests through which we passed showed how much of energy and perseverance was required to trace the road which was then forming. Now these obstacles would

* The inscriptions at Mulgiri consist of a few words in the square or Nagara character, and two lines of Cingalese, of little import and no value.

hardly be credited by any one who had not previously seen the country; for the shattered rocks and huge embankments were overgrown with vegetation, and the dense forest had almost disappeared from the vicinity of the road. In place of the rumbling ford and ferry of the Maha-oya, we crossed an elegant bridge at Mawenella, the design of Captain, now Lieutenant-colonel Brown, R.E.; and, instead of the clumsy ferry-boat at Peradennia, a light and elegant arch of satinwood, two hundred and five feet in length, spanned the Mahawelli-ganga. (This was constructed by Lieutenant-colonel Fraser, Deputy Quarter-master General.) Immediately adjoining the bridge, in a bend of the river, and four miles from Kandy, is the Botanical Garden, a pretty spot, which owes as much to nature as to art for its beauties.

The last time I passed this way, in 1828, the able officer, Captain Dawson of the Royal Engineers, who had traced and directed the formation of this road, was in rude health and buoyant spirits: now his lofty monumental column gleamed on the summit of the Kadeganawe pass, the most elevated part of the road, and one thousand seven hundred and thirty feet above the level of the sea; his intrepid spirit and iron frame had sunk beneath the severe trials he underwent in the zealous discharge of his public duties.

CHAPTER IX.

RELIGION OF CEYLON.

* * * Little else but dreams,
Conjectures, fancies, built on nothing firm.—MILTON.

Religion of Ceylon. — Buddhas. — Gautama Buddha —forbids Slavery. — Yakkas. — Nagas. — Worship of Gods. — Neerwané. — Buddhism established or renovated in Ceylon by Mehindu.

THE religion of Ceylon is properly that of Gautama Buddha; but his moral system is there found to be conjoined with the ancient superstitions of the aboriginal inhabitants, who never entirely abandoned the adoration of gods, demi-gods, devils, ancestors, and planets. Although demon worship is repugnant to the doctrine of Buddha, yet its unhallowed rites were always maintained either openly or in secret: it is probably in consequence of the decline of Buddhism that the devils' priests have become more audacious, and that of late their ceremonies have increased in favour with the Kandian people.

The Buddhists of Ceylon believe that, in periods of great moral depravity and mental debasement, a Buddha in prospect (a being who, by meritorious actions and blameless purity in his later transmigrations, had reached the most exalted of the heavenly mansions,) became incarnate to fulfill his own final transmigration; whilst at the same time he regenerated mankind, and restored religion. The twenty-fifth of those Buddhas whose names are preserved, and the fourth of the present Kalpa or great period of moral renovation, is the Gautama Buddha now worshiped in Ceylon.

There are authorities, although vague and unsatisfactory, for fixing the dates when Gautama's three immediate predecessors of this era became Buddhas; viz. Kakusanda, immediately after the commencement of the Kaliyuga, B.C. 3101. This Buddha arrived from the country ruled over by the King Kshêma; and from his capital of Kshemawattee-nuwara,* Lanka (Ceylon) was supplied with priests of the Buddhist religion. The coincidence

* Kshemawatte-nuwara is probably the same city, the name of which was afterwards corrupted into Saewatte-nuwara,—Gya,—to which pilgrimages were made, and where offerings were deposited to *deceased ancestors*. The great antiquity of Gya may be inferred from the manner in which it is mentioned in the Ramayana.

in name of the kingly patron of this Buddha, and the position of his capital in the upper provinces of Hindostan, with that generally assigned to the son of Noah, progenitor of the eastern nations, cannot fail to strike one as an extraordinary approximation to the records of Holy Writ. Another Buddha appeared at the conclusion of the 1002nd year of the Kaliyuga, or B.C. 2099; whom I suppose to have been Konagamma, the second Buddha of this era. The third Buddha's era, Kasyapa, may be fixed about B.C. 1014; for this date is supported by a great variety of concurrent testimony from China, Japan, Tartary, and Tibet. The records of these countries vary the time of a Buddha's appearance from B.C. 1036, to B.C. 950: the extremities of these dates may be the periods of his birth and death; and the intermediate dates may be the time of his becoming a Buddha.

Every Buddha, on attaining the object of his ambition, was invested by his followers with the innumerable titles of former Buddhas (many of these were appertaining to gods); and by visiting the same places, enjoining the same observances, retaining the same moral laws, and imitating all their actions, he identified himself with the meritorious deeds as well as with the moral doctrines of his predecessors, the earlier Buddhas. From these circumstances, it is not easy to particularise the acts of any individual Buddha; and the difficulty has been increased by native writers on the subject, who in general have preferred aimless dissertations to historical incidents.*

The scanty details of the earlier Buddhas are involved in the obscure theories or fictions in which Buddhists describe the form and duration of the universe, and the multiplied incarnations of Buddhas. In some of these works we find the calculations and dates to consist of numberless figures; and that the statements and descriptions are an interminable labyrinth of absurdities, seemingly without object, and certainly without amusement: some of these reveries appear to be the production of an unbridled fancy, whose only care had been to abstain from aught probable, possible, or comprehensible; adhering to the orthodox Buddhist text. "Thus the Buddhas are incomprehensible, their doctrines are incomprehensible, and the magnitude of the fruits of faith to those who have faith in these incomprehensibles is also incomprehensible."

As Gautama Buddha summed up his admirable and simple moral laws thus, "Abstain from all

* The parentage of all the twenty-five Buddhas (whose names are preserved) are recorded, as well as the places where they were born; and in respect to the three predecessors of Gautama, the sovereign who protected each is also mentioned, and the chief priests and priestesses whom they left in Ceylon.

sin, acquire all virtue, repress thine own heart,"* it is but natural to conclude that the present intricate system connected with Buddhism is like rubbish which has accumulated round a great but decaying fabric of religion. A system that discourages the gratification of animal passions, forbids trafficking in human beings (slavery), enforces strict morality with peaceable demeanour, and denounces warlike kings or quarrelsome individuals, would never have spread so rapidly and widely over Asia if its doctrines had not been clear, at least intelligible; but, like other religions, its purity has been impaired by the controversies, the commentaries, the deeds, and the writings of those whose duty it was to have preserved it inviolate.

So far as I can learn from any works which I have examined belonging to the Buddhists of Ceylon, I should infer that the geographical knowledge of their earliest teachers was extremely limited;

* "This is Buddha's injunction." From Kitelgama Dewamitta Unnanze's Summary of the Genuine Tenets of Buddhism; a tract composed in 1826 for the information and at the request of Mr. Sawers, judicial commissioner at Kandy, who at that time had the superintendence of the Buddhist church: the translation of this Epitome was made by the best Cingalese and English scholar in Ceylon, Mr. Armour, district judge of Tangalle. Mr. Armour, in his Introduction, states that this tract "has been acknowledged to embody the orthodox dogmas of the Buddhist faith" (of course as at present enduring in Ceylon).

that they knew little of those countries which lay beyond the great mountain range from whence flows the Indus, the Brahmaputra, and the Ganges. They seem to have assigned Mahameru and the Himalaya mountains, with their thrones of glass and peaks of gems, as the region of the gods; Jambodwipa, (or southward from these mountains, and confined between the Indus and the Brahmaputra,) as the habitation of mortals; and Patala, the lower region, (including Ceylon, and probably the countries beyond the mouths of the Ganges and Indus,) as the abode of Nágas and Asurs. If, happily, the country of Pándi (southern peninsula of India) escaped the name of Patala,* its inhabitants nevertheless shared the opprobrious epithet of Asurs (infidels) with their neighbours of Ceylon, in the periods antecedent to the appearance of Gautama Buddha.

* Patala is also a fanciful division (of Buddhist visionaries) in the interior of the earth's crust; this place they make an abode of Nágas, whom they admit to be Buddhists. Yet some early commentators, and the modern priesthood, will have them to be hooded snakes. The confusion arises possibly from two causes, the name of the country or class of people, which again is probably derived from their worship of the nága or hooded snake. Yet we find in several Cingalese works the details of Gautama Buddha's visit to the Nágas (in the present Nagpore country); and the memorials he left on the banks of the Narmada-ganga (Nerbudda river) on his way to Ceylon from Bahar: and in the same journey he visited Sacha-badda-parouette (probably Mount Samet).

The existing records of the life, writings, and ministry of Gautama are so minute and credible, that they may fairly claim to be admitted into genuine history. I shall, therefore, give a slight sketch of his life, and of some of the most remarkable events connected with his visits to Ceylon, then known by the name of Lanka. He was the son of the King Suddhódana by one of his Queens; was born at Kapilawastapura (or Kimbulwatpura), B.C. 623; and received the name of Prince Siddharta.

At the age of sixteen he was married to the Princess Yasodará (called also Subhadda-Kachchána): when he was twenty-nine years of age, his wife brought him a son, who afterwards received the name of Rahula, and became a priest. On the same day that his son was born, Siddharta forsook his family and country, and commenced a life of penance and meditation: this he continued for six years in the wilderness of Oorawella;* and during that period existed upon the wild fruit he picked up, or the alms that were offered to him. After this sojourn in the wilderness, having fasted for forty-nine days, he had a severe struggle with, but finally overcame, Marya† and a legion of demons (*i. e.* death, deadly sins,

* Where the remains of Buddhagya now are (in Bahar).

† Marya may be translated "lust, deadly sin, death."

and evil passions), and became a Buddha by the name of Gautama. As Gautama Buddha, he proceeded to commence his ministry, and first expounded his doctrines at the grove called Isipatana in the immediate neighbourhood of Baranás (now called Benares). In the ninth month after his sacred character was established, Gautama arrived at the town of Mahawelligam,* the capital of the Yakkas† in Ceylon; this place is then said to have occupied a space twelve miles in length and eight in breadth on the banks of the Mahawelli-ganga.

The majority of the Yakkas appear to have been converted to the faith of the Buddhas, and to have driven those who adhered to their ancient superstitions into the rocky island or islands called Yakgiri. Tradition places these islands to the south-east of Ceylon; and the legends, which are preserved on that coast, of sunken cities, may refer to some territory of which the Bass Rocks are the only visible remains. A portion of Gautama's hair, cut off when he became a Buddha, was enclosed in a golden casket, over which a dágoba (Myungana ‡) was built in the town of Mahawelligam:

* Where Myungana now stands in the district, and near the village of Beentenné.

† Yakkas, translated "devils, devil-worshippers."

‡ Myungana is still a sacred place of pilgrimage; its dágoba, originally built by the chief of the converted Yakkas, was afterwards enriched by the addition of the griwa (neck-bone) relic,

this relic is said to have prevented the return of the Yakkas (devils) whom Buddha had expelled, *i. e.* the worship he had superseded.

The second visit of Gautama to Ceylon was B.C. 581, on which occasion he reconciled two rival princes of the Nágas, Chulodra and Mahodra, who had been carrying on a destructive war. These chiefs were near relations; and their capitals of Kellania* and Wadenawágalla† were situated towards the western side of the island, in that division then called Naga-diwinia. On the termination of their feud, the throne for which the princes had contended was made an offering to the Buddha, and was afterwards enshrined by the Nágas in the dágoba of Kellania,‡ to be venerated as a memorial of their benefactor.

A third time Gautama returned to Ceylon, B.C. 577; and having revisited Kellania, from thence proceeded to Samanala (Adam's Peak), Diganakhya§

and enlarged to the height of twelve cubits: it was again increased by the King Chula Bhya to thirty cubits; and Dootoogaimoonoo, between 164 and 140 B.C. raised it to the height of ninety cubits.

* Kellania, situated four miles from Colombo.

† Wadenawágalla, in the district now called the Seven Korles.

‡ This dágoba still exists.

§ On the south-east of the island, near the south end of the Batticaloe district, is Diganakhya, a very large ruin overgrown with jungle.

in Ruhunu, the eight places at Anurádhapoora, and all others that had been sanctified by former Buddhas; then took his final departure from the island, and proceeded to the temple of Jaitawana-rama, in Saewat-nuwara * of Maghada.†

Gautama continued to the last day of a long life to be indefatigable in publishing his doctrines, and to be eminently successful in increasing his followers. He died in a forest outside the town of Kusinara-nuwara, near the Kukuta river, in the eighty-first year of his age, and B.C. 543. It is his moral doctrines that are recognised as the rule of conduct for Cingalese Buddhists; it is he who is still invoked by them as the present Buddha; and it is of his religion I speak, without reference to other forms of Buddhism, such as may be found in Japan, China, Tartary, and Tibet,—in which last place it appears to exist in one of the most degraded forms of worship which wickedness could invent, or weakness adhere to. I consider the

* Saewat-nuwara, in some Cingalese works said to be identical with Buddha-gya, which contains amidst its shapeless ruins the remains of Gautama's residence, as well as the wreck of those splendid temples which were built to commemorate his worth, or cover his relics.

† The Pali, or language in which the ancient sacred books of Buddhism are written, is still called by priests and learned Cingalese the Maghada language. The extent of the country of Maghada, no doubt, often varied; but appears to agree nearly with what is now called Bahar.

whole system of gods to be quite unconnected with the religion of Gautama;* and the superstitions of snake, demon, and planetary worship he openly condemned. But, as many of the sovereigns of Ceylon have been of continental families, and have ascended the throne, some by conquest, and others by election, it is natural to suppose that mere outward conformity (which those who succeeded without violence must have professed to the established religion) would not make them sincere Buddhists, nor prevent their encouragement of a system of gods nearly the same as those they had been accustomed to acknowledge. As to the Kings who reigned by right of conquest, we find, as might be expected, that some of them destroyed, pillaged, and polluted the sacred objects of Buddhist veneration.

The belief and practice of the Cingalese Buddhists with regard to the worship of the gods, is

* "In times designated Abudahotpaada, or intervals when Buddhas existed not, mankind, being ignorant of the doctrines of Neerwana, went in pursuit of vanities, like those who sought for refreshment from the miringo-jala (mirage), or fire from the glow-worm, and addressed themselves to the worship of Vishnu, Iswara, and other gods, and ascribed to trees and rocks, stocks and stones, the power of protecting and rewarding; fancying that they should thus obtain protection and happiness, whereas their erroneous practices only doomed them to torments more and more severe."—From Kitulgama Unnanze's Tenets of Buddhism, translated by Mr. Armour.

equally inconsistent: a Buddhist priest is considered superior to them, yet is only a mortal. Buddha forbids the killing even of the meanest insect, and commands peace, not only in deeds, but in words; yet the emblems and relics of the gods are those of war and slaughter, viz. shields, swords, spears, bows and arrows. Amongst the other gods we find Mahasen, a King of Ceylon, who died eight hundred years after Gautama: to him several temples have been raised; but the principal of these is near one of his gigantic public works, the tank of Minneria.* The less powerful successors of Mahasen, unable to imitate his designs, have proclaimed him a god: a less numerous people, unable to execute such works, pronounce them to be the performance of devils.

All religions must have some points in common; and, by founding arguments on these, learned and inquiring men have attempted to assimilate the mild and tolerant Buddhist with the haughty Brahmins, — those who denounced caste, and those who exist by it alone; the amiable sage, with the ambitious conqueror, — Gautama, with Sesostris, — the being who threatens warlike kings, and whose first commandment is, "From the meanest insect up to man, thou shalt not kill," with him whose life was spent in wars and carnage.

* From this he is often called Minneria-deiyo.

It is also to be remarked, that the religion of Gautama Buddha was disseminated without assistance from the sword, and ought to have been maintained without cruelty; for the use of corporeal inflictions as a stimulant to orthodoxy finds no support in the doctrines of Buddhism, although the history of Ceylon furnishes us with three examples of punishment inflicted for religion's sake, by an usurper, a reclaimed apostate, and a relentless zealot. The first of these, Goloo Abhá, who reigned from A.D. 248 to 261, branded sixty heterodox priests and banished them from the island. The second was Mahasen, who reigned from A.D. 275 to 301, and accompanied his return to orthodox Buddhism by the sacrifice of the teacher of his youth and the minister of his maturer years. The third, Udaya the First, soon after his accession in A.D. 891, put an end to a heresy by giving to the flames a house in which he had collected and secured the professors, as well as the books and records, of the blue-robed Buddhists.

The works which contain the principles of Buddhism have been lately discovered, disconnected from commentaries and discourses,* which appear

* Mr Turnour has succeeded in discovering the Pali Buddhist scriptures, separate from the dilated commentaries with which, heretofore, it was supposed they were irremediably incorporated. It is to be hoped that he will ere long give to the public an analysis of the real doctrine contained in these works;

to be often but the vapid records and confused visions of some hermit's brain, which he had persuaded others, and perhaps himself believed, to be the results of revelations and experience acquired in former transmigrations. It appears to me to be unjust to Buddhism, and contrary to common sense, to suppose that thousands of years of trials and expiation were to be rewarded with the most unsatisfactory of all terminations, viz. annihilation; yet this is now generally asserted to be the meaning of Neerwana. Not only Europeans, but the earliest Buddhist writers, may have erred in giving too definite a word to represent the meaning of a mystical expression belonging to a language which had probably ceased to be spoken before the doctrine of Buddha was recorded. It is also uncertain if we have just equivalents in English, or the Buddhists in their vernacular languages, for the subtle expression Neerwana, which may have been intended to remain a mystery of Buddhist doctrine. From a comparison of the many different epithets used by Buddhists as synonymous * with Neerwana,

an undertaking which, from the advantages of his position, as well as from personal acquirements, he is so well calculated for successfully accomplishing.

* Such, for instance, as Amurta, and many others. Amurta is used for Neerwana; and in the Rev. Mr. Clough's Cingalese dictionary we find the translation given, "immortal, imperishable, unfading; freedom from death; the final emancipation of the soul from the body."

I am of opinion that "having attained Neerwana" signifies not only that the spirit from that time forth is emancipated from the flesh, but that the spirit itself, having been gradually and finally purified, is at last untroubled by any passion or aspiration; it is then, and for ever, an essence of purity and virtue.

The images of Buddha are only represented in three positions, viz. sitting cross-legged, standing as if preparing to advance, and reclining on his side with his head resting on a pillow: he is generally represented clad in the yellow robe, but one of pomegranate-flower colour is also canonical. His statues are not placed in the temples as objects of worship, but to recall more forcibly the founder of their religion to the minds of its votaries. Corresponding to the mild tenets of Gautama's religion, are the offerings made in his temples: ornaments are presented to the wihare; but flowers, remarkable for fragrance and beauty, are alone offered before the figure of the Buddha.

Prior to the reign of Dewenepiatissa, which commenced B.C. 307, the religion of Gautama, although established, was greatly neglected; but Mehindoo then arrived, and Buddhism was renovated by his preaching, his example, and the presence of the numerous relics of Buddha which were forwarded to Ceylon by Dharmasoka, King of Maghada. The two principal of these memorials were, the right collar-bone of Gautama, and a branch of his sacred tree: the former reposes beneath the elegant, though now ruinous, structure of Thuparáma at Anurádhapoora; the latter still flourishes, to receive the veneration of those who journey to that holy place of pilgrimage.

Letters and writing (by that I understand the Pali language and square character commonly called Nagara*) were introduced by Mehindoo two hundred and thirty-seven years after Gautama's death; and this forms an era, called the establishment of religion, which is sometimes used to correct or corroborate the year of Buddha.

* In this character there are an immense number of inscriptions cut in rocks and on stone buildings in different parts of Ceylon.

CHAPTER X.

BUDDHA'S TOOTH IN THE PALACE OF KANDY.

Yet to the remnants of thy splendour past
Shall pilgrims, pensive, but unwearied, throng.—BYRON.

Buddha's Tooth, — taken from the Funeral Pile; — placed at Dantapoora; — removed to Patalipura. — Miracles. — Wars. — Juggernaut. — Tooth driven from the Continent of India, — finds Refuge in Ceylon. — It, or a Counterfeit, taken by the Portuguese, and burnt. — Tooth taken away by the Kandian Rebels, — re-taken by the British.

HISTORY OF THE DALADA,* OR TOOTH OF GAUTAMA BUDDHA, NOW KEPT IN THE MALIGAWA TEMPLE AT KANDY.

Two great contending parties, the Buddhist and Brahmin, professing irreconcilable principles, appear

* There are various native histories of the tooth, and of the offerings made to it. The oldest, called the Daladáwansa, which is still extant, is mentioned by Mahanámo, who wrote prior to A.D. 477. He bears testimony to the accuracy of its details regarding the conveyance of the Dalada to Ceylon, which event occurred about one hundred and fifty years before that priest compiled his history.

from the earliest ages* to have influenced society in Hindosthan. The Buddhists, whose system is essentially contemplative, humane, peaceful, and regulated by plain moral laws, have nevertheless unsuccessfully opposed the arbitrary classification and trammels of caste, bloody sacrifices, and the monopoly of superior rank and special sanctity claimed by Brahmins.

The historical works of Ceylon, including those which treat of the Dalada relic, enable us to fix, with much probability, the period of the most active persecution of the Buddhists, and the final success of the Brahmins. In the following abstract of its adventures, the trials and miraculous triumphs of the relic at the city of Paelalup are so far of value to general history, that they show the tenets of its persecutors and votaries. By the native histories of Ceylon we learn that the doctrines of Gautama Buddha were predominant in India for three or four centuries after his death;† after which they appear to have declined. In A.D. 209, the Brahmin Wytoolia attempted to introduce a change in the national religion of Ceylon; and this design was persevered in,‡ openly or insidiously,

* The Ramayan, also Cingalese accounts of Rawana, show that, even in the very early age in which that poem was written, these antagonist principles produced active enmity.

† As may be seen in the account of the three great religious convocations, &c. in Turnour's Mahawanso.

‡ Cingalese account of the Wytoolia and other heresies.

up to the period when the Dalada found refuge in Ceylon. From these and other concurrent circumstances, as well as facts mentioned in the histories of the relic, there is great reason to believe that the triumph of the Brahmins in India was not consummated until the expulsion of the Dalada from the continent, and the fall of Dantapoora in A.D. 309. From that time Brahminism in various shapes appears to have maintained its dominion in Hindosthan, with the exception of those places to which plunder and ambition lured the Mohammedan to conquest, and where the edge of the sword became his efficient argument for conversion.

Gautama Buddha's death took place in the eighty-first year of his age, and B.C. 543, near the town of Coosinara; and in the forest of sal-trees, near the spot where he expired, the magnificent funeral pile was prepared. Before the entire destruction of the mortal remains of his teacher, the priest Khaima rescued the Dalada from the flames, and it was then conveyed (as had been prophesied) to the country of Kálinga,* where for several centuries it was treated with all the veneration that had been shown to Buddha when alive. Towards the end of the third century, the King of Kálinga, Guhasiva, listening to the Achailakas (naked fana-

* Kálinga, an ancient division of India, comprehending Orissa, and a great extent of country along the north-west coast of the bay of Bengal.

tics), neglected the Dalada, and omitted the prescribed offerings; but he was recalled from apathy or infidelity by the remonstrances of his minister, who represented to him the unanimous belief of the people in the power of this relic. The Achailakas then repaired to Paelalup,* and complained to Panduwas, chief sovereign of India, that his tributary King, Guhasiva of Kálinga, neglecting Vishnu, Siva, and the other gods, worshiped only a piece of bone. On their representations, Panduwas ordered a large army to proceed to Kálinga under the command of Chyttyana Raja. This force, having advanced into the territories of Guhasiva, encamped before his capital of Dantapoora.† Chyttyana Raja was invited into the city by the King, and entertained as an honoured and friendly guest: former miracles regarding the Dalada were related, and new miracles performed, until at last the invader admitted the power of the relic. Chyttyana then departed for Paelalup, accompanied by Guhasiva bearing the Dalada in a splendid procession; for the commands of Panduwas to Chyttyana were clear and precise, viz. "Repairing to the Kálinga country, bring hither Guhasiva and the piece of human bone which he worships day and night." ‡

* Paelalup, Patalipura; modern Patna.

† Dantapoora;—Danta (tooth), poora (city).

‡ From Turnour's translation of the Pali History of the tooth.

Crossing rivers and mountains, in due time they reached Paelalup, where the King Panduwas received them, surrounded by his court, and immediately ordered the "piece of human bone" to be delivered into the hands of its enemies: then commenced what Buddhists term the "trials" of the Dalada, and which they assert ended by triumphant evidences of its superhuman nature.

The Achailakas were overjoyed at having obtained possession of the relic, and forthwith prepared in the yard of the palace a pit filled with glowing charcoal: into this the Dalada was thrown; and from thence, say the Buddhists, it burst unscathed, emitting rays which ascended through the skies and illumined the universe. The Dalada was afterwards buried deep in the earth, which was trodden down by elephants; but, spurning a subterraneous retreat and bonds of clay, it re-appeared in the centre of a gold lotus-flower. It was cast into a deep and filthy pool, which speedily became a clear pond covered with lotus-flowers: on one of these the relic was seen reposing. The Achailakas insisted that these wonders were only frauds and deceptions of the Buddhists; and, placing the Dalada on an anvil, prepared to crush it: the ponderous hammer was raised for its destruction; but, ere it could descend, the relic had sunk into the iron, and there remained safe and immoveable.

The enemies of Buddhism, seeing the effect produced by these miracles on the mind of the King, exclaimed that the Dalada must be a relic of some Avatar of Eiswara, Vishnu, or one of the gods; as no remains of the sage Gautama, or of any other mortal, could have supernatural power. The King replied, "If this be a relic of the gods, pray to them, and let their power release it from the anvil." The Achailakas having in vain supplicated the assistance of the gods in the task thus imposed on them, the King permitted the Buddhists to prove the truth of their faith as connected with this relic of Gautama.

Then Subhadra, (a lineal descendant of Anepidhu, who built the Jaitawana temple for Buddha,) having made great offerings to the Dalada, and recapitulated the meritorious acts and successive transmigrations of Buddha, was rewarded by seeing the relic disengage itself from the iron, and still farther acknowledge the faith of the votary by the effulgence which spread around. The Dalada then floated in water placed in a golden cup which was held by Subhadra.

The prime minister and the nobles were satisfied; the people already believed. These miracles confirmed the wavering, and converted the unbelievers; amongst others the King Panduwas, who discarded the heretics, made great offerings to the wihares, and entreated forgiveness from Buddha. In his supplications the King did not fail to point out that these trials of the Dalada were the means of procuring a triumph to true religion, by showing its power; and that it was for this laudable purpose he had allowed the temporary indignities to be offered to the tooth. "Gems" said the Raja, "are of acknowledged perfection after they have passed through the fire; and gold becomes more valuable after its purity has been subjected to proof."

Shortly after these events, Ksheeridara, King of Saewat-nuwara, assembled an army, and demanded that the Dalada should be delivered up to him: on the refusal of this proposal, Ksheeridara advanced against Paelalup, and beneath the walls of the city sustained a complete defeat from the army of Panduwas. The relic was now restored to Guhasiva, who returned to Kálinga, and again placed it in the great temple of Dantapoora. Panduwas, after these events, resigned the throne of India to his son, became a Buddhist priest, and died in retirement.

After the return of Guhasiva, the son of the King of Oodaini (a zealous Buddhist) arrived at Dantapoora, made great offerings to the Dalada, and became the husband of Hemamálâwa (called also Ranawali), a daughter of the King of Kálinga. After the defeat of Ksheeridara by Panduwas, his nephews* collected a great army which they directed against Kálinga, and finally appeared before Dantapoora. Apprehensive of the power by which he was assailed, Guhasiva directed his daughter and son-in-law (now called Dantakumara) to escape from the city. Disguised as Brahmins, and in possession of the Dalada, they departed; and, having crossed a large river to the southward of the town, concealed the relic amongst the sands. From thence, with the Dalada concealed amongst the hair of Hemamáláwa, they contrived to reach a ship, in which they awaited the issue of an impending battle. A red flag was to be displayed if there no longer were hopes of success for the besieged; in which case the guardians of the relic were directed to proceed to Ceylon, (which island had been foretold as its final resting-place,) and to deliver it to the King of that island. Accordingly, when the red flag, the signal of defeat and desperation, was displayed on Dantapoora,† the Prince and Princess proceeded towards their destination. Eventually, with their invaluable charge,

* Mr. Turnour says Ksheeridara was killed in battle in the campaign against Panduwas.—Account of the tooth in the Bengal Asiatic Journal, 1837.

† Dantapoora, city of the tooth. Very many circumstances combine to point out Pooree, or Juggernaut, as identical with Guhasiva's capital; and that the sanctity of that place in the estimation of the Buddhists originated in its having contained

they safely reached Ceylon. Since then, for upwards of fifteen hundred years, it has shared the vicissitudes of those who, along with it, swayed the destinies of the island. It has had its wanderings and returns, captivities and exiles, degradation and triumphs; and now rests, after two thousand years of travel, in one of the richest shrines of superstition.

the Dalada for a period of upwards of eight centuries. Amongst other reasons I shall observe—

1. Guhasiva's country, Kálinga, comprehends the site of Juggernaut.

2. The name of Juggernaut, Jhagat-natha, (lord of the universe,) an appellation of Buddhas, which Gautama himself assumed; for it is said, that on the day he became Buddha, as well as when he was about to expire, he exclaimed, "O universe, I am thy lord!"

3. The position of the city, its proximity to the sea, with the sands before it, and the river to the southward of it.

4. Even now, its guardians say Juggernaut is Bhagawan, which is a generic name for a Buddha; and Bhagawá is one of the most common epithets applied to Gautama Buddha.

6. "To the Buddhists of Tibet; Allahabad, Benares, Durjodum, Gaya, Saugor Island, and Juggernaut are objects of devout pilgrimage: but the two last are deemed of pre-eminent sanctity; while Gaya, the birth-place of their great legislator, is only of secondary rank."—(Hamilton's Gazetteer, article Tibet.)

7. But the most remarkable fact is to be found in Stirling's History of Orissa, who relates the tradition of the taking and destroying Jaggannáth and Puri by the invader Rakta Bahu (the red-armed), and the rage of the conqueror at the escape

The Dalada arrived in Ceylon A.D. 309, in the reign of Kitsiri Maiwan, who received the royal escort and their precious charge with all the honour and respect which a devout King and a numerous and believing people could bestow: his subjects vied in the richness of the offerings which they made on such an auspicious event, and the King dedicated the whole island to the Dalada.

Since its arrival in Ceylon, the account of this relic forms an important part in the Cingalese chronicles, and may be traced in the history of their Kings; which, however, is silent regarding one of its adventures recorded by Rebeiro, who irreverently pronounces it to be the tooth of an ape. He states, that in A.D. 1560 it was taken

of a relic. This happened in the reign of Subhan Deo, who succeeded to the throne A.D. 318; a very near approximation to the date of the capture of Dantapoora, which, according to Cingalese history, took place A.D. 309. Mr. Stirling proceeds to say, after describing this capture of Jagannáth, "Possibly the tradition which I have described above, may have some connection with the fierce religious disputes which raged between the worshipers of Brahma and Buddha about the period in which the invasion of foreigners and the flight of Jagannáth is placed; and which, as is well known, terminated in the expulsion of the latter from the continent of India."

8. All castes are privileged to mix within the sacred limits of Juggernaut; I believe they are even blameless for eating together: this certainly savours of a Buddhist origin and arrangement.

from the Cingalese * by Constantine de Braganza, who refused an immense ransom offered for it by them, and caused it to be publicly burned. Sir Thomas Herbert mentions, that Constantine refused three hundred thousand ducats; but that another tooth was forged so well that the priests were deceived and purchased it at a high price.

If the appearance of the Dalada could have warranted the Portuguese historian in his assertion that it was the tooth of an ape, it must have risen from its ashes, not only unimpaired, but greatly increased in size. However, the counterfeit is stated by Sir Thomas Herbert to have been so well executed as to deceive the priests; and the Cingalese say, the Dalada was not captured by the Portuguese, but at that time remained concealed at Delgamma, in Saffragam. In either case, it is reasonable to suppose that whatever became of the Dalada, if a substitute was prepared, it would be an exact resemblance of the original; and not the least curious fact connected with this antique is, that the original promoter of the imposition (which passed it as a tooth of Gautama) did not procure some old man's tooth, and thus deprive sceptics of at least one strong argument against its authenticity.

* Rebeiro says, it was taken at Yapana (Jaffna). This is probably a mistake for Yapahoo, the ruins of which capital may still be seen in the Seven Korles.

When, in A.D. 1815, the British became rulers over the whole of Ceylon, and proprietors of the Dalada, we might expect that its wanderings were at an end; but, previous to the rebellion of 1817, it was surreptitiously removed by certain priests appointed to officiate at its sanctuary. Towards the conclusion of the rebellion it was again recovered, having been found with a priest who was seized in the Mátalé district. The first Adikar remarked on this event, "that, whatever the English might think of the consequence of having taken Kappitapola (and other chiefs of the rebellion), in his opinion, and in the opinion of the people in general, the taking of the relic was of infinitely more moment." And Dr. Davy, who was in the country at the time, says, "The effect of its capture was astonishing, and almost beyond the comprehension of the enlightened."

The next occasion on which the Dalada attracted public attention was, at its public exhibition in Kandy on the 28th of May 1828, the first time for fifty-three years; and of this splendid festival I have already spoken.*

* For preparing the description of the Dalada which I have given in the account of the great Kandian festival of 1828, I had the best opportunities, having gone to Kandy and remained there during its public exhibition. I also repaired to Kandy and was present when it was privately shown to Sir Robert and Lady Horton and party, amongst whom was Baron Von Hugel.

In 1834, a plan was discussed by some disaffected persons for again removing the Dalada, and then renewing those scenes from which the Kandian country suffered so grievously in 1818; but their proceedings were watched, their purpose prevented, and themselves exposed.

THE DALADA OF SAIRUWAWILLA.

Many Buddhists reject as apocryphal the account of the Soma dagoba at Sairuwawilla, which asserts that a Dalada relic is contained in that monument; yet, as the King of that most orthodox country, Siam, was anxious to become its possessor, and the arguments against its authenticity must have been set at nought by those who reared this great pile in honour of it, I shall subjoin a very short account of this tooth, which, in permanence of place and obscurity of destiny, offers so striking a contrast to the vicissitudes of the great (Kandian) Dalada relic.

Abhya, a Prince of Girinuwara, having quarrelled with his more powerful relations, left his country, and sought refuge with Saiva, a tributary King, residing at Sairuwawilla. The Prince was accompanied by numerous followers, and his Queen Soma, by whose advice he commenced building a dagoba. When the building had reached a proper height, a priest, called Mehindoo, fulfilled a promise he had formerly made, by giving a Dalada relic to Abhya, who, having deposited it in a space left in the centre of the building, completed the work B.C. 180, and named it the Soma dagoba.

Sairuwawilla is situated in a remote part of a little-frequented district, Cotiar, and between the two branches into which the Mahawelli-ganga separates before reaching the sea.

At the request of the King of Siam, the Kandian King, Radjadhi-raja Singha, in 1797, made an attempt to gain possession of this relic, the repository of which was within the territories taken by the British from the Dutch Government in the preceding year. For this purpose, a Kandian chief with a few trusty persons were clandestinely sent into the British territory, and safely reached the secluded ruins of the Soma dágoba, and the other buildings of Sairuwawilla (which one of the party described to me as lying on the opposite side of a tank, but connected with the dágoba by a causeway through the water). Seeing how hopeless an undertaking it was for so small a party to attempt to penetrate to the relic, they returned to Kandy, and no farther attempt was made to obtain this tooth for the Buddhists of Siam.

CHAPTER XI.

HISTORY OF THE PORTUGUESE IN CEYLON.

Portuguese first land in Ceylon. — Treaty. — Fort of Colombo commenced. — Natives defeated, — surround Colombo. — Successful Sortie. — Cingalese Prince crowned in effigy at Lisbon. — Unsuccessful Policy of the Portuguese. — Wimala Dharma defeats De Souza, and captures Donna Catherina. — Hieronymus de Azivedo defeated. — Attempt to assassinate the Cingalese King. — Character of Wimala Dharma. — Constantine de Saa defeated and killed. — De Melo and Bottado defeated and killed. — Raja Singha. — Portuguese Forts and Territory taken by the Dutch.

SUMMARY OF THE HISTORY OF PORTUGUESE AFFAIRS IN CEYLON, FROM A.D. 1505 UNTIL 1658.

From the time when the Portuguese first landed in Ceylon, A.D. 1505, until their expulsion by the Dutch in 1658, we may look in vain in any record for traits of sound judgment or common justice in their conduct towards the natives of the island. The Portuguese were ever ambitious to increase their territories in Ceylon, and to extend the Roman Catholic religion: yet a vile policy forbade permanent success to their great political schemes; and if they managed to withdraw worshipers from Buddhism, it was only to replace one superstition by another, which, preached by fanatics, and enforced by those who disregarded every moral obligation, was miscalled Christianity.

A few of the most prominent incidents in the history of Portuguese dominion in Ceylon will be sufficient to show the nature of their policy; and, notwithstanding the unscrupulous conduct of many of their governors or commanders, the abilities and courage of some of them, and the cruelties of others, their measures in general remain alike unredeemed by good intentions or successful execution.

In the year 1505, Lorenzo de Almeida, (son of Francisco de Almeida, viceroy of Goa,) while in command of nine vessels, was accidentally driven on the coast of Ceylon; and has not unfrequently been called the discoverer of the island, even by those who record the notices of it to be found in ancient writers, as well as the visits of Marco Polo in the thirteenth, and Sir John Mandeville in the fourteenth century. The Portuguese asserted that Don Lorenzo concluded a treaty with the Cingalese monarch (Dharma Prákrama Bahoo the Ninth), who agreed to pay an annual tribute of two hundred and fifty thousand pounds' weight of cinnamon; in return for which, the King of

Portugal was to defend his Cingalese Majesty from every enemy. The Portuguese historian * adds, that a pillar, on which were cut the arms of Portugal, was erected to commemorate the conclusion of this treaty; but it was more probably intended as an evidence of discovery, to be followed by forcible possession at some future period, if the Cingalese monarch should be found unable to resist the arms of his new ally, his Faithful Majesty. The treaty itself must have been an invention of the Portuguese commander, or some qualified evasion of his demands by the Cingalese monarch, who probably never intended to execute, and certainly could not have fulfilled such a contract. That the engagement with regard to cinnamon was not expected to be performed, or never existed, may be inferred from the fact that the Portuguese did not return to Ceylon until twelve years after this treaty is said to have been executed; and, in the sixteenth century, such an immense quantity of cinnamon would have been too valuable an addition to the income of any European monarch, to allow of its remaining so long unclaimed.

In 1518, Lopez Suaar Alvarengo arrived in Ceylon with a large fleet, and commenced erecting a fort; but was interrupted by the natives, whom he attacked and routed. The Portuguese say, that

* Ribeiro.

after this defeat the Cingalese King agreed to sanction the erection of a fort at Colombo; also, to pay annually six elephants, some precious stones, and one hundred and twenty thousand pounds' weight of cinnamon. The existence of this treaty is doubted by Ribeiro; but, whether the Cingalese gave the permission, or want of power prevented their successful opposition to the work, a fort at Colombo was finished in 1519, and enlarged and strengthened in 1520. The insolent and aggressive proceedings of the Portuguese again brought on hostilities, in which the natives were defeated; but reassembled in such numbers as compelled their enemies to take refuge in the fort, which was immediately besieged. After being shut up for five months within their walls, the Portuguese received a reinforcement of fifty men from Goa; and, although after this increase their force only amounted to three hundred soldiers, their commander, Lopez de Bretto, made a sortie, entirely defeated the numerous horde by which he had been so long blockaded, and compelled their King to sue for peace.

In 1524, orders were sent from Portugal to destroy the fort of Colombo: it was in consequence abandoned, with the exception of a factor, secretary, and fifteen men; but the defences must have been preserved, as this small force successfully resisted a great body of Malabars, who came by sea from the continent of India and attacked the post.

The King of Ceylon, Bhuwaneka Bahoo the Seventh, finding that the succession of his adopted son and intended successor would be disputed, determined to place him under the protection of the King of Portugal; and, in furtherance of this object, two Cingalese ambassadors were sent to Europe, bearing with them a figure of the young Prince and a golden crown. With much pomp and ceremony, in the hall of the palace at Lisbon, A.D. 1541, the effigy of the Cingalese Prince was crowned by the Portuguese monarch.* On the death of Bhuwaneka Bahoo, who was accidentally shot by a Portuguese gentleman in a boat on the river Kellania, he was succeeded by the youth who had been acknowledged in Portugal, and who was now supported by the forces of that kingdom in Ceylon. He had been educated by the Portuguese as a Christian; and in their history is known by the name of Don Juan, but in the Cingalese annals is called Dharma Pala. Notwithstanding the influence of his European allies, and the assistance they afforded him, Don Juan was compelled to seek protection in the Portuguese fortresses; while the real sovereign power over the Cingalese was possessed by Raja Singha of Seetawaka.† The Por-

* Ribeiro. † Raja Singha the First, of Cingalese history.

tuguese then assisted Kónappoo Bandar, who had been educated by them at Goa, and received the Christian name of John, to raise the inhabitants of the mountainous districts against the tyranny of Raja Singha: this service he successfully accomplished; but his European patrons, jealous of his influence and abilities, placed over him another Prince, Don Philip, whom they styled King. Impolitic as ungrateful, they still continued Kónappoo in command of the native army and the auxiliary Portuguese force; but their conduct had changed him from a useful ally into a determined enemy. Tempted by ambition, and stimulated by injuries, he poisoned his rival, Don Philip; disarmed the Portuguese troops who were then at Ganarooa, three miles from Kandy; and then proceeded to attack Raja Singha. Before their armies met, Raja Singha, who, even in extreme old age,* had lost nothing of the savage cruelty that distinguished his earlier years, threatened to inflict on Kónappoo the same torture as that under which his father had expired. Kónappoo's father, by order of this Raja Singha, had been buried in the ground up to his neck; and, after enduring this torture for some time, his sufferings were terminated by rolling stones against his head.† The threats of this enthroned monster only inflamed his opponent's

* One hundred and twenty years. † Ribeiro.

rage and thirst for revenge; and from his sudden onset the forces of Raja Singha fled in irretrievable disorder. That monarch died immediately after his defeat; and Kónappoo became King of Ceylon by the name of Wimala Dharma, A.D. 1592.

Soon after these events, Pedro Lopez de Souza was sent from Goa in command of a strong force; and, on his arrival in Ceylon, took the field against Wimala Dharma, with a well-appointed army, which numbered fifteen hundred Europeans, exclusive of half-castes and native auxiliaries. De Souza brought from Manár, and proclaimed as Queen, Donna Catherina, a Princess of the Cingalese royal family; who, possessed of spirit and ability, would have been generally acceptable to the Cingalese people, had it not been for the insolent rapacity and wanton cruelty of the allies by whom she was accompanied, but who, nevertheless, carried her victorious into the Kandian capital.

These successful operations of De Souza were mainly attributable to the zealous co-operation of a native Prince, whom the Portuguese commander first insulted, and then assassinated. After this deed, De Souza was deserted by all the Cingalese who had espoused the cause of Donna Catherina; whilst the army of Wimala Dharma rapidly increased, until at Wellané he surrounded, attacked, and finally defeated the Portuguese forces. De

Souza died of his wounds; and those of his army who escaped the slaughter were made prisoners, and compelled to work for the King. Donna Çatherina remained in the power of the conqueror, who united his right of possession to her hereditary claims on the crown of Ceylon by a marriage, which gave great satisfaction to their native subjects, and was celebrated with all the magnificence that the country could afford.

Three years after the defeat of De Souza, Don Hieronymus De Azivedo arrived in Ceylon, bringing with him from Goa a force deemed sufficient to restore the affairs of the Portuguese in Ceylon, and to revenge the death of their late commander. Don Hieronymus with his army advanced to Wellané, and was there attacked by Wimala Dharma, who gained a complete victory, and pursued his enemies to the walls of Colombo. In consequence of one of the Cingalese chiefs, who had been taken prisoner, being put to death by the Portuguese as a traitor, the King of Ceylon caused several of his prisoners to be trodden to death by elephants; and despatched others to Colombo, after having had them mutilated and disfigured. For this act, being one of retaliation, as well as for their defeat, the Portuguese army blamed their general; and, worked up to fury by the sight of their maimed companions, they rushed upon Azivedo, who only escaped from the daggers of his own soldiers by the intrepidity of some priests. De Azivedo next entered into a conspiracy to procure the assassination of Wimala Dharma, but the eager villany of the Portuguese general allowed him to become the dupe of Cingalese cunning; and the five Portuguese, who were to have been the assassins of the monarch, became the victims of his severity, and suffered death by torture.

The following description of Wimala Dharma is gathered from Ribeiro. He was tall and well-formed; a great general, and an able politician; feared and beloved by all, he recompensed liberally and punished severely; distrusting the Portuguese, and despising the natives, he was neither heathen nor Christian; and, having no religion, his own interest and ambition formed the rules for his conduct.

In 1630, Constantine de Saa invaded Ouva; and was there defeated and slain by the Cingalese under the command of three Princes, sons of Donna Catherina, viz. Vijeya Pála and Kumara Singha, her sons by Wimala Dharma, and Raja Singha, her son by Sennerát, her second husband, a brother of Wimala Dharma.

In 1638, the Portuguese force, amounting to two thousand three hundred regular troops and six thousand natives, again invaded the Kandian country, made themselves masters of its capital, and exercised many acts of wanton cruelty. After being deserted by their native allies, the Portuguese retired three miles to a small fortification on the bank of the Mahawelli-ganga, called Ganarooa, where they were surrounded, attacked, and defeated by the Cingalese under Prince Raja Singha. The Portuguese commanders, De Melo and Bottado, were killed; only seventy prisoners were taken, and none escaped from this disastrous rout.

"On the day that the fort at Gannoroowé was taken, Raja Singha, who exposed himself very much, had a narrow escape of his life: a Kaffer aimed at him, and sent a bullet through his cap; the Prince returned the fire with effect.* For very many years the cap was kept as a court-curiosity; and the gun which the Prince used may be in existence even now, for it was in the late King's armoury. It was left-handed, as the Prince was; there was this inscription on it: 'This is the gun with which Raja Singha killed the Kaffer who fired at him at Gatambe.†'" The heads of his fallen enemies were cut off, and piled before the young Prince Raja Singha, afterwards King by the same name, Raja Singha the Second. This is the same monarch whose character, manners, and appearance are so well described by Knox,

* Extract from Dr. Davy's "Ceylon." † Near Ganarooa.

who was his captive for twenty years. Despite the cruelties of this Raja Singha, and the consequent rebellions of his subjects, he maintained his authority, repelled the Portuguese, reigned half a century, and died a natural death at eighty years of age, A.D. 1685.

The Portuguese had erected seven forts in different parts of the maritime provinces; these, one after another, fell before the rising power and greater energy of the Dutch: in 1656, Colombo surrendered to them. and in 1658, Jaffna, the last possession held by the Portuguese in Ceylon, was taken, and their garrisons were sent prisoners to Batavia.

The Portuguese, on several occasions, claimed a legitimate right to the sovereignty of the island in virtue of bequests from native princes, who, unable to maintain themselves as Kings, bequeathed what they never had enjoyed; and which had they possessed, they could have had no right to bestow.

CHAPTER XII.

HISTORY OF THE DUTCH IN CEYLON.

The Dutch visit Ceylon. — Admiral Spilbergen. — Sibald de Weerd — is killed. — Cingalese King's Letter. — Boschouder. — Coster murdered. — Adrian Vanderstel killed. — Dutch take Kandy; — abandon the Kandian country; — surrender their Possessions in Ceylon to the British.

SUMMARY OF THE HISTORY OF DUTCH AFFAIRS IN CEYLON, FROM A.D. 1602 TO A.D. 1796.

IN 1602, Admiral Spilbergen arrived on the coast of Ceylon, near Batticaloe: the native chief of the district there being unable to furnish a cargo of spice, and thus obtain by barter the goods he had seen and coveted, determined to attempt gaining possession of the ship by stratagem. In this design he was frustrated by the vigilance of the admiral, who determined to visit the Cingalese King, and proceeded on his journey through Beentenne. On his arrival at Kandy, the King, Wimala Dharma, received him graciously, treated him with confidence, and, anxious to support a power hostile to the Portuguese, granted permission to the King of Holland to build a fort in any part of the island. The firm and judicious conduct of Spilbergen, and his having captured (soon after his return from Kandy) three small Portuguese vessels, — one of which, with its cargo, he presented to the Cingalese King, — impressed that monarch and his followers with a favourable opinion of the Dutch nation.

In the same year Sibald de Weerd arrived at Batticaloe, and proceeded to visit the Kandian King, who received and entertained him with marked respect. After his return to the ships, De Weerd proceeded to Acheen, and on his way back to Ceylon captured four Portuguese ships, which, with their cargoes, he restored to their owners: this, and several other acts, excited in Wimala Dharma (who had arrived at Batticaloe) suspicions of the fidelity of his new ally. Soon after this event, De Weerd, in a fit of intoxication having insulted the King, was murdered, and many of his followers shared his fate. Wimala Dharma expressed regret for the destruction of the attendants, but said that De Weerd deserved his death. Valentyn gives a copy of the King's letter, addressed to the officer who had succeeded to the command of the Dutch ships. "He who drinks wine is good for nothing; God has executed justice: if you desire peace, let there be peace ; if war, war."

In the reign of Sennerát, the brother and successor of Wimala Dharma, A.D. 1612, Boschouder arrived from Holland, and on the part of the Dutch Government concluded an alliance, offensive and defensive, with the Cingalese King, who distinguished Boschouder by many honourable titles, employed him in the highest offices, and treated him with entire confidence. About this time the Dutch had commenced building a fort at Cotiár, but were surprised and massacred by a party of Portuguese; who, in returning from this service, were pursued by the Cingalese, and defeated near the borders of the Seven Korles. In 1613, Boschouder, still in the Cingalese King's employment, quelled an insurrection of the natives, and took prisoner the chief who headed the rebels. He also defeated a Portuguese fleet, and took several vessels that turned out rich prizes. Boschouder after these events returned to Holland, and by a supercilious behaviour disgusted his countrymen. Equally displeased and indignant with them, he proffered his services to the King of Denmark, and died on his way returning to India in command of a Danish ship and yacht. In 1638, Adam Westerwold with five hundred men took Batticaloe from the Portuguese, and concluded an advantageous commercial treaty with the Cingalese King, Raja Singha the Second.

In 1639, the Dutch obtained possession of Trinkomalee; and, in 1640, took Negombo and Point de Galle from the Portuguese.

Coster, who at that time commanded the Dutch troops, then proceeded to Kandy; and there, having made himself obnoxious to the King, was ordered to quit the country. Coster departed from Kandy, and was murdered on the road to Batticaloe.

Raja Singha, having at last discovered that the Dutch were equally powerful as the Portuguese, and in no way more desirable as neighbours, forbore to assist in pressing the latter to extremities, and withdrew all assistance from the former, in hopes that their mutual wars would exhaust the resources of both, and prevent either from farther aggressions on the Cingalese territories. The Portuguese then recovered Negombo; but it was taken from them a second time by the Dutch forces under the command of Francis Carron, who caused the fortifications to be strengthened.

In 1646, the Dutch having carried off several elephants belonging to the Kandian King, with whom they were then at peace, he avenged himself for the insult by attacking a party of Dutch who were crossing through the Seven Korles under the command of Adrian Vanderstel, who was killed, and many of his men were made prisoners. Raja Singha caused the Dutch commander's head to be cut off, tied in a silken bag, and sent it in that way to Negombo, from which garrison the party had proceeded to seize the royal elephants.

On the final expulsion of the Portuguese in 1658, the Cingalese King was convinced of what he had long dreaded, viz. that the Dutch had no intention of fulfilling any promise they had made of restoring to him either fortresses or territory which they had wrested from the Portuguese. On their parts, the Dutch repeatedly, but in vain, attempted to regain the favour of Raja Singha, who received their rich presents, detained some of their ambassadors, dissembled his feelings, and retained his hatred. One of the ambassadors thus detained, having determined to regain his liberty or lose his life, proceeded to the palace in full dress, entered the audience-hall, took a formal and respectful leave, the same as if the King had been present, and then proceeded on his journey. Raja Singha directed the chiefs to furnish him with supplies, and he arrived safe at Colombo.

In 1672, a French fleet under Monsieur De la Haye anchored at Trinkomalee, and from thence sent an ambassador to Kandy: the King directed that their ships should be supplied with provisions, and promised that assistance should be given to enable the French to build a fort near the bay of Cotiár. This work had not proceeded far when the French fleet was defeated, and the fort taken, by the Dutch under Admiral Van Goens. The French ambassador who had proceeded to Kandy, Monsieur Laisne de Nanclars de Lanerolle, having defied the customs and observances of the court, was beaten and imprisoned, as well as his followers, by order of the King. When Knox made his escape (nine years after this), they were still detained, and the ambassador continued as haughty and uncompromising as ever.

The Dutch and natives continued to regard each other with mutual jealousy; and the former gradually extended their territory, and strengthened their posts around the coasts of the island. On the 19th of February 1763, a Dutch force, sent by the Governor, Von Eck, after considerable opposition and some loss, took possession of Kandy, and sent out detachments, which penetrated into the surrounding districts of Mátalé, Dombara, and Walapané, to the extent of twenty miles around the capital. The Dutch, however, found themselves unable to retain their conquests, which they soon abandoned, and then found it necessary to conclude a treaty with the Kandian King. The terms of this arrangement, highly disadvantageous to the Dutch, afford a convincing proof that at the time it was concluded their affairs had miserably retrograded; but, as the Kandian Government were unable to enforce the observance, the Dutch continued to evade the performance of the most obnoxious articles of this convention.

From this time, the Kandians and Dutch continued to regard each other with suspicion and hatred, until the maritime provinces of Ceylon were taken possession of by the British forces in 1796; at which time the Kandian King, Rajadhi Raja Singha, attempted, by assisting the British, to revenge the long course of injury and oppression which his countrymen had suffered from the mercenary and encroaching spirit of Dutch colonial dominion.

CHAPTER XIII.

THE CINGALESE LANGUAGE AND LITERATURE.

I was made aware that they
Were the Kings pre-Adamite
Of that giant race of might
Who o'er earth held regal sway.
They traced up their line to heaven;
To those watchers who came down,
And forsook their heavenly crown.—READE.

Cingalese Language and Literature.— Nágara. — Cingalese.— Elu.— Cingalese Books. — Writing. — Poetry.— Eras used in Cingalese Works. — Formation of the present World. — Descent of Mankind.— The first King.

THE CINGALESE LANGUAGE AND LITERATURE.

Two distinct written characters have been employed in Ceylon; one of these has not only been obsolete for generations, but even its alphabet was unknown: this is called the Nágara, and is remarkable for the square or angular form of its letters. The Cingalese character now in use, on the contrary, is equally remarkable for its circularity. The Nágara for many ages has only existed in the numerous stone inscriptions that are scattered over Ceylon, and still remain untranslated; but as the alphabet lately restored by Mr. Prinsep,* and published in his most valuable journal, appears to be nearly identical with the Ceylon Nágara, there is little doubt that any Pali scholar may now investigate the secret of these writings. This form of letters was probably brought into Ceylon from Patalipura by Mehindoo B.C. 307; and it may be doubtful whether it ever was in use, unless amongst the priesthood.

The Cingalese written character is particularly neat; and it is wonderful with what expedition a practised native writer proceeds with his work, and how straight he preserves the lines, although he has no support for the leaf except his left hand. Cingalese writings were always executed on leaves of the palmyra or tala trees: the former, being narrow, were used for ordinary messages and common deeds; but the talapat was always employed for books of value. The leaves of a handsome Cingalese book are about two and a half inches in breadth, and twenty inches in length: they are placed between boards of the same size,

* This alphabet is of the letters employed in the inscriptions in various parts of India; and was published in 1837, in the Asiatic Society Journal, Calcutta.

neatly lackered, and the whole is connected together by being strung on a cord; to receive which the leaves and boards are perforated with two holes in the middle of the leaf, and four inches from each end. The Cingalese writing is performed with a long, sharp-pointed style, by which the leaf is scratched or graved; and, to any person unaccustomed to the operation, it is even difficult to see the letters after they are formed: the whole is then made visible by rubbing over the leaf with a strong-scented, dark-coloured oil, prepared from charred gum; when this is again wiped off, the indented letters only are left black. The imperishable nature of the tala-leaf, and the properties of the oil used in blackening the writing, which is a preservative from the attack of insects, are the reasons why native books may be found of very great age, and in good preservation.

The language employed in Cingalese books is not the same as that usually spoken, nor is it generally understood; it is properly called Elu,* but more commonly "High Cingalese:" it does not approximate so near the Sanskrit as the colloquial language,† of which nine out of every ten words

* Mr. Clough, author of the Cingalese Dictionary, thinks Elu was the language of Lanka (Ceylon) prior to the Cingalese conquest.

† The common Cingalese Mr. Clough supposes was introduced by the Singha conquerors.

are derived from Sanskrit, or Pali.* The greater intricacy is not more striking than the greater regularity of the Cingalese language as compared to the dialects of Europe; and the proportion of natives who can read and write their own difficult character may astonish, and might shame, nations who have looked on the Cingalese as illiterate savages.

The Cingalese are fond of poetry; but their most voluminous writer of poems in Cingalese is Gasco,† a Portuguese, who in early youth was taken prisoner by the Kandians, and afterwards rose to the highest native situation under the King, Raja Singha the Second. His poems are in no wise exempt from the defects which are so marked in the poetry written by natives of Ceylon; they are in general confused in arrangement, intricate in construction, and obscure in meaning; greater stress being laid on the sound and position of letters, than in elucidating the subject, or exciting the imagination of the reader.

The eras made use of in Cingalese works, and from which the dates in this work are all reduced to B.C. (before Christ) and A.D. (the Christian era), are—

* Introduction to Clough's Cingalese Dictionary.

† Particulars of this poet's fate will be found in another place.

The Kaliyuga, which commenced 1631 years before the death of Gautama Buddha, is B.C. 2174.

The era of the death* of Gautama Buddha, B.C. 543, is generally used in Pali, and also in Cingalese historical works.

The era of the establishment of religion is B.C. 237; and marks the time when Mehindoo renovated the Buddhist religion, and brought many valuable relics of Gautama to Ceylon.

The era of Saka, although seldom used in books, is generally employed in all deeds and grants of land, as well as every other secular document. It is the same as that of King Sálivahana, so well known on the continent of India, and whose era, as fixed by the Cingalese, corresponds to A.D. 78. The natives, or their historians, ignorant of the origin of this era, or unwilling, when it was imposed upon them, to record the real merits of the case, account for the establishment of this era by the following legends.

During a grievous famine, a Buddhist priest arrived at the house of Saka, a man of the Goya (cultivator) caste, at the time when he had only one meal of rice left to support himself and his family; this he ordered to be prepared, and with-

* Before or soon after the death of Gautama, the period of his becoming a Buddha, viz. B.C. 588, is occasionally employed as an era, but not in historical works.

out hesitation offered it to the holy man. To reward this sacrifice to hospitality, and obedience to the injunctions of Buddha, the handful of rice became inexhaustible, and during the continuance of the famine supplied Saka, his family, and neighbours. The conduct of Saka being thus manifestly approved by the gods, the people raised him to the throne of the kingdom, — what kingdom the legend does not say; and the whole is a fiction, evidently composed on account of its moral, and as an admirable commentary on the ordinance which enjoins giving alms to the priesthood.

The famine above alluded to is said not only to have devastated a great part of the continent of India, but also to have carried off multitudes of people in Ceylon; and its origin at Sagalla-nuwara* is stated to have been as a punishment for the crimes of the King and the vices of his people, who had irritated the gods, particularly by the murder of a Brahmin, of which deed of violence the following account is given. The King of Sagalla-nuwara, Mehindoo, having conceived a violent passion for the wife of a Brahmin, desired his emissaries to involve the husband in some offence, and have him removed. Soon after these instructions had been given, as the Brahmin was proceeding on a journey into a neighbouring dis-

* Near the present town of Mirsa-poor.

trict, one of the King's cattle was placed in a ravine through which the Brahmin had to pass, and at a spot where the animal could neither return nor clamber up the banks. The Brahmin was seized, and put to death, for stealing from the royal herd. Temptation and persecution alike failed to effect the purpose which the King had in view: the widow vowed to destroy herself on her husband's funeral pile, and, previous to her voluntary immolation, she sprinkled the soles of her feet with charcoal; then, three several times throwing water towards the heavens, she imprecated a curse on the King and country. Twelve years of drought and famine scourged that country, and avenged the unjust death of the Brahmin; and, to punish the impiety of various other nations, the famine extended to them and endured for various periods: in Ceylon it continued for a space of three years.

Besides their continued histories, and the religious Buddhistical works, the Cingalese have books on grammar, medicine, astrology, origin of caste, geography of the island, many detached fragments of history, and portions said to be Buddhistical revelations. As a specimen of the latter, I shall give their account of the creation of the world.

If this history of the creation of the world and of man, or rather of the re-construction of the former and descent of the latter, was preserved by tradition, however inaccurate, it is curious for its antiquity: if it is the invention, miscalled revelation, of a philosopher, it at least shows deep reflection: above all, it is interesting from the coincidence of some of its statements with the facts of creation as recorded by Moses; a coincidence the more extraordinary, as it seems to argue a common origin, but not a copy. In this work we find an account of the fall of man from a more perfect being to his present state, by progressive stages, occasioned by increasing wickedness; in the Mosaic account the crime is single, the event sudden. By both accounts the punishment is interminable as regards the race of beings which peopled the earth, as well as their posterity.

Again, we have the Kalpauruksha (tree of life?)*

* In the month of June 1831, there was a festival and Kalpauruksha at Banderapola near Mátalé. At a range of buildings prepared for the priests and people, an immense tree was fixed in the ground; many of its branches had been left unlopped, and additional artificial ones added: this formed the *tree;* its *fruit* was the offerings of the people who came from all parts with their gifts. Whatever they offered was in some way attached to the Kalpauruksha; and a more motley accumulation of animate and inanimate, worthless and valuable objects than those which dangled from its branches, or were attached to its stem, cannot be imagined. At night, during the whole continuance of the festival, priests relieved each other, preaching to the people, who flocked to the revival of an ancient and almost obsolete custom of their religion.

or, as translated by Cingalese, "the tree producing all things necessary or desirable," by which the progenitors of the race of man existed. After this tree became extinct, the race became mortal. We also find several succeeding days or generations in which there was light, but previous to the creation of the sun and moon. Another coincidence might be found according to some translations of the Bible, ch. vi. verses 2 and 3 of Genesis.

ACCOUNT OF THE CREATION.

The whole world, its rocks and mountains, were destroyed by fire, and with its oceans and atmosphere formed one chaotic mass. (This destruction and a subsequent re-creation of the world have repeatedly happened before, and may be expected to happen again, but by a different agency.) Then the gods caused a great storm; the rain descended, and increased from drops until it fell in sheets of water covering thousands of miles, and until everything was concealed by the waters. A great wind now arose, and violently agitated the flood, which was absorbed or dissipated, until the earth became visible. The air is beneath the waters, and the waters are beneath the adamantine crust, which is the visible world; in which portions of land are scattered through the waters, like lotus-leaves on the surface of a pond.

The world was still in darkness when the Bambas* descended from the celestial regions, and light which emanated from their bodies illuminated the earth. They lived as those creatures did in the place from whence they had descended, and to which they still retained the power of returning. The flavour of the new-formed earth was sweet; the Bambas first tasted, then ate of it; but, evil passions having been engendered in them, the earth lost its savour and became bitter. This is one period.

In the second period, a species of mushroom sprang from the earth, and was the food of the Bambas; but, as a punishment for their increasing wickedness, this supply also failed.

In the third period, the Bambas were nourished by various small plants, which at last became extinct.

In the fourth period, the Kalpauruksha (tree of life?) sprang up, and produced everything desirable; until, from the wickedness of the Bambas, the tree became extinct.

In the fifth period, the earth produced a species

* Bambas are described as not very different from angels: not omnipotent, yet possessing supernatural powers; pure as compared to mortals, yet not perfect, being liable to err. The Cingalese believe that the small detached rocks which are to be found scattered on the surface of many of the rocky mountains are Bambas, who in former eras were thus transformed.

of rice, which having eaten, the Bambas became transformed: they lost the power of returning to the celestial mansions; light was no longer diffused from their bodies, — they were mortal, — the earth once more in darkness. It was at this time they were formed into different sexes, and new passions appeared. Hitherto the sins of the Bambas consisted in enviousness, covetousness, ambition: to these were now added lasciviousness and other wicked inclinations; which, acting on beings who no longer possessed divine attributes, produced all the crimes of mortals, and all the sufferings of mortality. In misery and darkness mankind thought of their former power and glory, and now called for light: soon after the sun arose, and this day was called Irida (Sunday); the moon appeared the next day, and it was called Handuda (Monday); and so in successive days appeared planets whose names have attached to the days, thus: — Anguharuada (Mars, Tuesday); Budadu (Mercury, Wednesday); Brahaspoti (Jupiter, Thursday); Sikura (Venus, Friday); Senasura (Saturn, Saturday).

From the prevalence of crime, life and property were insecure; and mankind, having consulted together, determined to choose from amongst themselves one to whom they would give authority over all, to award justice and inflict punishment.

That the individual so chosen might be powerful and independent, all agreed to contribute to his support, and assist in maintaining his dignity. The person chosen was Surayia Kumara, afterwards styled Maha-Sammata-Raja (the great King elected by the people).

One million three hundred thousand years are said to have elapsed from the first descent of the Bambas until the election of Maha-Sammata-Raja;* from whom there is an attempt to trace the descent of the Buddhist sovereigns of India, including the family of Gautama Buddha, and the branch of it which furnished a conqueror to Lanka,† and fixed on it the name of Singhala

* He appears to be the same as Menu.

† Vijeya of the Singha race.

CHAPTER XIV.

HISTORY OF THE ISLAND PRIOR TO THE CINGALESE CONQUEST, B.C. 543.

What vast foundations in the abyss are there,
As of a former world! Is it not where
Atlantic kings their barbarous pomp displayed;
Sunk into darkness with the realms they swayed,
When towers and temples, thro' the closing wave,
A glimmering ray of ancient splendour gave?

ROGERS.

Traditions of Lanka prior to the Cingalese Conquest, B.C. 543. — *Wars of Rama and Rawana.* — *Partial submerging of the Island.* — *Date of the Flood.* — *The Ramayana.*—*Quotation.* — *Adventures of Seeta.* — *Deification of Rama.*

As several of the places I visited, and the anecdotes concerning them, relate to the wars of Lanka in the days of Rama and Rawana, I shall give a short account of that period, and the few other events that are recorded previous to the commencement of Cingalese history, B.C. 543

To the days of Rawana, we have to look back through the "long withdrawing vale" of time, which forty centuries cast their shades across; and in the haze of farthest distance to trace the outline of events that are partly obscured by the clouds of fiction. Poetry, although a deceptive medium (and too often confused by mythology), has still had a preserving power: without it we should be as ignorant of the history of Rawana, as we are of that long period which intervenes between his death and the era of Gautama Buddha, B.C. 543.

The rape of a Princess, followed by a long and destructive war, the siege of a city impregnable by open assault, and the final recovery of the fair cause of quarrel, are the principal events common both to the Iliad and the Ramayana. It is these poems that have preserved to us a knowledge of the victories of Achilles and Rama; although time has effaced all traces of the strength of Troy, and ocean rolls above the riches of Sri Lanka-poora.

In all accounts of the contentions and wars of Rama and Rawana, the principal actors are either exalted into gods, or branded as demons: this fact, combined with many circumstances in their history, may assure us that they were champions of adverse faiths, and fought for religion, as well as for love and empire. From the position he now holds,

Rama was certainly a champion of the Brahmins;* while Rawana adhered to the antagonist principles of the Buddhas (predecessors of Gautama Buddha), and was also a votary of the Bali † and Yakka ‡ superstitions.

Although Rawana is depicted as a monster, and denounced as a cruel tyrant, by Valmika and Kalidás, in the Ramayana and Raghuwanzae, yet from their own details we should infer that Rama was the aggressor, and that Seeta was carried away as an act of retaliation: so, in their long and doubtful strife, had victory sanctified the cause of Rawana, the virtues attributed to the deified hero might have attached to the victorious demon, and Lanka's tyrant would have been a god of India.

The partial submerging of Ceylon is stated in

* Rama is called "the friend of Brahmins." — Ramayan, Book I. section i.

Rawana, "the mighty hero, the King of the Rakshases."—Ramayan, Book I. section i.

Rama says, "Where, O Brahmin, is thy sacrifice which is to be protected? and where are the Rakshases who are to be slain by me?"—Ramayan, Book I. section xxviii.

Rama, killing all the sacrifice-destroying Rakshases, was adored by the Rishis.—Ramayan, Book I. section xxviii.

From these, and many similar passages, it would appear that the Rakshases were the opponents of bloody sacrifices, of which the Brahmins were the promoters.

† Bali, planetary. ‡ Yakka, demon.

Cingalese records to have occurred soon after the death of Rawana, and B.C. 2387. Previously to this event, Lanka is asserted to have been five thousand one hundred and twenty miles in circumference; it was then reduced by that judgement to two thousand nine hundred and ninety-two miles. By the farther encroachment of the sea in the reign of Panduwas, the second King of the Mahawanzae,* and afterwards by the more extensive calamity in the reign of Dewenepiatissa, and his feudatory Kellania Tissa,† Ceylon was reduced to nine hundred and twenty-eight miles in circumference, which, Cingalese topographical works ‡ assert, is the present extent § of the island. From the Ramayana it might be inferred that the island of Mainaca, to the westward of Mánar, had sunk below the level of the ocean, or been overwhelmed, prior even to the era of Rama; but that tradition then preserved its name, and noted the fate which had befallen it.

The Raja Walia fixes the death of Rawana B.C. 2387;‖ and the very extensive submerging of the

* Who reigned from B.C. 504 until B.C. 474.

† In the third century before Christ.

‡ Kadaimpota and Lanka-Wistrie.

§ The circumference of Ceylon is about eight hundred miles.

‖ Raja Walia, a Cingalese history, says, that from the wars of Rawana until the era of Buddha was 1844 years. Buddha's era 543 B.C. + 1844 = 2387.

coasts and low country of Lanka is said to have occurred soon after: this near coincidence with the date of the flood, according to the most eminent chronologers B.C. 2348, is remarkable, and nearly agrees with the period of the reign of Yaou in China, in whose time the deluge is said by Confucius to have happened; or according to Mangtze, "At the time of Yaou the deluge had not entirely subsided." Yaou commenced his reign B.C. 2337.*

The reduced extent of the circumference of Lanka after this first catastrophe is not very different from the statement of its size given by Eratosthenes,† and preserved by Pliny. Eratosthenes states its length to be seven thousand stadia, and its breadth five thousand.

As the same authorities that mention these different irruptions of the sea, and consequent diminution of the size of the country, allude to the several thousand islands attached to the kingdom of Lanka which have disappeared in these successive visitations,‡ it is no unnatural conjecture

* Gutzlaff's History of China.

† Eratosthenes wrote full two centuries before the Christian era.

‡ "Meya performed his devotions in Salmala, a country a little to the eastward of Lanka." This is quoted from Davies' Astronomical Computation of the Hindus. There is now no country near Ceylon to the eastward; but Cingalese traditions

that the Maldive and Laka-dive islands were at one time dependencies on Lanka, when its capital of Sri Lanka-poora was in longitude 75° 53′ 15″ E. Laka-diva is the Elu (old Cingalese) name of the island, from which Lanka is probably derived; and its derivation might then be accounted for as Laka, the ten thousand, and diva, islands. This position would also serve to explain the immense extent of territory said to have been overwhelmed by the sea; although many persons find an easier solution of these records, by total disbelief, or by considering them as the exaggerated statements of oriental writers. Yet the ancient geographers and historians of the west have recorded what all those of the east asserted,* viz. that Ceylon was formerly of much greater extent than it is at present. That the sea has encroached on the Coromandel coast, at no great distance from the northern point of Ceylon, is sufficiently proved by the remains of a city in the destruction of which ocean seems to have been stayed midway: for ages its baffled waves have been unable to secure, and earth has had no

agree that there were islands there after the commencement of Cingalese history, B.C. 543; and it was to them the Yakkas were banished soon after the introduction of Buddhism.

* "The dimensions of Lanka are equal to one-twelfth part of the equatorial circumference of the earth."—Davies' Astronomical Computation of the Hindus.

power to reclaim, the site and ruins of Maha-Balipoor.

The names of many places in Ceylon afford support to the histories of the Ramayana; and the Cingalese traditionary legends of the wars of Rawana may be considered either as the uncollected materials, or shattered fragments, of an ancient history. From these different sources is compiled the following sketch of that remote period, when gods of India were mortals in Lanka. In the conduct of these deified personages, as recorded by their panegyrists, we search in vain for higher qualifications to distinguish those who are worshiped from their adversaries who are execrated; and can only conclude that the former were endowed with virtues, and exalted into demi-gods, by "history's purchased page" and Brahmin priestcraft.

When we remember that the Ramayana is the oldest of epic poems,* we may receive with doubt its detail of events; but must regard with admiration a work which contains such passages as the following extract, and can only regret that as yet so little of the Ramayana has been made accessible

* Valmika was a contemporary of his hero; and his (Rama's) era, I have already stated, is fixed by Cingalese accounts as 2387 B.C. Sir William Jones states the period of Rama's actions as about 1810 B.C., and says, "Rama, who conquered Silan, a few centuries after the flood."

to the English reader.* Rama, while consoling his younger brother Bharata, after the death of their aged parent, the King Dasha Ratha, proceeds:—"All compounded substances hasten to decay; all that are elevated must fall; all things compacted will be dissolved; and all who live must finally die: as there is no other fear respecting ripe fruits besides their falling, so death is the grand thing feared by all who are born. As a large and firm edifice, when become old, falls into ruins, so the aged, subjected by death, sink into dissolution. The night once past never returns; the waters of Yamoona run to the sea; days and nights are passing away: the time of life appointed for all living is constantly wasting, as the rays of the sun in the summer dry up the moisture of the earth. Grieve for thyself!—why shouldst thou grieve for others? What has that man to do with what continues, or with what passes away, whose life is every moment departing? Death always accompanies us; death stays with us; after having travelled to the greatest distance, death ends our course: wrinkles are already in the body; grey hairs cover the head; decrepitude seizes on man. Why should man be anxious for future enjoyments? Men rejoice when

* The English translation, from which this passage is extracted, is that of Cary and Marshman. It was only continued to the end of the 144th section. The poem contains 620 sections.

the sun is risen; they rejoice also when it goes down, while they are unconscious of the decay of their own lives. They rejoice on seeing the face of a new season, as at the arrival of one greatly desired; yet the revolution of seasons is the decay of human life. As pieces of drift-wood, meeting in the ocean, continue together a little space; thus, wives, children, relatives, and wealth, remaining with us for a short time, separate, and their separation is certain: no one living can escape the common lot; he who mourns his departed relatives has no power to cause them to return. One standing on the road would readily say to a number of persons passing together, 'I will follow you;' why then should a person grieve when travelling the inevitable road which has been assuredly trodden by all his predecessors? Viewing the end of life, which resembles a cataract rushing down with irresistible impetuosity, every mind ought to pursue that which is connected with its own happiness, even virtue."

In the earliest ages of which tradition has preserved any memorials, the inhabitants of Lanka appear to have been subdued by Brahmin warriors, whose conduct and success probably extended their power, and commanded greater respect amongst their own followers and in their native countries. These feelings afterwards increased into veneration, and finally ended in the worship of conquerors, such as Ramachandra, now an Avatár of Vishnu, but first a Prince of Oude, and conqueror of Lanka.

Previous to that event, Lanka, divided into three kingdoms, was under the sway of the Kings Malee, Sumalee, and Maliawan, who, as well as their subjects, are called Asurs, and enemies of the gods.* The country at that period is described as being of immense extent, unequalled fertility, and containing prodigious wealth. Vishnu,† in his wars against the Asurs, having killed Malee and Sumalee, Maliawan, accompanied by his daughter, escaped into the forests; and Kubheran, or Kuweran, ruled over Lanka. This King ‡ was son of the Brahmin Vishravas, of the race of Pulastya, and afterwards became an object of worship as Kuweran, god of riches; but he was driven from the throne by his half-brothers, Rawana,§ Kumbakarna, and Weebeeshana, the three sons of Vish-

* From the Cingalese, Rawana Katháwai.

† Some incarnation previous to Rama.

‡ "Cuvera, the Indian Plutus, one of whose names is Pulastya."—Sir William Jones. Cuvera is also called a chief of Yakshas.

§ "Where Rawana remains, there the sun loses his force; the winds through fear of him do not blow; the fire ceases to burn; the rolling ocean, seeing him, ceases to move its waves. Vishravana (Cuvera), distressed by his power, has abandoned Lanka and fled."—Ramayana, Book I. section xiii.

ravas, by Maya, daughter of Maliawan the Asur. The epithet "Asur" appears to have been bestowed by Brahmins on the infidel inhabitants of Lanka and southern India: they also appear to employ it as a term of disparagement to giant, demi-god, and devil, infidel or innovator.

Rawana is said to have distinguished himself by the practice of severe austerities, and the performance of virtuous actions, until he established himself as King of Lanka and Pandi * (southern India): then, corrupted by prosperity, he disregarded alike the Brahmins and Buddhist priests, and aspired to render himself sovereign King over all India. He embellished his capital of Sri Lanka-poora with many noble palaces, and fortified it with seven walls strengthened by towers; the whole being surrounded by a ditch of great breadth, supplied with water from the ocean.† Several of Rawana's kindred having been destroyed, and his sister, Soorpanukha, being insulted and mutilated by Rama Prince of Yodhya (Oude), Rawana revenged himself by surprising and secretly carrying off Seeta,

* One of Rawana's capitals was Caveripoora.—Kadaimpota, a Cingalese work.

† The ditches of Sri Lanka-poora being filled with salt-water (like the present leways of Ceylon), shows that no very great convulsion of nature was required to overwhelm a city in such a position.

the beauteous wife of Rama, and detaining her concealed in the forests of the interior of Lanka.*

The cause of the disappearance of Seeta, and the place of her captivity, having been discovered by Rama, he collected an army with which he passed into Lanka, advanced against Rawana, and laid siege to his capital.† After a war of varied success and twelve years' duration, Rawana was defeated and slain; while the conquering Rama, having rescued his devoted Seeta, and placed Weebeeshana on the throne of Lanka, returned in triumph to Oude to reign a king and die a god.‡

* The forests called Asoka Arameya (the asoka groves) constitute the region about Nuwara-ellia.

† It is believed by the Hindus that Rawana's Queen (Wandódaree) invented the game of chess during the tedious siege of Sri Lanka-poora. The name of this game, and the designation of the different pieces, are words common to the Cingalese language; but, like most of its expressions, are originally Sanskrit. The game itself is called Chaturanga, the four forces or members of which an army is composed.

PIECES.

Sanskrit.	*Translation.*	*English Game.*
Raja	King	King.
Mantri	Minister	Queen.
Hasti	Elephant	Bishop.
Aswa	Horse	Knight.
Ratha }	{ War-chariot }	{ Castle.
Roka }	{ Ship }	{ Rook.
Padátika	Foot-soldier	Pawn.

‡ As Ramachandra, an Avatár of Vishnu. Rama and his brother Laksmana are both worshiped in Ceylon by the same

Weebeeshana assisted Rama against his brother Rawana; and the crown of Lanka, with a place amongst the gods, were the rewards of his treason.

Rama appears to have owed his success mainly to the wisdom and power of his continental ally Sugriwa; and a chief who, notwithstanding his eminent services, has suffered deification in the undignified form of a monkey, and under the name of Hanuman.

The traditions say that the defeat and death of Rawana were but parts of that judgment which his wickedness and the impiety of the Rakshases had provoked. The doom extended to their country, whose fairest provinces sank beneath the ocean,* while the waves of oblivion closed for ever above the pride and wealth of Lanka-poora. Its name, however, survives as the meridian point of Indian astronomers;† and in legends of Ceylon

name, Saman; the statues of the former are painted blue, and the latter yellow.

* "Silan was peopled time out of mind by the Hindu race; and formerly, perhaps, extended much farther to the west and to the south, so as to include Lanka or the equinoctial point of the Indian astronomers."—Sir W. Jones.

"Many of the people in the distant provinces of India believe that Ceylon is destroyed."—Introduction to Roberts' translation of a Hindu Book of Fate.

† Colonel Lambton has fixed the meridian of Lanka as 75 53′ 15″ east of Greenwich; this is nearly three degrees to the westward of any part of Ceylon.

and the continent of India it is maintained that the splendour of Lanka's brazen battlements still gleams from the depth of ocean,* and illumines the sky above, just at the time when day has ceased, and before night has closed in darkness :

> " So gleams the past, the light of other days,
> Which shines, but warms not with its powerless rays."

---

* Statement of a Fakir :—He says, he went to Ramiseram, but did not go to Ceylon (Singuldwip), from whence (he says) the glitterings of Lanka are seen. He further says, he was told that in it (Singuldwip) is the seat of Rawan, and Hanuman's twelve watch stations. (Communicated by Mr. Duncan, vol. v. Asiatic Researches.)

"Lanka :—According to some Hindu accounts, it is distinct from Ceylon, from which island Lanka is said to be just visible."—Wilson's Sanskrit Dictionary.

APPENDIX.

TURNOUR'S* EPITOME OF CINGALESE HISTORY.

INTRODUCTION.

To the Editor of the Ceylon Almanac.

SIR,—In compliance with your request, I have the pleasure to send you a chronological list of the Kings of Ceylon, compiled from the native annals extant in this island.

In the comparatively short period that this colony has been a British possession, several histories, besides minor historical notices of Ceylon, have already been published in English.

The individuals to whom we are indebted for those works, unacquainted themselves with the native languages, and misguided by the persons from whom they derived their information, have concurred in representing that there were no authentic historical records to be found in Ceylon.

CORDINER affords no information regarding them; and falls at once into an anachronism of 471 years, by applying the following remark to the Buddha worshiped in Ceylon: "Sir W. Jones, on taking the medium of four several dates, fixes the time of Buddha, or the ninth great incarnation of Vishnu, in the year 1014 before the birth of Christ."

PERCEVAL asserts, that "the wild stories current among the natives throw no light whatever on the ancient history of the island: the earliest period at which we can look for any

* The Honourable George Turnour, Ceylon Civil Service.

authentic information is the arrival of the Portuguese under Almeida, in 1505."

Bertolacci, in his valuable statistical work, states "We learn *from tradition* that Ceylon possessed in former times a larger population and a much higher state of cultivation than it now enjoys: although we have no data to fix with any degree of certainty the exact period of this prosperity, yet the fact is incontestable. The signs which have been left, and which we observe upon the island, lead us gradually back to the remotest antiquity."

Philalethes, professedly writing "The History of Ceylon *from the earliest period*," which is prefixed to the last edition of Knox's historical relation of the island, dates the commencement of the Wejayan dynasty in A.D. 106, instead of B.C. 543; and is then reduced to the necessity of adding, "Without attempting to clear a way, where so little light is afforded, through this labyrinth of chronological difficulties, I shall content myself with exhibiting the succession of the Cingalese sovereigns, with the length of their reigns, as it appears in Valentyn."

Davy appears to have been more accurately informed; but, dependent on the interpretations of the natives, who are always prone to dwell on the exaggeration and fictions which abound in all oriental literature, has been induced to form the opinion, that "the Singhalese possess no accurate record of events; are ignorant of genuine history; and are not sufficiently advanced to relish it. Instead of the one, they have legendary tales; and instead of the other, historical romances."

To publish now, in the face of these hitherto undisputed authorities, a statement containing an uninterrupted historical record of nearly *twenty-four centuries*, without the fullest evidence of its authenticity, or at least acknowledging the sources from which the data are obtained, would be to require the public to place a degree of faith in the accuracy of an unsupported document, which it would be most unreasonable in me to expect. I must therefore beg, if you use at all the paper I now send you, that it be inserted in the detailed form in which it has been prepared by me, together with this letter in explanation.

The principal native historical record in Ceylon is the Maha Wanse. It is written in Pali verse. The prosody of Pali grammar prescribes not only the observance of certain rules which regulate syllabic quantity, but admits of an extensive licence of permutation and elision of letters, for the sake of euphony. As the inflexions of the nouns and verbs are almost exclusively in the ultimate syllable, and as all the words in each verse or sentence are connected, as if they composed one interminable word, it will readily be imagined what a variety of constructions each sentence may admit of, even in cases where the manuscript is free from clerical errors; but, from the circumstance of the process of transcription having been almost exclusively left to mere copyists, who had themselves no knowledge of the language, all Pali manuscripts are peculiarly liable to clerical and other more important inaccuracies; many of which have been inadvertently adopted by subsequent authors of Singhalese works, materially altering the sense of the original. It is, I presume, to enable the reader to overcome these difficulties, that the authors of Pali works of any note, composed in verse, usually published a commentary also, containing a literal rendering of the sense, as well as explanations of abstruse passages.

The study of the Pali language being confined, among the natives of Ceylon, almost entirely to the priesthood, and prosecuted solely for the purpose of qualifying them for ordination, their attention has been principally devoted to their voluminous religious works on Buddhism. I have never yet met with a native who had critically read through and compared their several historical works, or who had, till lately, seen a commentary on the Maha Wanse; although it was the general belief that such a commentary did still exist, or at least had been in existence at no remote period. By the kindness of the provincial chief priest of Saffragam, I was enabled in 1827 to obtain a transcript of that commentary, from a copy kept in Mulgirigalla wihare, a temple built in the reign of Saidaitissa, about 130 years before the birth of Christ; and, when brought with me to Kandy, I found that the work had not before been seen by the chief or any one of the priests of either of the two establishments which regulate the national religion of this island.

It had heretofore been the received opinion of the best-informed priests and other natives, that the Maha Wanse was a national state record of recently-past events, compiled at short intervals by royal authority, up to the reign in which each addition may have been made; and that it had been preserved in the archives of the kingdom.

The above-mentioned commentary has not only afforded valuable assistance in elucidating the early portion of the Maha Wanse, but it has likewise refuted that tradition, by proving that Maha Naama Terronnanse, the writer of that commentary, was also the author of the Maha Wanse from the commencement of the work to the end of the reign of Maha Sen, comprising the history of Ceylon from B.C. 543 to A.D. 301. It was compiled from the annals in the vernacular language then extant, and was composed at Anooraadhapoora under the auspices of his nephew Daasen Kelliya, and the minister Deegha Sandana, between A.D. 459 and 477. It is still doubtful whether Maha Naama was not also the author of the subsequent portion, to his own times. As the commentary, however, extends only to A.D. 301, and the subsequent portion of the work is usually called the Sooloo Wanse, I am disposed to infer that he only wrote the history to A.D. 301.

From the period at which Maha Naama's work terminated, to the reign of Praakrama Bahoo in A.D. 1267, the Sooloo Wanse was composed, under the patronage of the last-named sovereign, by Dharma Kirti Terronnanse at Dambedeniya. I have not been able to ascertain by whom the portion of the history from A.D. 1267 to the reign of Praakrama Bahoo of Kurunaigalla was written; but from that reign to A.D. 1758, the Maha or rather Sooloo Wanse was compiled by Tibbottoowewe Terronnanse, by the command of Kirti-Sree, partly from the works brought during his reign by the Siamese priests, (which had been procured by their predecessors during their former religious missions to this island,) and partly from the native histories, which had escaped the general destruction of literary records in the reign of Raaja Singha I.

The other works from which the accompanying statement has been framed, and which have supplied many details not contained in the Maha Wanse, are the following; which are written in Singhalese, and contain the history of the island also, from B.C. 543, to the period at which each work was written.

The POOJAAWALLEYE, composed by Mairoopaada Teronnanse, in the reign of Praakarama Bahoo, between A.D. 1267 and 1301.

The NEEKAAYSANGRAHA, or SAISANAAWATAARA, by Daiwarakhita Jaya-Bahoo Teronnanse, in the reign of Bhuvaneka Bahoo in A.D. 1347.

The RAAJA RATNAIKARA, written at a more recent period (the exact date of which I have not been able to ascertain) by Abbayaraja Teronnanse of Walgampaaye.

The RAAJAWALLEYE, which was compiled by different persons at various periods, and has both furnished the materials to, and borrowed from, the Maha Wanse.

Lastly, WILBAAGEDERA MUDIYANSE's account of his embassy to Siam in the last century.

From these native annals I have prepared hastily, and I am aware very imperfectly, an Epitome of the History of Ceylon, containing its chronology, the prominent events recorded therein, and the lineage of the reigning families; and given, in somewhat greater detail, an account of the foundation of the towns, and of the construction of the many stupendous works, the remains of which still exist, to attest the authenticity of those annals.

The materials from which this statement is framed were collected by me (assisted in the translation from the Pali by my native instructors) some years ago, when it was my intention to have arranged them for publication. Subsequent want of leisure, and the announcement of the proposal of publishing in England the translation of the greater part of the works noticed by me, have deterred me from prosecuting that project. By the last accounts received from home, the translation was in an advanced stage for publication. Its appearance in this country may, therefore, now be early looked for.

In the mean time, the circulation of this abstract of the History of Ceylon may be the means of making the translation more sought for when it arrives; and at the present moment, when improved means of communication are being established to Anooraadhapoora and to Trincomalie, traversing the parts of the island in which the ruins of the ancient towns, tanks, and other proofs of the former prosperity of Ceylon are chiefly scattered, this statement will perhaps be considered an appropriate addition to your Almanac for the ensuing year.

I am, Sir, your faithful obedient servant,

GEORGE TURNOUR,

Kandy, September 14th, 1832. *Ceylon Civil Service.*

EPITOME

OF THE

HISTORY OF CEYLON.

*** The names of places printed within brackets signify the seat of Government. The names printed in italics are those of subordinate or contemporar Princes. The dates denote the period of accession of the Kings.

1. Wejaya. [Tamana-nowera.] B.C. 543. Bud. 1. Reigned 38 years.

Son of Singha-bahoo and Singha-walli, the twin children of a daughter of the King of Waggoo. He was expelled from his father's kingdom Laala, and embarked with seven hundred followers: attempted to land at Sooppaarakapatana, in Dambadiva, but was repelled by the natives. He landed on this island on the day of Budha's death — which is the epoch of the Budhistical æra — (April B.C. 543): formed a settlement at Tamana, and made it the seat of his government. He married, first, Koovaini, the daughter of a native Prince, by whom he had two children: he repudiated her, and married, secondly, a Princess from the Paandi country, in Dambadiva, who was accompanied by many male and female attendants; the latter were given in marriage to the King's followers: — he died without issue by the second marriage.

2. Oopatissa 1st. [Oopatissa-nowera.] B.C. 505. Bud. 38. Reigned 1 year.

Minister of Wejaya: built a city at Ella Sattara, called it Oopatissa-nowera. He brought over from Saagalnowera, in Dambadiva, Panduwaasa, son of the late King's brother Somittra, and placed him on the throne in that city.

3. Panduwaasa. [Oopatissa-nowera.] B.C. 504. Bud. 39. Reigned 30 years

Nephew of Wejaya: married Bhaddakachaana, a Princess of Kimbulwatte-nowera, in Dambadiva, who was followed to the island by six brothers: had issue ten sons, and a daughter, named Oommaada Chittra. In this reign a great part of Raamanaaga (situated between the continent and this island) was overflowed and lost in the sea.

Raama. [*Raamagoona.*]
Roohoona. [*Roohoona.*]
Diggaina. [*Diggaamaddulla.*]
Oorawelli. [*Mahawelligama.*]
Anooraadha. [*Anooraadhapoora.*]
Wejitta. [*Wejittapoora.*]

Brothers of Panduwaasa's Queen, and the children of Amitoodana, the paternal uncle of Budha: most of these Princes took their name from the place at which they respectively settled.

4. Abhaya. [Oopatissa-nowera.] B.C. 474. Bud. 69. Reigned 20 years.

Eldest son of Panduwaasa, who reigned in tranquillity for twenty years, till his nephew disputed the throne.

Interregnum. B.C. 454. Bud. 89. Continued 17 years, during the wars between the preceding and succeeding Kings, which terminated by the former surrendering the sovereignty to the latter.

5. Pandukaabhaya. [Anooraadhapoora.] B.C. 437. Bud. 106. Reigned 70 years.

Son of Oommaada Chittra: he put to death nine of his maternal uncles: married Soowana Paali, the daughter of one of those uncles: made Anooraadhapoora his capital; greatly embellished it: formed the tanks Jayaawewa and Abhayawewa. His son, Ganatissa, appears to have participated in this reign, and to have raised his own son, Mootaseewa, to the throne soon after the King died.—Ganatissa, in most books, is not noticed as a reigning sovereign, and Mootaseewa is called the son of Pandukaabhaya.

6. Mootaseewa. [Anooraadhapoora.] B.C. 367. Bud. 617. Reigned 60 years.

Son of Ganatissa: he formed the extensive suburbs and the garden Maha-Maiwoona round Anooraadhapoora: left ten sons and two daughters.

7. Devenipeatissa. [Anooraadhapoora.] B.C. 306. Bud. 237. Reigned 40 years.

Second son: induced Dharmaasooka, sovereign of the many kingdoms into which Dambadiva was divided, and whose capital was Pattilipatta, to depute his son, Mihindoo, and his daughter, Sangamitta, with several other principal priests, to Anooraadhapoora, for the purpose of introducing the religion of Budha. They arrived in the year 237, the first of this reign, and eighteenth of that of Dharmasooka. They established Budhism, propagating its doctrines *orally*. The bo-tree was brought and planted at Anooraadhapoora, on the spot where the sacred trees of former Budhas had stood. The right jaw-bone of Budha was obtained from Sackrayaa himself, and a cup full of other relics from Dharmaasooka. The King built the wihare and daagoba, called Toohpaaraamaya, in which the jaw relic was deposited; sixty-eight rock-temples, with thirty-two priests' chambers, on Mihintallai, the Maha wihare, the Issaramooni wihare, the Saila-chytiya daagoba, and the Tissa-raamaya daagoba and wihare, and formed the Tissa-wewa tank. Anoola, the principal Queen, and many inferior wives of the King, assumed priesthood. The Queen, fearing that the King's next brother, Mahanaaga, would oppose the succession of her infant son to the throne, attempted to poison him; but the young Prince, happening to be with his uncle, ate the poisoned fruit, and died. Mahanaaga, dreading the resentment of the reigning family, fled to Roohoona. There is no date given from the arrival of Wejaya till the establishment of religion, as the fractional parts of the year in each reign are not mentioned: there is an error of one year at the accession of this King; date adjusted.

Mahanaaga. [*Maagama.*]

Next brother to Devenipeatissa: fled to the Roohoona division, and founded Maagama, a subordinate principality, and built many wihares in that division; and erected the daagoba at Mayangana, in Bintenne, thirty cubits high.

Jataalatissa. [*Kellania.*]

Son of Mahanaaga: settled at Kellania, at that time four gows distant from the mouth of the Kellaniaganga.

Gotaahbhaya. [*Maagama.*]

Son of Jataalatissa: went to Maagama to succeed his grandfather, leaving Kellanitissa to reign at Kellania, whose relationship to Gotaahbhaya is not stated.

Kellanitissa. [*Kellania.*]

In this reign a great part of the coast adjacent to Kellania was overflowed by the sea; nine hundred and seventy-nine villages of fishermen, four hundred and seventy of pearl-divers, were submerged; reducing the distance from Kellania to the sea to one gow.—His daughter, Wihara Daivi, married Kaavantissa.

Kaavantissa. [*Maagama.*]

Son of Gotaabhaya: he had by Wihara Daivi two sons, Dootoogaimoonoo and Saidaitissa; built many edifices in different parts of his kingdom.

8. Oottiya. [Anooraadhapoora.] B.C. 266. Bud. 277. Reigned 10 years.

Fourth son of Mootaseewa. Mihindoo died in the eighth year of this reign; was buried with great pomp, his ashes being enshrined in many daagobas at Mihintellai: Sangamitta died the following year.

9. Mahaseewa. [Anooraadhapoora.] B.C. 256. Bud. 287. Reigned 10 years.

Fifth son: improved the public edifices.

10. Suratissa. [Anooraadhapoora.] B.C. 246. Bud. 297. Reigned 10 years.

Sixth son: built many temples in the provinces: he introduced and kept in his service a body of foreign cavalry. Two brothers, Malabars, who commanded that cavalry, murdered him, and assumed the government.

11. Sena and Goottika. [Anooraadhapoora.] B.C. 236. Bud. 307. Reigned 22 years.

These usurpers were overcome, and put to death by Aséla.

12. Aséla. [Anooraadhapoora.] B.C. 214. Bud. 329. Reigned 10 years.

Ninth son of Mootaseewa:—these children were the issue of different Queens. Supposing him to have been born even the year his father died, this King must have been one hundred and two years old when dethroned by Elaala.

13. Elaala. [Anooraadhapoora.] B.C. 204. Bud. 339. Reigned 40 years.

A Malabar: invaded the island with a great army from Sollee, and subdued the whole of it, excepting the Roohoona division; threw up thirty-two fortifications, and probably founded Mantotta: plundered and injured the temples of Budha: he was vanquished after a protracted war, and slain in battle by Dootoogaimoonoo, who raised a splendid tomb over his valiant enemy at Anooraadhapoora, which, as well as the ruins of many of his forts, still exist.

14. Dootoogaimoonoo. [Anooraadhapoora.] B.C. 164. Bud. 379. Reigned 24 years.

Son of Kaavantissa, King of Maagama: attacked Elaala with an army raised in Roohoona, and overcame the Malabars; took their thirty-two forts; put Elaala to death in battle, and expelled the invaders from the island. He made Anooraadhapoora his capital; erected Mírissewettiya daagoba, one hundred and twenty cubits high; Ruwanwelli daagoba, one hundred and twenty cubits high; the Lowa-maha-paaya (brazen palace for priests), one hundred and twenty cubits square, the same in height, raised on sixteen hundred stone pillars, having nine stories, containing one thousand apartments, and covered with metal, from which it derived its name; and many other buildings. The splendid stone canoe, twenty-five cubits long, to contain prepared beverage for the priests, was also made by his order; and the Mayangana daagoba, of thirty cubits high, was encased in another eighty cubits high. His son, Saali-koomaaraya, was excluded from the throne for marrying a celebrated beauty beneath his rank: succeeded by his brother.

15. Saidaitissa. [Anooraadhapoora.] B.C. 140. Bud. 403. Reigned 18 years.

Brother: formed twelve tanks, &c.; erected Digganakhya daagoba and Diggaawewa tank in the Batticalow, Mulgirigal wihare in the Matura district, and other edifices, before his accession to the throne, while governing the Roohoona division.

16. Toohl, or Thullathanaka. [Anooraadhapoora.] B.C. 122. Bud. 421. Reigned 1 month and 10 days.

Son of Saidaitissa: murdered by Laiminitissa, his elder brother, whose descendants repeatedly usurped the throne at subsequent periods.

17. Laiminitissa 1st, or Lajjitissa. [Anooraadhapoora.] B.C. 122. Bud. 421. Reigned 9 years and 8 months.

Brother: improved many edifices both at Anooraadhapoora and in the Roohoona division.

18. Kaloonna, or Khallaata-naaga. [Anooraadhapoora.] B.C. 112. Bud. 431. Reigned 6 years.

Brother of Toohl: built a terrace round the brazen palace, and the square in which Ruwanwelli daagoba stands: put to death by his minister, Maharantaka, who was executed by the King's brother and successor.

19. Walagambahoo 1st, or Wattagaamini. [Anooraadhapoora.] B.C. 104. Bud. 439. Reigned 5 months.

Brother. The island invaded by seven Malabars, who landed at different ports, defeated the King, and compelled him to take refuge in the mountains, in the fifth month of his reign, and in the 439th year, 9th month, and 10th day after the death of Budha. One of the Malabars carried off Budha's cup (a relic), another the King's wife: the other five remained in the island (date adjusted—error two years).

20. (Total 14 years and 7 months.)

Pulahattha. [Anooraadhapoora.] B.C. 104. Bud. 439. Reigned 3 years.

Deposed and put to death by his successor.

Baayiha. [Anooraadhapoora.] B.C. 101. Bud. 442. Reigned 2 years.

Deposed and put to death by his successor.

Panaymaara. [Anooraadhapoora.] B.C. 99. Bud. 444. Reigned 7 years.

Deposed and put to death by his successor.

Piliyamaara. [Anooraadhapoora.] B.C. 92. Bud. 451. Reigned 7 months.

Deposed and put to death by his successor.

Daathiya. [Anooraadhapoora.] B.C. 91. Bud. 452. Reigned 2 years.

Deposed and put to death by the deposed King. The kingdom was in a state of complete anarchy during the whole period of the Malabar rule.

21. Walagambahoo 1st (*restored*). [Anooraadhapoora.] B.C. 89. Bud. 454. Reigned 12 years and 5 months.

While wandering in disguise, he discovered many caves and situations eligible for the formation of rock-temples, where he afterwards built wihares. He brought together five hundred of the principal and most learned priests, at a cave in Matale called Aloolenne, and, *for the first time, had the tenets of Budhism reduced to writing;* which occurred in the 217th year, 10th month, and 10th day, after they were promulgated *orally* by Mihindoo. He succeeded at length in raising an army in the Maayaa division of the island, and vanquished the usurpers of his throne. He restored the former religious edifices, and built Abhaayagiri daagoba, one hundred and eighty cubits high, at Anooraadhapoora. To commemorate the recovery of his Queen from captivity, he erected a daagoba, one hundred and forty cubits high, and called it after her, Soowana-raamaya daagoba; the Damboolla wihare, and other wihares.

22. Mahadailitissa, or Mahachoola. [Anooraadhapoora.] B.C. 77. Bud. 466. Reigned 14 years.

Son of Kaloonna: protected the priesthood, and built several wihares.

23. Chora Naaga. [Anooraadhapoora.] B.C. 63. Bud. 480. Reigned 12 years.

Son of Walagambahoo: an impious and tyrannical prince; he destroyed eighteen wihares, and was put to death by his own people.

24. Koodatissa. [Anooraadhapoora.] B.C. 51. Bud. 492. Reigned 3 years.

Son of Mahadailitissa: poisoned by his wife Anoola.

25. Anoola (*Queen*). [Anooraadhapoora.] B.C. 48. Bud. 495. Reigned 5 years and 4 months.

Widow of Koodatissa. She successively married, and raised to the throne, the following ministers, whom she got rid of by poison, in the periods mentioned opposite to their respective names: Balat-Sewama, 1 year 2 months; Wattooka, a Malabar, 1 year 1 month; the Prohitta Bramin, 6 months; Sukkoo, an astrologer, 11 months; Ballatissa, 1 year 3 months. She reigned alone 4 months, (unable, it is said, to induce any one to share her bed and the throne with her any longer,) and was herself put to death by her first husband's son.

26. Makalantissa, or Kaalakannitissa. [Anooraadhapoora.] B.C. 42. Bud. 501. Reigned 22 years.

Second son of Koodatissa: protected himself from violence in youth by becoming a priest: he restored order in the kingdom; built a rampart 7 cubits high round the town, a stone daagoba at Mihintallai, and formed several tanks.

27. Baatiyatissa 1st, or Bhaatikaa Bhaya. [Anooraadhapoora.] B.C. 20. Bud. 523. Reigned 28 years.

Son: a prince of great piety, enabled by Sackraya to enter the Ruwanwelli daagoba.

28. Maha Dailiya Maana or Daathika. [Anooraadhapoora.] A.D. 8. Bud. 551. Reigned 12 years.

Brother: built Saigiri daagoba, on the summit of Mihintallai, and made eighteen hundred stone steps to it.

29. Addagaimoonoo, or Aamanda Gaamini. [Anooraadhapoora.] A.D. 20. Bud. 563. Reigned 9 years and 8 months.

Son: built Ridi wihare: totally prohibited the destruction of life in the animal creation, yet was put to death himself by his brother and successor.

30. Kinihirridaila, or Kanijaanitissa. [Anooraadhapoora.] A.D. 30. Bud. 573. Reigned 3 years.

Brother: a cruel and impious prince.

31. Kooda Abhaa, or Choolaabhaya. [Anooraadhapoora.] A.D. 33. Bud. 576. Reigned 1 year.

Son of Addagaimoonoo: he built Salugalla wihare on the Goonaa Oya.

32. Singhawallee, or Seewalli. [Anooraadhapoora.] A.D. 34. Bud. 577. Reigned 4 months.

Sister: put to death by her cousin Elloona, in the fourth month of her reign.

33. Elloona, or Ila Naaga. [Anooraadhapoora.] A.D. 34. Bud. 577. Reigned 6 years.

Maternal nephew of Addagaimoonoo: ascended the throne by deposing Singhawallee. The natives revolted against his authority and imprisoned him: he was miraculously rescued by his state elephant, and enabled to escape beyond sea: he returned with an army after an absence of three years, and recovered his throne.

34. Scnda Moohoona, or Chanda Mukha Seewa. [Anooraadhapoora. A.D. 40. Bud. 583. Reigned 8 years and 7 months.

Son: he formed the tank at Minigiri, and dedicated the land irrigated by it to the wihare at that place.

35. Yasa Siloo, or Yataalakatissa. [Anooraadhapoora.] A.D. 49. Bud. 592. Reigned 7 years and 8 months.

Brother: deposed and put to death by Subha, who usurped the throne.

36. Subha. [Anooraadhapoora.] A.D. 56. Bud. 599. Reigned 6 years.

An usurper: he was called Balataa the Powerful: himself deposed, and put to death by Wahapp.

37. Wahapp, or Wasabha. [Anooraadhapoora.] A.D. 62. Bud. 605. Reigned 44 years.

A descendant of Laiminitissa: enjoyed a long and prosperous reign. Among other great undertakings, he formed sixteen tanks, and built a wall round Anooraadhapoora, sixteen gows in circumference.

38. Waknais, or Wanka Naasika. [Anooraadhapoora.] A.D. 106. Bud. 649. Reigned 3 years.

Son: built Mahamangulla wihare. The island invaded by the Solleans, who carried off twelve thousand of its inhabitants into captivity.

39. Gajaabahoo 1st, or Gaaminee. [Anooraadhapoora.] A.D. 109. Bud. 652. Reigned 22 years.

Son: invaded the Sollee country; obtained restitution of the sacred cup, carried off in the reign of Walagambahoo; and brought away twelve thousand natives of that country, in addition to the Singhalese seized by the King of Sollee in the reign of Waknais. The natives were restored to their families; the Solleans were settled in

Alutkur korle. He was attended in this expedition by the famed warrior Neela-yodhaya. He formed Gaaminitissa tank, and dedicated the lands to Abhayaagiri wihare.

40. Mahaloomaana, or Mallaka Naaga. [Anooraadhapoora.] A.D. 131. Bud. 674. Reigned 6 years.

Maternal cousin: built Abatoora and other wihares.

41. Baatiyatissa 2d, or Bhaatikatissa. [Anooraadhapoora.] A.D. 137. Bud. 680. Reigned 24 years.

Son: built several wihares, and formed many tanks.

42. Choolatissa, or Kanitthatissa. [Anooraadhapoora.] A.D. 161. Bud. 704. Reigned 18 years.

Brother: improved the brazen palace, Abhayaagiri and Rajamaha wihares, and other edifices.

43. Koohoona, or Choodda Naaga. [Anooraadhapoora.] A.D. 179. Bud. 722. Reigned 2 years.

Son: murdered by his successor.

44. Koodanaama, or Kooda Naaga. [Anooraadhapoora.] A.D. 181. Bud. 724. Reigned 1 year.

Nephew: deposed by his brother-in-law.

45. Kooda Sirinaa, or Siri Naaga 1st. [Anooraadhapoora.] A.D. 182. Bud. 725. Reigned 19 years.

Brother of Koodanaama's wife: repaired the brazen palace, reducing it to five stories, and embellished the Ruwanwelli daagoba.

46. Waiwahairatissa, or Wairatissa. [Anooraadhapoora.] A.D. 201. Bud. 744. Reigned 22 years.

Son. A great schism was created in the 752nd year, 4th month, 10th day of Budha, in consequence of the priests of Abhayaagiri wihare adopting as the tenets of Budhism the doctrines put forth by one Wytooliya: the books were burnt after a solemn inquiry. The King improved many wihares: — murdered by his successor.

47. Abha Sen, or Abhatissa. [Anooraadhapoora.] A.D. 223. Bud. 766. Reigned 8 years.

Brother: built a hall in front of the brazen palace.

48. Siri Naaga 2d. [Anooraadhapoora.] A.D. 231. Bud. 774. Reigned 2 years.

Son of Waiwahairatissa.

49. Weja Indoo, or Wejaya 2nd. [Anooraadhapoora.] A.D. 233. Bud. 776. Reigned 1 year.

Son: put to death by his successor.

50. Sangatissa 1st. [Anooraadhapoora.] A.D. 234. Bud. 777. Reigned 4 years.

Of the Laimini family: improved many religious edifices, and placed a pinnacle of glass on the top of Ruwanwelli daagoba: he was poisoned.

51. Dahama Sirisanga Bo, or Sirisanga Bodhi 1st. [Anooraadhapoora.] A.D. 238. Bud. 781. Reigned 2 years.

He was probably of the original royal stock, as his successor is expressly distinguished as of the Laimini race. A great famine and plague occurred during this reign, attributed to the malignity of the red-eyed demon. It was to appease this demon that a devil-dance was instituted, which is kept up to this day. Goolooabhaa became a competitor for the throne, which the King yielded without a struggle. He afterwards became a priest, and in that disguise found an asylum in Attanagulla wihare. Whether he made any attempt to recover his kingdom is not stated, but the reigning King set a great reward on his head. He was murdered by a peasant, who produced his head to the King, and received the reward: the head was buried at Attanagulla, over which the usurper raised a daagoba, which is still standing.

52. Goloo Abhaa, Gothaabhaya, or Meghawarna Abhaya. [Anooraadhapoora.] A.D. 240. Bud. 753. Reigned 13 years.

Of the Laimini race: he improved the brazen palace, enlarged the cupola of Toohpaaraamaya. The Wytooliya doctrines were again embraced by the Abhayaagiri priests; in consequence of which three hundred orthodox priests quitted it, and settled in Dakoonoogiri wihare: one of these gave rise to the Sangilli community of priests in the 795th of Budha. The apostate priests were branded on their backs, and sixty of them were banished the island; some of these settled at Kaaweripatnam in Sollee.

53. Makalan Detootissa 1st. [Anooraadhapoora.] A.D. 253. Bud. 796. Reigned 10 years.

Son: educated by Sangamittra, a disguised professor of the Wytooliya, but the King adhered to the orthodox faith; completed the building of seven stories commenced by his father, formed many tanks, built the Badulla and other wihares, and removed the jaw relic to Mihintallai.

54. Maha Sen. [Anooraadhapoora.] A.D. 275. Bud. 818. Reigned 27 years.

Brother: came to the throne in 818; also educated by Sangamittra, and converted by him to the Wytooliya. He published a prohibition against any alms being given to the orthodox priests, by which means alone they subsisted in those days, and ought, according to the rules of their religion, to subsist at all times. They wandered about Anooraadhapoora for three days starving, and then dispersed in the Roohoona division of the island, to which the heresy had not extended. Enraged at this non-compliance, the King, at the instigation of Sangamittra and his minister Soohoona, pulled down the brazen palace and three hundred and sixty-three other principal temples, with the view of using the materials in constructing temples for the Abhayaagiri priests, and destroying the old establishment. Saigiri wihare was taken possession of by the banished priests, who had returned. The King was subsequently brought to a sense of his impiety by a new minister, Meghawarnaabhaya. Sangamittra was beheaded by the Queen's order, and Soohoona was trampled to death by the infuriated populace. The King rebuilt the brazen palace, Maha wihare, and some of the other temples he had destroyed, and recalled the scattered priests. He erected Jaitawanaaraama wihare and daagoba, one hundred and forty cubits high; and formed the great tank at Mennairia, and, by damming up the Karaganga, turned its stream into it. He also formed sixteen other great tanks, and cut the Tallawattuella canal, by which means he formed 20,000 fields which he dedicated to the Denanakha wihare; whereby the rice-grounds got the name of Dan-talawa (Gantalawe or Kandelly). He sent a deputation to bring the Dalada relic from King Ghoohasewa of Dantapoora in Kalingoo. Before it arrived he died, in 844. 9. 20. of Budha. With his reign the first portion of the work called the Maha Wanse terminated; and, owing to the decline in the greatness, wealth, and prosperity of the kingdom, and not from any change of dynasty, the ensuing Kings, whose history was compiled at a subsequent period, are designated the Sooloowanse or inferior dynasty—(date adjusted—error 12 years).

55. Kitsiri Maiwan 1st, or Keertisree Megha Warna. [Anooraadhapoora.] A.D. 301. Bud. 844. Reigned 28 years.

Son. The Dangistra Dalada relic (or right canine tooth of Budha, now kept in Kandy,) arrived in the 9th year of this reign from Dantapoora, brought by the daughter and son-in-law of Ghoohasewa. They were settled in Keerawelle in the Four Korles. The King completed the rebuilding of the brazen palace, and construction of Jaitawanaaraama daagoba, eighteen wihares, and several tanks.

56. Detootissa 2d. [Anooraadhapoora.] A.D. 330. Bud. 873. Reigned 9 years.

Brother: carved many images with his own hands, and repaired several neglected temples.

57. Bujas, or Budha Daasa. [Anooraadhapoora.] A.D. 339. Bud. 882. Reigned 29 years.

Son: ordained that every division of ten villages should have a medical practitioner, an astrologer, a devil dancer, and a preacher. He raised the Maha wihare to five stories; erected the Monoorpopaya, the piriwenna of the same name, and several other wihares: a great proficient in the medical art.

58. Oopatissa 2nd. [Anooraadhapoora.] A.D. 368. Bud. 911. Reigned 42 years.

Son: he built a splendid temple at Hattanagal, and covered it with gilt copper tiles: he also built Paloowatta piriwenna, and formed the Toopaawewe, (probably near Pollonnaroowa,) and other tanks. A great famine prevailed in this reign.

59. Maha Naama. [Anooraadhapoora.] A.D. 410. Bud. 953. Reigned 22 years.

Brother. Buddhaghoso, a very learned and renowned priest, came from Dambadiva: he composed commentaries on the gaathaawas of Budha; and added to those gaathaawas of his own, with commentaries on them.

60. Senghot, or Sotthi Sena. [Anooraadhapoora.] A.D. 432. Bud. 975. Reigned 1 day.

Son: poisoned on the day of his accession by Princess Singharaadoo, who married Laiminitissa.

61. Laiminitissa 2nd, or Chatagaahaka. [Anooraadhapoora.] A.D. 432. Bud. 975. Reigned 1 year.

Of the Laimini race: ascended the throne by marrying Singharaadoo: formed the Chatagaahaka tank.

62. Mitta Sena, or Karalsora. [Anooraadhapoora.] A.D. 433. Bud. 976. Reigned 1 year.

His relationship to preceding Kings is not stated: he was raised to the throne by the minister of Chatagaahaka: built a wall round Mayangana daagoba at Bintenne. The island was invaded by certain Malabar chieftains, who captured the capital, and put the King to death.

63. Paandu. [Anooraadhapoora.] A.D. 434. Bud. 977 Reigned 5 years.

A Malabar: the native Princes and chiefs left the Pihitee division of the island, and crossed the Mahawelliganga to Roohoona.

Paarinda Kooda. [Anooraadhapoora.] A.D. 439. Bud. 982. Reigned 16 years.

Brother: engaged in war with Dhaatu Sena.

Khudda Paarinda. [Anooraadhapoora.] A.D. 455. Bud. 998. Reigned 2 months.

Son of Paandu; killed in war by Dhaatu Sena.

Daatthiya. [Anooraadhapoora.] A.D. 455. Bud. 998. Reigned 3 years.

Brother of Paandu; killed in war by Dhaatu Sena.

Pitthiya. [Anooraadhapoora.] A.D. 458. Bud. 1001. Reigned 7 months.

Brother of Paandu: killed in war by Dhaatu Sena.

Total 24 years and 9 months.

64. Daasenkelliya, or Dhaatu Sena. [Anooraadhapoora.] A.D. 459. Bud. 1002. Reigned 18 years.

Several members of the royal family settled themselves in disguise in secluded parts of the island during the usurpation of Subha. From one of these was descended Dhaatu Sena: he had two sons, Dhaatu Sena and Seelatissa; the former was brought up a priest under his maternal uncle, Mahanaama Teronnanse. He relinquished priesthood, and became a competitor for the throne. After a protracted war, he extirpated the Malabars, and established his authority over the whole island: he repaired and improved many tanks and edifices; and cut the Handaganaawa canal in Bintenne, which was fed from the Mahawelliganga. His uncle, Mahanaama, under his auspices, composed, with the assistance of other priests, the Maha Wanse, or Deepa Wanse. He had two sons, Kaasyapa and Moogallaana; and a daughter, married to the minister. The minister and the eldest son conspired against the King, and put him to an ignominious death: Moogallaana fled to Dambadiva.

65. Seegiri Kasoomboo, or Kaasiyappa 1st. [Seegiri-galla Nowera.] A.D. 478. Bud. 1020. Reigned 18 years.

Son: he abandoned Anooraadhapoora, and fortified himself on an inaccessible rock, which, from being ornamented with figures of lions, obtained the name of Seehagiri, to which he removed the treasures and regalia of the empire: committed suicide on the field of battle on being defeated by his brother.

66. Moogallaana 1st. [Anooraadhapoora.] A.D. 495. Bud. 1038. Reigned 18 years.

Brother: fled to Dambadiva on the murder of his father, to escape the vengeance of his reigning brother, for having aided their parent: returned with an army, and landed and fortified himself at Colombo; he then waged war against, and defeated his brother in battle near his own capital; and executed the minister, and upwards of one thousand persons concerned in the murder of his father. The Kaisa-dhaatu relic (lock of Budha's hair) was brought from Dambadiva to Anooraadhapoora, which the King made his capital.

67. Kumaara Daas, or Kumaara Dhaatu Sena. [Anooraadhapoora.] A.D. 515. Bud. 1056. Reigned 9 years.

Son: a Prince of great learning. It was in this reign that the poet Panditta Kaalidaas (not Rishi Kaalidaas, the Shakspeare of the East) visited Ceylon. The King, who frequented the house of a courtesan much sought for her wit and fascination, inscribed on the walls of her room two verses; adding, that he would grant the prayer of any individual, whatever that prayer might be, who completed the stanza. Kaalidaas, who visited her soon after, seeing these lines on the wall, perfected the stanza. To secure the reward to herself, she murdered Kaalidaas, and buried him under the floor of the room. The murder was detected, and the corpse taken up and burnt with great pomp. The King, in his mental agony, threw himself on the funeral pile

68. Kirti Sena. [Anooraadhapoora.] A.D. 523. Bud. 1065. Reigned 9 years.

Son: murdered by his successor.

69. Maidee Seewoo, or Seewaka. [Anooraadhapoora.] A.D. 532. Bud. 1074. Reigned 25 days.

Maternal uncle: murdered by his successor.

70. Laimini Oopatissa 3rd. [Anooraadhapoora.] A.D. 532. Bud. 1074. Reigned 1 year and 6 months.

Brother-in-law, and son of Moogallaana: he lost his sight; his son-in-law Seela-kaala became a competitor for the throne, and was opposed by the King's son Kaasyapa, who was vanquished, and committed suicide: the King died of grief.

71. Ambaherra Salameawan, or Seela-kaala. [Anooraadhapoora.] A.D. 534. Bud. 1077. Reigned 13 years.

Son-in-law. The Wytooliya doctrines were again introduced into the kingdom by a trader, who imagined himself to be importing an orthodox book. The King, also in ignorance of its tendency, showed the book to the Abhayagiri priests, who contrived to propagate its tenets; until an eminent priest, Jhoti Paali, detected and exposed its fallacies. This schism originated in the 1088th of Budha, in the 852d of the establishment of religion, and the 12th of his reign. (Date adjusted—error one year.)

72. Daapuloo 1st, or Daatthaapa Bodhi. [Anooraadhapoora.] A.D. 547. Bud. 1090. Reigned 6 months and 6 days.

Second son: murdered a younger brother, and committed suicide on being defeated in battle, while engaged in war with his elder brother.

73. Dalamagalan, or Moogallaana 2d. [Anooraadhapoora.] A.D. 547. Bud. 1090. Reigned 20 years.

Elder brother: formed a bank across the Kolong, or Malwattu Oya, and turned the stream into the tanks of Galwewe and Boogawewe. Some of his near relations were poisoned by his wife.

74. Kuda Kitsiri Maiwan 1st, or Keertisree Mégha-warna. [Anooraadhapoora.] A.D. 567. Bud. 1110. Reigned 19 years.

Son: a minor, raised to the throne by his mother; her authority was opposed and overthrown. The King was put to death by his successor. In some books this reign is reduced to nineteen days.

75. Senewee or Maha Naaga. [Anooraadhapoora.] A.D. 586. Bud 1129. Reigned 3 years.

Descended from the Mooriya or Okkaaka branch of the royal family, who had settled in the Roohoona division: a pious Prince; repaired and endowed many temples.

76. Aggrabodhi 1st, or Akbo. [Anooraadhapoora.] A.D. 589. Bud. 1132. Reigned 34 years.

Maternal nephew: restored order in the country before the ninth year of his reign: formed the Kooroondoowewe and many other tanks: cut a great canal to the Mennairia tank: built the Maha-naama piriwenna, and many other religious edifices; and settled a schism. Twelve poets of great genius flourished in his court.

77. Aggrabodhi 2d, or Soola Akbo. [Anooraadhapoora.] A.D. 623. Bud. 1166. Reigned 10 years.

Son-in-law: brought back the jaw relic to Toohpaaramaya: repaired the brazen palace: formed fourteen great tanks.

78. Sanghatissa. [Anooraadhapoora.] A.D. 633. Bud. 1176. Reigned 2 months.

Brother: opposed by the Senewirat, or minister; and, being defeated in battle, he and his eldest son fled. A younger son was captured, and his feet and hands were chopped off. The fugitives also were subsequently taken and decapitated.

79. Boona Moogalan, or Laimini Bonaaya. [Anooraadhapoora.] A.D. 633. Bud. 1176. Reigned 6 years.

The Senewirat. The northern part of the island was afflicted by a general sickness. In that state of the country, the King was attacked by the Asiggaaheka of the Roohoona division, overcome, and put to death: his son escaped to Dambadiva.

80. Abhaseggaaheka, or Asiggaaheka. [Anooraadhapoora.] A.D. 639. Bud. 1182. Reigned 9 years.

Maternal grandson of the deposed King: his uncle landed in the northern division of the island, and was defeated and killed: the captives of his army were bestowed as slaves on temples.

81. Siri Sangabo 2d. [Anooraadhapoora.] A.D. 648. Bud. 1191. Reigned 6 months.

Son: driven out of the island by his successor, a descendant of the royal family, after a civil war.

82. Kaloona Detootissa, or Laimini Katooreya. [Anooraadhapoora.] A.D. 648. Bud. 1191. Reigned 5 months.

Of the Laimini family. The deposed King returned with a Malabar army, and unsuccessfully disputed the succession, till a reinforcement arrived from the continent, when the reigning King, in despair, committed suicide in his camp: his Queen assumed the priesthood.

Siri Sangabo 2d (*restored*). [Anooraadhapoora.] A.D. 649. Bud. 1192. Reigned 16 years.

Recovered his kingdom by the aid of a foreign army, and the assistance of his relations in the island. He formed some tanks, and built a palace at Pollonnaroowa: was again expelled the kingdom; returned a second time, and established himself in the Roohoona division, where he died, after a residence of sixteen years.

83. Daloopeatissa 1st, or Datthopatissa. [Anooraadhapoora.] A.D. 665. Bud. 1208. Reigned 12 years.

Of a younger branch of the Laimini family: expelled the King: committed many acts of injustice, and plundered the temples and daagobas: he was also for a short time obliged to seek an asylum on the continent, being overcome by Kaasiyappa: he returned, and was killed in battle.

84. Paisooloc Kasoomboo, or Kaasiyappa 2d. [Anooraadhapoora.] A.D. 677. Bud. 1220. Reigned 9 years.

Brother of Siri Sangabo 2d: he declined being crowned during the year that his predecessor was expelled the kingdom, as his elder brother was still living in Roohoona: he appointed his maternal nephew his heir.

85. Daapuloo 2d. [Anooraadhapoora.] A.D. 686. Bud. 1229. Reigned 7 years.

The appointed heir conceded the throne to his own father, who was a descendant of the Okkaaka branch, settled in Maagama. This King attempted to expel his Malabar subjects from the capital: they conspired against him, and invited over the son of Datthopatissa from the continent, to which he had fled with his father. The King returned to Roohoona, and died there three years afterwards.

86. Daloopeatissa 2nd, or Hattha-Datthopatissa. [Anooraadhapoora.] A.D. 693. Bud. 1236. Reigned 9 years.

Son of Datthopatissa: invaded the island from the continent: a righteous Prince.

87. Paisooloo Siri Sangabo 3rd, or Aggrabodhi. [Anooraadhapoora.] A.D. 702. Bud. 1245. Reigned 16 years.

Brother: reigned in peace, and performed many acts of charity: built and repaired several temples and tanks: he established himself in the latter part of his reign at Pollonnaroowa, where he died: the government devolved on his minister, Pottakutta, a Malabar, who selected a successor, and conveyed the regalia back to the capital.

88. Walpitti Wasidatta, or Dantanaama. [Anooraadhapoora.] A.D. 718. Bud. 1261. Reigned 2 years.

Of the Okkaaka family: raised to the throne by the minister.

89. Hoonoonaru-riandala, or Hatthadatha. [Anooraadhapoora.] A.D. 723. Bud. 1263. Reigned 6 months.

Of the original royal family; likewise selected by the minister: also demised in a few months.

90. Mahalaipanoo, or Maanawamma. [Anooraadhapoora.] A.D. 720. Bud. 1263. Reigned 6 years.

Of royal descent: fled in his youth to Dambadiva, and found an asylum in the court of Naraseeha: he distinguished himself in that sovereign's service, in his wars with King Koodoowarte: he subsequently obtained assistance from Naraseeha, and invaded Ceylon; but was defeated and repelled: he returned with a larger force, routed the King's troops, made the King prisoner, and decapitated him on the field of battle. Pottakutta fled; but was subsequently poisoned in his seclusion.

91. Kaasiyappa 3rd, or Kasoomboo. [Anooraadhapoora.] A D. 726. Bud. 1269. Reigned 3 years.

Son: he appointed his brother's son, Aggrabodhi, his successor.

92. Aggrabodhi 3rd, or Akbo. [Anooraadhapoora.] A.D. 729. Bud. 1272. Reigned 40 years.

Nephew. His son, Seelamaiga, repeatedly disturbed the peace of the country by opposing his father's authority, whom he succeeded under the title of Aggrabodhi.

93. Aggrabodhi 4th, or Kuda Akbo. [Pollonnaroowa.] A.D. 769. Bud. 1312. Reigned 6 years.

Son: formed several tanks, and resided partly at Pollonnaroowa: he survived his sons, and appointed his successor.

94. Mihindoo 1st, or Salamaiwan. [Pollonnaroowa.] A.D. 775. Bud. 1318. Reigned 20 years.

Of royal descent. The early part of his reign was disturbed by internal wars: he built a palace, the Rattana-prasaada (in which a splendid golden image of Budha was enshrined), and other temples at Pollonnaroowa:

he repaired the Toophaaramaya and other edifices at Anooraadhapoora, and formed the great registers (Lekammittiyas).

95. Daapuloo 3rd. [Pollonnaroowa.] A.D. 795. Bud. 1338. Reigned 5 years.

Son: he suppressed an insurrection, and governed the northern part of the island during his father's reign: after his accession, he took up his residence near Mennairia for some time, to improve the works connected with the lakes: he repaired the brazen palace and the daagobas at Anooraadhapoora; built hospitals, and a college for medical students at Pollonnaroowa: to prevent the perversion of laws after his demise, he caused those he had administered to be embodied into a code: his daughter married Mihindoo Koomareya, Prince of Roohoona.

96. Mihindoo 2nd, or Dharmika-Seelamaiga. [Pollonnaroowa.] A.D. 800. Bud. 1343. Reigned 4 years.

Son: a righteous King: he completed the Rattana-prasaada, which is stated to have been several stories high.

97. Aggrabodhi 5th, or Akbo. [Pollonnaroowa.] A.D. 804. Bud. 1347. Reigned 11 years.

Brother: emulated the piety of his father and brother, devoting his time and attention entirely to religious observances.

98. Daapuloo 4th, or Kuda Daapulla. [Pollonnaroowa.] A.D. 815. Bud. 1358. Reigned 16 years.

Son: repaired and embellished the edifices attached to the Bo-tree and Jaitawana-raamaya wihare: his cousins, Aggrabodhi and Mihindoo, the sons of Mihindoo, Prince of Roohoona, were brought up in his court: he left a son.

99. Aggrabodhi 6th. [Pollonnaroowa.] A.D. 831. Bud. 1374. Reigned 3 years.

Cousin: his brother, Mihindoo, and the late King's

son, made an ineffectual attempt to oppose his succession, and were obliged to fly the island.

100. Sena, or Mitwella Sen. [Pollonnaroowa.] A.D. 838. Bud. 1381. Reigned 20 years.

Son: he had three sons, Mihindoo, Kaasiyappa, and Udaya. The island was invaded by the King of Paandi in person, who fortified himself at Mahapellegama. The King attacked him there; and, being defeated, fled to the Malayaa division. His sons, Mihindoo and Kaasiyappa, raised a second army; which also being defeated, Mihindoo committed suicide on the field of battle: his brother fled. The invaders captured the capital, sacked it, and despatched the spoils, including the golden images, the temple jewels, the Jayaberra (drum of victory), and the sacred cup, to the Paandi country. A treaty ensued, and the Paandi sovereign quitted the island, on receiving a large sum of money. The King, thereafter, succeeded in re-establishing his authority over the whole island, and formed the Toopaahwewa. Another heresy was introduced during this reign from the Wijraparwatte (mountain) in Dambadiva, and therefore called the Wijrawaadiya, in the year 1144 of religion, or 1362 of Budha. These dates do not agree; to make them accord, the latter should be 1381, which shows an error of at least four years: date adjusted.

101. Kaasiyappa 4th, or Maagayin Sen. [Pollonnaroowa.] A.D. 858. Bud. 1401. Reigned 33 years.

Son. A son of the King of Paandi had waged war against his own father; and, being defeated, found an asylum in Ceylon. To avenge the insult offered in Sena's reign, the King espoused the cause of the fugitive Prince, and invaded Paandi. In conjunction with the exiled Prince's party, the army laid the country waste, and captured the capital, Madura. The King of Paandi was put to death, and his rebel son raised to the throne. The Singhalese army returned, bringing back the plunder taken from

Ceylon, together with a great additional booty. In this reign the heresy of the Neela-patta-dara (blue robe) was introduced into the island from the continent.

102. Udaya 1st. [Pollonnaroowa.] A.D. 891. Bud. 1434. Reigned 35 years.

Brother: repaired and embellished the brazen palace and Ruanwelli daagoba at Anooraadhapoora: formed an embankment across the Minemaikalan-ganga, and diverted its stream into the Mennairia lake.

103. Udaya 2d. [Pollonnaroowa.] A.D. 926. Bud. 1469. Reigned 11 years.

Son. His brother, Mihindoo, who governed Roohoona, threw off his allegiance: the King attacked him there; and, being defeated, fell back on his capital, pursued by Mihindoo, who was there made prisoner, and put to death. The King formed a canal of irrigation from the Mahawelli-ganga: he threw embankments across the Kolong, or Malwattu Oyas, and thereby formed several tanks.

104. Kaasiyappa 5th. [Pollonnaroowa.] A.D. 954. Bud. 1497. Reigned 10 years.

Maternal nephew and son-in-law. Mihindoo, Prince of Roohoona, attempted to bring Mayaa under his authority: he was defeated by the King, who subsequently bestowed one of his daughters on him. The King chiefly devoted his time to religious observances, and to the improvement of religious edifices, both at Anooraadhapoora and Pollonnaroowa.

105. Kaasiyappa 6th. [Pollonnaroowa.] A.D. 954. Bud. 1497. Reigned 10 years.

Son-in-law. The Kings of Paandi and Sollee were engaged in war: the former sought aid from Ceylon. The King's son, Sekka Sena, was sent with an army, which embarked at Mantotte, and joined the Paandi King at Madura. The Sollean King evacuated Paandi. Before the allied army could invade the enemy's country,

Sekka Sena died, and the Singhalese troops were recalled by the King, and the command of them in the island was given to his youngest son, Siddharta, alias Udaya.

106. Daapuloo 5th. [Pollonnaroowa.] A.D. 964. Bud. 1507. Reigned 7 months.

Eldest son: died in the seventh month of his reign.

107. Daapuloo 6th. [Pollonnaroowa.] A.D. 964. Bud. 1507. Reigned 10 years.

Relationship not stated. The King of Paandi, vanquished by the King of Sollee, fled from the continent, and landed at Mantotte: he was well received by the King, and established near Anooraadhapoora. In consequence of the detection of certain intrigues among the chiefs, in which the exiled King was probably implicated, he was obliged to quit the island, and depart for Kairalla, leaving his crown and regalia in Ceylon.

108. Udaya 3d. [Pollonnaroowa.] A.D. 974. Bud. 1517. Reigned 3 years.

Brother: a tyrannical Prince. The chiefs and people conspired against him: the leaders of the revolt sought security by becoming priests; they were, nevertheless, seized, decapitated, and their heads were thrown into the streets; whereupon the populace rose against the King, besieged his palace, seized his courtiers, and subjected them to the same fate: by the intervention of the priesthood, the King made such concessions as induced the people to return to their allegiance.

109. Sena 2d. [Pollonnaroowa.] A.D. 977. Bud. 1520. Reigned 9 years.

Relationship not stated: he appointed his "faithful friend," Udaya, his heir.

110. Udaya 4th. [Pollonnaroowa.] A.D. 986. Bud. 1529. Reigned 8 years.

Relationship not stated: appointed Sena his heir. The King of Sollee sent a mission to treat for the regalia of the exiled King of Paandi: the application being rejected, he sent an army to enforce the demand: the King, being defeated, fled to Roohoona; but, uniting his forces to those of the Prince of that province, he defeated the invaders, and obliged them to quit the island.

111. Sena 3d. [Pollonnaroowa.] A.D. 994. Bud. 1537. Reigned 3 years.

Relationship not stated: he appointed Mihindoo his successor.

112. Mihindoo 3d. [Pollonnaroowa.] A.D. 997. Bud. 1540. Reigned 16 years.

He repaired the edifices on Adam's Peak, which the Solleans had demolished: patronized the religious institutions of the country: married a Princess of Kalingoo, by whom he left two sons and a daughter.

113. Sena 4th. [Pollonnaroowa.] A.D. 1013. Bud. 1556. Reigned 10 years.

Son: ascended the throne in the twelfth year of his age: his brother was appointed his heir, and the government was administered by his father's minister, Sena. By the intrigues of the courtiers, that minister's mother and two brothers were put to death; he raised an army and drove the King to Roohoona. The Queen Dowager and the Malabars retired to Pollonnaroowa; a reconciliation ensued: the King returned to his capital, and died there at an early age, a victim to excessive use of ardent spirits: he left a son.

114. Mihindoo 4th. [Anooraadhapoora.] A.D. 1023. Bud. 1566. Reigned 36 years.

Brother: ascended the throne at Anooraadhapoora. The foreign population, settled in the island, had increased to such an extent, that they had gained the ascendency over the native inhabitants, and the King had lost his authority over both. In the tenth year of his reign he was besieged in his palace: he escaped in disguise to Roohoona, and fortified himself at Ambagalla, where his son, Kaasiyappa, was born; he, thereafter, removed to Kappagolla-nowera. The Solleans invaded the island twenty-six years after the King's flight from the capital, which they occupied; and, following him into Roohoona, captured him and the Queen, whom, with the regalia, they transferred to Sollee. A Sollean viceroy administered the government, making Pollonnaroowa his capital. The King died in the twelfth year of his captivity.

Interregnum [Pollonnaroowa.] A.D. 1059. Bud. 1602. Continued 12 years.

The island was governed by the Sollean viceroy during the King's captivity: an army of ten thousand men was sent from Sollee to assist the viceroy in subduing Roohoona and capturing Prince Kaasiyappa; but he was defeated. On hearing of the demise of his father, the Prince proclaimed himself King of Ceylon, under the title of Wikramabahoo; and was making great preparations to expel the Solleans, when he died.

Maha Lai, or Maha Laala Keerti. [*Roohoona.*]

Wikrama Paandi. [*Kalutotta.*]

Jagat Paandi, or Jagati Paalie. [*Roohoona.*]

Praakrama Paandi, or Praakramabahoo. [*Roohoona.*]

The relationship of these Kings to each other, or to preceding rulers, not always stated. During the whole of this period, which comprises the interregnum in Pihitee, the island was in a state of complete anarchy, owing to the constant invasions and irruptions of the Malabars. Different members of the royal family took up the reins of the government of Roohoona, as they were abandoned by, or snatched from, each predecessor. At the termination of Praakrama Paandi's reign, no royal candidate for the crown appearing, it was assumed by the minister Lokaiswera.

Lokaiswera. [*Kaacharagama.*]

The minister: a descendant of Maanawamma: he left a son, Kerti, who subsequently assumed the title of Wejayabahoo.

115. Wejayabahoo 1st. [Pollonnaroowa.] A.D. 1071. Bud. 1614. Reigned 55 years.

Son: he was proclaimed in his infancy on the demise of his father Wikramabahoo; and an embassy was sent to Siam for pecuniary aid to re-establish the Budhistical dynasty, which aid was afforded. In the mean time, Kaasiyappa, a Prince of royal descent, aided by a brother, became a competitor for the throne: he was defeated and slain; his brother escaped. The news of this victory, together with the oppressions of the Solleans, made the natives flock to the standard of Wejayabahoo, who thereupon proclaimed war against the Solleans. After a protracted and desultory warfare, a general action was fought under the walls of Pollonnaroowa. The Solleans, being defeated, threw themselves into the town, which was carried by storm, after a siege of six weeks, and given up to the sword. The King's authority was soon recognized over the whole island after the capture of the capital, and the fame of his actions extended over all Dambadiva. Ambassadors arrived from the sovereigns of India and of Siam; and learned priests were sent by Anuradha, King of Arracan. At the audience given to the ambassadors, the first place in precedence was assigned to the envoy of the Budhist sovereign of Siam; and the insult was quickly avenged by the King of Sollee, by cutting off the nose and ears of the Singhalese envoy accredited to his court. Each monarch then prepared to invade the country of the other. The Sollean army embarked first, and landed at Mantotte, where the Singhalese army was assembled for embarkation. Having defeated it, and the country in the rear being unprotected, the enemy marched at once on the capital, from which the King fled; it was occupied by the enemy, who demolished the palace. The King, however, soon re-assembled his army, which, under the command of his son Weerabahoo, expelled the Solleans from the island. In the 45th year of his reign he invaded Sollee; from which, however, he was obliged to make a hasty retreat. The King then turned his attention to internal improvements: he formed and repaired many tanks and temples, and restored the Mennairia canal, which had been destroyed during the Sollean interregnum. He survived his martial son Weerabahoo, but left other children.

116. Jayaabahoo 1st. [Pollonnaroowa.] A.D. 1126. Bud. 1669. Reigned 1 year.
117. Wikramabahoo 1st. [Pollonnaroowa.] A.D. 1127. Bud. 1670. Reigned 22 years.
Maanaabarana. [*Roohoona.*]
118. Gajaabahoo 2d. [Pollonnaroowa.] Reigned 20 years.
Siriwallaba, or Kitsiri Maiwan [*Roohoona.*]

Total 22 years.

Jayaabahoo (a brother of Wejayabahoo 1st) was opposed by Wikramabahoo, a younger son of the late King, which led to great internal commotions, in which Maalaabarana and Gajaabahoo, the grandsons, and Serewallaba, the brother of the late King, took part. They were subsequently reconciled, each retaining the portion of the island he then held, in which he exercised an imperfect authority. Wikramabahoo's capital was Pollonnaroowa; he adopted Praakrama, the son of Maalaabarana. On his demise, Gajaabahoo took possession of the capital, and bestowed his daughter on Praakrama. The said Praakrama, from the great services he had rendered the country, became the favourite of his reigning relations, and the idol of the people. These Princes subsequently disagreed among themselves, and Praakrama openly aimed at the sovereignty. He first drove Gajaabahoo from the capital into Saffragam. The conflict was again renewed, and the capital was regained by Gajaabahoo. The priests then interfered and mediated between them. They met Gajaabahoo at Mandalaagiri wihare, who consented to resign the sovereignty to Praakrama, and caused that abdication to be engraven on a rock near that temple. He retired to the "River City," where he died in the 20th year of his reign. It is not defined from what date his reign commenced; if reckoned from the demise of Wejayabahoo, the error in the chronology is six years.

119. Praakramabahoo 1st. [Pollonnaroowa.] A.D. 1153. Bud. 1696. Reigned 33 years.

Crowned King of Pihitee, at Pollonnaroowa, in 1696, on the abdication of Gajaabahoo. He immediately took the field in person to reduce the provincial chiefs to subjection. His father, who was similarly engaged in Roohoona, effected his object first, and sent his minister Mihindoo to invade Pihitee. In the absence of Praakrama with his army in the northern districts, both Pollonnaroowa and Anooraadhapoora fell into the hands of Maanaabarana. A furious war ensued, which terminated in the father being compelled to recross the Mahawelli-ganga. On his death bed, by the advice of his ministers and the priests, he forgave his son, sent for him, and caused him to be crowned King of Roohoona. The King returned to his capital, and reduced the whole island to complete subjection: re-established the ordinances of Budhism; built a rampart round the city, a palace seven stories high, and two edifices of five stories for priests and devotees; formed the garden Manda-Oodeyana, and erected in it the coronation-hall of three stories; and built a temple for the Dalada relic. He married, secondly, a daughter of Kitsiri Maiwan, which Queen built the Rankot daagoba. At this period the greater streets of Pollonnaroowa extended seven gows, and the lesser streets four gows from the town through its suburbs. He sent a minister to Anooraadhapoora, to repair the neglected edifices and tanks near that city.

In the eighth year of his reign, the chiefs of Roohoona revolted, and were subdued by the minister after a protracted struggle, which occasioned a great destruction of lives and property: a severe example was made among the insurgents, by impaling, beheading, and other executions. The minister remained in that part of the island, and founded the town of Mahanaaga-poora at Gintotta.

The King of Cambodia and Arramana had committed many acts of violence on Singhalese subjects: he had plundered some merchants trading in elephants; had inflicted indignities on the Singhalese ambassador, whom he banished to the Malayan peninsula, maimed and mutilated: he had intercepted ships conveying some Princesses from Ceylon to the continent. In the sixteenth year of his reign, to avenge these insults, the King "equipped in five months several hundred vessels," which sailed from the port of Pallawatotta on the same day, with an army on board, commanded by Demilla Adikaram, fully provisioned and provided for twelve months. The expedition landed in Arramana, vanquished the enemy, and obtained full satisfaction.

The King next turned his attention to the chastisement of Koolasaikera, King of Paandi, for the countenance and aid he had always afforded to all invaders of Ceylon: a powerful army was sent under the command of the minister Lanka-naatha, which subdued Rammissaram and the six neighbouring provinces, drove the King from his capital, and placed his son Weerapandoo on the throne. The names of all the chiefs who opposed or submitted to the invading army are given. Koolasaikera made three attempts to recover his kingdom, with the aid of the King of Sollee. Being defeated in all, and seven gows of the territory of Sollee also being subdued, he surrendered himself, and made the required concessions. He was restored to his kingdom, and the conquered portion of Sollee was made a principality for Weerapondoo. Lanka-naatha returned with a great booty, and received an extensive grant of land for his services.

During the remainder of his reign,—the most martial, enterprising, and glorious in Singhalese history,—the King occupied himself in internal improvements. He repaired the religious and other public edifices at Pollonnaroowa, Anooraadhapoora, Seegiri, and Wijittapoora, and constructed others; among them, the Ruanwelli daagoba, at Kirrigama in Roohoona, to the memory of his Queen. He cut many canals for the purpose of diverting rivers into the great tanks: among them the Goodaaviree canal, to divert the waters of Kara-ganga into "the sea of Praakrama;" the Kaalinda canal, to conduct the waters of the Mennairia lake to the northward; and the Jaya-ganga canal, to conduct the waters of the Kalaawewe tank to Anooraadhapoora.

120. Wejayabahoo 2d. [Pollonnaroowa.] A.D. 1186. Bud. 1729. Reigned 1 year.

Nephew: also a Prince of great promise. He composed in Pali a letter of great merit to the King of Arramana, soliciting him to depute learned and pious Budhist priests to Ceylon, to decide on certain controverted points of doctrine in their mutual faith. Before the mission arrived, the King was put to death by one Mihindoo, whom he had selected as his successor, in a dispute regarding a herdsman's daughter.

121. Mihindoo 5th, or Kitsen Kisdaas. [Pollonnaroowa.] A.D. 1187. Bud. 1730. Reigned 5 years.

Not of the royal family: put to death.

122. Kirti Nissanga. [Pollonnaroowa.] A.D. 1192. Bud. 1735. Reigned 9 years.

Relationship not stated: he came from the Kalingoo country; built several wihares, and gilt seventy-three images at Dambulla wihare, which temple thereby got the name of Rangiri Dambulla: his son Weerabahoo was put to death on the night of his accession by a minister, as being unworthy of succeeding his father. In the Maha Wanse he is stated to have died a natural death.

— Weerabahoo. A.D. 1201. Bud. 1744. Reigned 1 day.

123. Wikramabahoo 2d. [Pollonnaroowa.] A.D. 1201. Bud. 1744. Reigned 3 months.

Brother of Kirti Nissanga: put to death.

124. Chondakanga. [Pollonnaroowa.] A.D. 1201. Bud. 1744. Reigned 9 months.

Nephew of Kirti Nissanga: his eyes were put out by the minister Kirti, who married the widow of Praakramabahoo.

125. Leelawatee. [Pollonnaroowa.] A.D. 1202. Bud. 1745. Reigned 3 years.

The widow of Praakramabahoo: her husband governed the kingdom in her name, till she was deposed by Saahasamallawa.

126. Saahasamallawa. [Pollonnaroowa.] A.D. 1205. Bud. 1748. Reigned 2 years.

Of the Okkaaka race: he was himself deposed by the influence of the minister Neekanga, who set up the sister of Kirti Nissanga.

127. Kalyaanawati. [Pollonnaroowa.] A.D. 1207. Bud. 1750. Reigned 6 years.

Sister of Kirti Nissanga.

128. Dharmaasooka. [Pollonnaroowa.] A.D. 1213. Bud. 1756. Reigned 1 year.

Of royal extraction: placed on the throne at the age of three months.

129. Nayaayanga, or Neekanga [Pollonnaroowa.] A.D. 1214. Bud. 1756. Reigned 17 days.

The above-named minister usurped the throne by the aid of a Sollean force: put to death by his minister Manoda, who restored the deposed Queen to the throne.

— Leelawatee (*restored*). [Pollonnaroowa.] A.D. 1214. Bud. 1757. Reigned 1 year.

Again dethroned by a foreigner.

130. Lokaiswera 1st. [Pollonnaroowa.] A.D. 1215. Bud. 1758. Reigned 9 months.

Usurped the throne by means of a foreign army, and was deposed by the ex-Queen.

— Leelawatee (*restored*). [Pollonnaroowa.] A.D. 1216. Bud. 1759. Reigned 7 months.

Restored for the second time, and again deposed by means of a foreign army.

131. Paandi Praakramabahoo 2d. [Pollonnaroowa.] A.D. 1216. Bud. 1759. Reigned 3 years.

A usurper. Maagha invaded the island from Kalingoo with an army of 24,000 men; conquered the whole of it; captured the King, and put his eyes out.

132. Maagha. [Pollonnaroowa.] A.D. 1219. Bud. 1762. Reigned 21 years.

A Malabar: he broke open and plundered many religious edifices, and destroyed all those not adapted for his purposes or the accommodation of his army; demolished the national edifices of the capital, and destroyed all literary records that could be collected by him.

133. Wejayabahoo 3d. [Dambadiniya.] A.D. 1240. Bud. 1783. Reigned 24 years.

Descendant of Siri Sangabo 1st. He recovered the Maaya division of the island; made Dambadiniya his capital; restored Budhism; brought the Dalada relic from Kotmale, where it was concealed during the foreign usurpation; repaired the Kellania daagoba.

134. Kalikaala Saahitya Sargwajnya, or Pandita Praakramabahoo 3d. [Dambadiniya.] A.D. 1267. Bud. 1809. Reigned 35 years.

Son: ascended the throne in 1809: completed the conquest of the island; but in the eleventh year of his reign the island was invaded by an army of Javakoo (the general appellation of the Malays), under the command of Chandrabanoo, who were repelled by the King's relation Weerabahoo. The King invited over to the island the celebrated Budhist priest Dharmakirti from Tambaratta. He founded the town of Siriwardhnapoora in the Seven Korles, and removed the Dalada relic to it. He improved internal communication by building many bridges, which are all named: the largest being "two hundred and eighty cubits long, to communicate with Saalaagama," which is not stated to be over a river; the next in size, across the Kalloo-ganga, of eighty-six cubits, on the road from Adam's Peak to Bentotte. To carry on these public works, he delegated his authority to his son Wejayabahoo, who assumed the name of Bosat, and was assisted by the King's nephew Weerabahoo. For the great works they executed at Pollonnaroowa, Yapahoo, and Kurunaigalla, the son was crowned King at Pollonnaroowa, and the government of that division was entrusted under him to Weerabahoo. The Dalada relic was removed to that city. Chandrabanoo again invaded the island, assisted by the Paandians and Solleans, and met with a signal defeat. In this reign, the Maha Wanse was compiled to this period, from the reign of Maha Sen, by Dharmakirti Terunnanse, and the Poojaawalliya by Mairoopaada Terunnanse.

135. Bosat Wejayabahoo 4th. [Pollonnaroowa.] A.D. 1301. Bud. 1845. Reigned 2 years.

Son: murdered by Mitta Sena, a minister, in an intrigue in which they were both engaged with the same woman. According to the Maha Wanse, he employed a slave to commit the murder, with the view of usurping the throne. Mitta Sena fled to Dambadiva to raise forces to oppose the King's brother.

— *Bhuwanekabahoo.* [*Yapahoo, or Subhapabattoo.*]

136. Bhuwanekabahoo 1st. [Yapahoo, or Subhapabattoo.] A.D. 1303. Bud. 1847. Reigned 11 years.

Brother: happened to be at his brother's court when he was murdered, and immediately fled to Yapahoo, which had been his place of residence. Mitta Sena despatched a force after him: though overtaken, the King succeeded in escaping to Yapahoo. In the mean time, Mitta Sena was assassinated by Takkoora, one of the King's officers. The army immediately declared for the King, and brought him back to Pollonnaroowa, where he was crowned. The King returned to Yapahoo, taking the Dalada relic with him, and made that his capital: subsequently an army sent by Koolasaikera, the King of Paandi, commanded by Aareya-Chakkra Warti, took Yapahoo, and carried off the Dalada relic, and presented it to his sovereign.

137. Praakramabahoo 3d. [Pollonnaroowa.] A.D. 1314. Bud. 1858. Reigned 5 years.

Son of Bosat Wejayabahoo. Not having the means of coercing the King of Paandi to restore the Dalada relic, he went to treat for that purpose in person. His mission was successful: he brought the relic back in great state, and placed it at Pollonnaroowa, which he made his capital.

138. Bhuwanekabahoo 2d. [Kurunaigalla, or Hastisailapoora.] A.D. 1319. Bud. 1863. Reign not stated.

Son of Bhuwanekabahoo 1st: made Kurunaigalla his capital, to which he removed the Dalada relic.

139. Pandita Praakramabahoo 4th. [Kurunaigalla, or Hastisailapoora. Reign not stated.

Relationship not stated: devoted his time exclusively to religious observances, and to the building and embellishing sacred edifices at Kurunaigalla. Many religious and historical works, among them the Maha Wanse were compiled under his auspices.

140. Wanny Bhuwanekabahoo 3d. Reign not stated.

141. Wejayabahoo 5th. [Kurunaigalla, or Hastisailapoora.] Reign not stated.

They are only noticed for their piety, and the protection they afforded the national religion.

142. Bhuwanekabahoo 4th. [Gampola, or Gangaasiripoora.] A.D. 1347. Bud. 1890. Reigned 14 years.

Relationship not stated: ascended the throne in 1890: he founded Gampola, made it his capital, and settled a religious controversy in 1896.

143. Praakramabahoo 5th. [Gampola, or Gangaasiripoora.] A.D. 1361. Bud. 1904. Reigned 10 years.

Nothing stated.

144. Wikramabahoo 3d. [Partly at Kanda, or Sengaddagulla Nowera.] A.D. 1371. Bud. 1914. Reigned 7 years.

Cousin of the preceding King. In this reign, the minister Alakaiswara built the city of Jayawardhanapoora at Kotta, which spot he selected from its insulated position, and its neighbourhood to Colombo, a place frequented even at that time by trading vessels. Aareya-Chakkra Warti again invaded the island, and threw up fortifications at Colombo, Negombo, and Chilaw. Alakaiswara expelled him from all of them.

145. Bhuwanekabahoo 5th. [Gampola, or Gangaasiripoora.] A.D. 1378. Bud. 1921. Reigned 20 years.

Nothing recorded of him beyond the length of his reign.

146. Wejayabahoo 6th, or Weerabahoo. [Gampola, or Gangaasiripoora.] A.D. 1398. Bud. 1941. Reigned 12 years.

Relationship not stated: he expelled some gangs of Malabars who were pillaging the country: endowed many religious edifices, and corrected a laxity of discipline among the priests.

147. Sree Praakramabahoo 6th. [Kotta, or Jayawardhanapoora.] A.D. 1410. Bud. 1953. Reigned 52 years.

Relationship not stated: reduced the eighteen pattoos of the Wanny under subjection, and removed the Dalada relic to Kotta, which he made his capital: murdered.

148. Jayaabahoo 2nd. [Kotta, or Jayawardhanapoora.] A.D. 1462. Bud. 2005. Reigned 2 years.

Son of Maddaye Daivi, daughter of the preceding King. Bhuwanekabahoo, a descendant of the royal family, settled at Yapahoo, attacked Kotta, and put the King to death.

149. Bhuwanekabahoo 6th. [Kotta, or Jayawardhanapoora.] A.D. 1464. Bud. 2007. Reigned 7 years.

Relationship not stated: he held previously the government of Yapahoo, from Sree Praakramabahoo.

150. Pandita Praakramabahoo 7th. [Kotta, or Jayawardhanapoora.] A.D. 1471. Bud. 2014. Reigned 14 years.

Adopted son of the last King: deposed, and put to death by his successor.

151. Weera Praakramabahoo 8th. [Kotta, or Jayawardhanapoora.] A.D. 1485. Bud. 2028. Reigned 20 years.

Brother of Bhuwanekabahoo the Sixth: he raised an army, by which he deposed his brother, at Ambulagalla: his reign is represented to have been peaceful and prosperous: he had by his first marriage four sons, Dharma Praakramabahoo, Raaja Singha, Wejayabahoo, and Raygama Bandara; also, a daughter: he then married the younger sister of his wife, and had two sons, Sakallawalla Abhaya and Tamwalla Abhaya.

152. Dharma Praakramabahoo 9th. [Kotta, or Jayawardhanapoora.] A.D. 1505. Bud. 2048. Reigned 22 years.

Son: his reign was disturbed in the early part by the competition of his brothers, whom he succeeded in reducing to submission. The Portuguese first visited the island, and were permitted to trade.

153. Wejayabahoo 7th. [Kotta, or Jayawardhanapoora.] A.D. 1527. Bud. 2070. Reigned seven years.

Brother: he had issue jointly with his late brother, Raaja Singha, three sons, Bhuwanekabahoo, Raygam Bandara, and Maaya Dunnai. He married, secondly, a

Princess from Keerawella, and adopted her younger brother, Daiva Raja Koomaraya. Finding this adoption opposed, he attempted to put his three sons to death. The two elder fled to Yapahoo, and the youngest to Oudarata, where he was received by Jayaweera, who governed the mountain division. That Prince furnished Maaya Dunnai with an army; who, joining his forces with those of his two elder brothers, attacked and plundered Kotta, and on the same night got an obscure individual, Salama, to murder their father. The eldest son was proclaimed next day.

— *Jayaweera Bandara.* [*Gampola.*]

154. Bhuwanekabahoo 7th. [Kotta.] A.D. 1534. Bud. 2077. Reigned 8 years.

Son of the preceding King: he suppressed an insurrection raised by Weera Suriya Bandara, son of Weera Praakrama's daughter. His brother, Maaya Dunnai, settled at Seetaawaka, and built that town. The younger brother, Raygam Bandara, settled at Raygam. The King adopted as his heir Dharmapaala, his daughter's son by Weedeye Raja. Maaya Dunnai opposed this adoption, in which opposition he was supported by his brother, Raygam Bandara. Unable to cope with their united forces, the King placed his son under the protection of the Portuguese, and sent Salappoo Aratchy to Portugal with a golden image of the young Prince to ask for aid: the Prince was christened at Lisbon, in effigy, by the name of Don Juan, after Don Juan of Austria, in 2083; and an auxiliary force was sent with the Aratchy to the island. The King was accidentally killed, being shot through the heart by a Portuguese gentleman while on a water party on the Kellania with his European friends.

Maaya Dunnai. [*Seetaawaka.*]

Raygam Bandara. [*Raygam.*]

Jayaweera Bandara. [*Kanda Nowera.*]

155. Don Juan Dharmapaala. [Kotta.] A.D. 1542. Bud. 2085. Reigned 39 years.

Grandson: raised to the throne by the Portuguese, who brought Wilponte Alphonso Perera, a Roman priest, from Goa, purposely to baptize the King. A number of chiefs and people followed his example in apostacy. He was vigorously opposed by Raaja Singha throughout his reign, who ultimately obtained the ascendency. The King never recovered his authority beyond those parts which were under the immediate control of the Portuguese.

A Malabar. [*Yapahoo.*]
Portuguese. [*Colombo.*]
Weediye Raaja. [*Pailainda Nowera.*]
Raaja Singha (short time). [*Awissawelle.*]
Idirimaaney Suriya. [*Seven Korles.*]
Wikramabahoo. [*Kanda Nowera.*]

Descendant of Siri Sangabo: a great favourite of the nation.

156. Raaja Singha 1st. [Seetaawaka.] A.D. 1581. Bud. 2124. Reigned 11 years.

Son of Maaya Dunnai, of Seetawaka. In the course of his wars with Don Juan, he captured Kotta, and laid siege to Colombo, which he was obliged to raise, in consequence of the Portuguese bringing Koonappoo Bandar from Goa, and sending him with an army to Oudarata, to make a diversion in their favour. He was a descendant of the branch of the royal family that had settled at Peradeniya, and had been sent in his childhood to Goa. The King subsequently relinquished Budhism, and became a convert to the Braminical faith: he built the Bairaindi kowille at Awissawelle, and bestowed the shrine of Adam's Peak on some Aandee Fakiers: he extirpated the priests of Budha, and destroyed the books containing the tenets of their religion wherever they could be found. He also put to death every member of the royal family he could get into his power. He died while engaged in war with Koonappoo Bandar, at Kukal-bittrawella, in 2135.

Jaya Suriya. [*Seetaawaka.*]

Weediye Raaja's Queen. [*Seetaawaka.*]

His relationship to Raaja Singha is not stated: he succeeded him at Seetaawaka, and was put to death. Raaja Singha's sister, who had married Weediye Raaja, ascended the throne. She was made prisoner by Don Juan and the Portuguese; and her daughter, five years old, was sent to Goa.

157. Wimala Dharma. [Kanda Nowera.] A.D. 1592. Bud. 2135. Reigned 35 years.

On the death of Raaja Singha, Koonappoo Bandar proclaimed himself sovereign of the island under this title. The Portuguese marched against him, taking with them, as the candidate for the throne, Donna Catharina daughter of Weerabahoo, the expelled King of Kandy. The King defeated the invading army, took the Princess prisoner, and united her right to his own by marrying her. Since the landing of the Portuguese, the relic had been removed for security from Kotta, to Delgamoowe in Saffragam. The King transferred it to Kandy; and by bringing priests from Arracan, in 2140, renewed the Upasampada ordination in the island. He died, leaving issue two sons, Wijayapaala and Koomara Singha.

158. Senaaratena, or Senerat. [Kanda Nowera.] A.D. 1627. Bud. 2170. Reigned 7 years.

Brother of the late King: he had been a priest. By marrying Queen Catharina, he ascended the throne, and assumed the guardianship of the two Princes: he was forced by the Portuguese to quit Kandy, and retire to a wilderness (Nowera-Elliye), and from thence to Bintenna, where Raaja Singha was born. He returned to Kandy on the retreat of the Portuguese. Before the King died, he assigned Mátale and Ouvah to the two elder Princes, and the rest of the island to his own son.

159. Raaja Singha 2nd. [Kanda Nowera.] A.D. 1634. Bud. 2177. Reigned 50 years.

Son. Koomaara Singha died soon after his father. Wijayapaala made war against the King: being defeated, he repaired to Colombo and embarked for Goa. The King himself carried on a successful war against the Portuguese during his father's reign. At seventeen years of age he defeated a Portuguese army, and took their general, Don Constantino, prisoner. After he assumed the government himself, he drove the Portuguese from all their possessions, excepting the fortified towns on the sea-coast: from these, also, he expelled them by a treaty entered into with the Dutch, at Dennaanaka, or Digaawewa, near Batticalow, which was taken to Holland by two of his chiefs to be ratified. An auxiliary force arrived, and Colombo was taken in 2199, and the whole of the coast was transferred to the Dutch, excepting Batticalow and Putlam. Married a Princess of Madura.

Koomaara Singha. [*Ouvah.*]

Wijayapaala. [*Matelle.*]

160. Wimaladharma Suriya 2nd. [Kanda Nowera.] A.D. 1684. Bud. 2227. Reigned 22 years.

Son. Religion had been greatly neglected during his father's martial and tyrannical reign. The Upasampada order was almost extinct, which he renewed by bringing over learned priests from Arracan; and he improved the religious establishments: also married a Princess of Madura.

161. Sreeweera Praakrama Narendra Singha, or Koondasaala. [Kanda Nowera.] A.D. 1706. Bud. 2249. Reigned 33 years.

Son. The ordinances of Budhism had again fallen into such neglect that the Upasampada order had become completely extinct. By the advice of Welliwitte Samanairoo, he exerted himself to prevent the extinction of religion itself, by keeping up the Samanairoo order: built a palace at Koondasaala; the Naathadewalla, in Kandy: encouraged literature. He married a Princess of Madura, whose brother succeeded him, the Singhalese royal family being extinct.

162. Sreewijaya Raaja Singha, or Hanguranketta. [Kanda Nowera.] A.D. 1739. Bud. 2282. Reigned 8 years.

Brother-in-law: by the advice of the same Welliwitte, he sent a deputation of chiefs to Siam, to bring over learned priests to restore Upasampada and the other neglected ordinances of Budha. The vessel was wrecked: one of the chiefs and two of the followers only escaped, who reached their destination, but only succeeded in bringing a single book on religion. Welliwitte then prepared to depart himself with a retinue of Samanairoo priests. He was dissuaded by the King, who consented to send a suitable mission. Wilbaagedere Mudiyanse and Doraneagama Mudiyanse were selected: they sailed in 2288. The latter was detained by illness at Batavia. Wilbaagedere Mudiyanse fulfilled the object of his mission; and, when on the point of returning with the Siamese priests, he heard of the death of his sovereign. The Siamese King would not allow his priests to proceed to their destination until the wishes of the new sovereign of Ceylon were known. Wilbaagedere Mudiyanse returned to the island without them. The King built a palace at Hanurangkettu: died without issue: he had married also a Princess of Madura, whose brother succeeded him.

163. Kirti Sree Raaja Singha. [Kanda Nowera.] A.D. 1747. Bud. 2290. Reigned 33 years.

Brother-in-law of the late King, who died without issue: he again despatched Wilbaagedere Mudiyanse, with three other chiefs, on the same mission. They sailed in a Dutch ship from Trincomalie in July 2293, and arrived at the court of King Dhaarmaka in the following June. In December they left that court, accompanied by the Siamese priests and two ambassadors, to embark for Ceylon. The ship was stranded, and they were obliged to return, and to wait till the Dutch could prepare another vessel. They then embarked, and landed at Trincomalie in August 2296. The ordinances of Budha were restored in their original purity. Welliwitte was placed at the head of the church with the title of Sanga Raaja, and made chief of Adam's Peak. The Siamese priests returned, after a residence in the island of six years. The King afterwards entered into hostilities with the Dutch, who drove him to Meda Maha Nowera from Kandy, which they occupied. The Dutch abandoning that position, and retreating to the coast, a peace ensued. Under his auspices the Maha Wanse was compiled, from the reign of Praakramabahoo of Kurunaigalla to 2301, by Tibbootoowewa Terrunnanse. The King died in consequence of a fall from his horse.

164. Raajaadhi Raaja Singha. [Kanda Nowera.] A.D. 1780. Bud. 2323. Reigned 18 years.

Brother: co-operated with the English in the capture of the sea-coast in 2339.

165. Sree Wickrema Raaja Singha. [Kanda Nowera.] A.D. 1798. Bud. 2341. Reigned 17 years.

Son of the late King's wife's sister: deposed by the English in the seventeenth year of his reign: imprisoned at Vellore, where he died in 2375, leaving a son, born during his captivity.

EXPLANATORY NOTES.

Dambadiva, or Jamboodweepa is applied, according to the native literature of this island, to India in its most extended signification; and is sometimes used even in the sense of the Terra Cognita of the Ceylon Budhists.

Waggoo and Laala were subordinate kingdoms or principalities of Madhyadaisaya, or the Magadha empire, which comprised South Bahar and the Gangetic provinces.

Kalingoo consisted of the southern parts, including Kalingapatnam at least, if not the whole of the present Northern Circars.

Paandi was composed of the southern provinces of the peninsula of India, of which Madura was the capital. Sollee adjoined Paandi on the north, and probably included a considerable portion of the present Tanjore and Mysore.

Siam and Cambodia retain their former names. Rakkando, or Arakkando, is Arrakan. Ramaanaya, or Arramana, comprises probably the provinces situated between Arrakan and Siam.

The ancient divisions of Ceylon were :

Pihitee Ratta, bounded on the west, north, and east by the sea; on the south by the Mahawelli-ganga and Dedoro Oya rivers; it was also sometimes called Raaja Ratta, as the ancient capitals were situated in it.

Roohoona Ratta, bounded on the west and north by the Mahawelli-ganga and Kaloo-ganga (or Caltura) rivers; and on the east and south by the sea. The mountainous portion of it was called Malayaa Ratta.

Mayaa Ratta, bounded on the north by the Dedoro Oya; on the east by the Mahawelli-ganga and the mountains; on the south by the Kaloo-ganga; and on the west by the sea.

Almost all Pali proper names, whether geographical, or of persons, have some specific signification. In the translation of these names into vernacular dialects, their meaning, and not their sound, has been generally preserved. Thus, Pulutti Nuggera is Pollonnaroowa : Subba Pubattoo is Yapahoo in the Seven Korles; which European authors, guided by the sound only, have converted into (Yapana) Jaffna, and thereby made that place one of the ancient capitals of the island: Hastisailapoora is Kurunaigalla: Jayawardhanapoora is Kotta: Siriwardhanapoora and Senkadagalla Nowera are the former names of Kanda Nowera, or Kandi: and Maha-waalooka-ganga is the Mahawelli-ganga river.

Owing to this peculiarity in the native languages, almost every sovereign is designated by more than one appellation; and it requires much patient investigation to identify the ancient names of innumerable tanks and other ruins, scattered through the present deserted parts of the island, with those they now bear in the vernacular dialects. We are ourselves augmenting this confusion of names by pursuing the same course in many instances in which the meaning of a proper name is obvious. Instead of adopting the native designations, we have given to provinces the appellations of Seven Korles, Four Korles, and Three Korles; and to mountains the names of Elephant and Yam rocks, and Peacock mountain, &c.

The ancient measures of distance and space, quoted in the Epitome, are the following: the yoodoona, equal to four gows; the gow, equal to four hatackmas; and an hatackma is considered to be about one English mile. It is, however, rather the distance that can be walked within one Singhalese hour (24 minutes), at the ordinary native travelling pace, than a given measure of distance. Hence an hatackma is found to be much longer in the level than in the mountainous parts of the country. A cubit, or rather what is called a carpenter's cubit, is found to be equal to two feet three inches.

NOTES BY THE AUTHOR ON Mr. TURNOUR'S EPITOME.

The following extract from Crawford's "Embassy to Ava" is a remarkable confirmation of the Cingalese history in the time of Praakramabahoo the First, the 119th King.

"The last temple which we visited at Pugan is called Dammaran-kri, the etymology of which I have not been able to ascertain. The building of this handsome edifice is ascribed to a King who reigned in Pugan from 1151 of Christ to 1154, and who is commonly known in Burman story by the epithet of Kula-kya. 'Kula' is a term applied by the Burmans to the inhabitants of every country lying west of their own, whether European or Asiatic; and, in the sense in which they use it, is not very remote from the word 'barbarian,' as it was applied by the Greeks to strangers. 'Kya' is, to fall, or be dethroned; and it is stated that the epithet is derived from the circumstance of this Prince having lost his life and throne by the hands of a foreigner from the west; and we may suspect, most probably, by those of some Hindu adventurer."

The following is the translation of an inscription in the ancient Cingalese characters, which I copied from a rock in the midst of a rice-field, near the bank of the stream below Makulamadda, in Mátalé. It will be perceived that this inscription has reference to one of the most obscure periods of Cingalese history; and that Mr. Turnour has been unable to fix the length of time that the 138th, 139th, 140th, and 141st Kings reigned. This memorial shows that No. 139, Praakramabahoo the Fourth, was alive in A.D. 1359, and that it was the fifteenth year of his reign; which, therefore, commenced A.D. 1344, and gives the length of his predecessor's reign, twenty-five years: it also leads to the conclusion that Praakramabahoo the Fourth had been dethroned; but that his successors were not acknowledged in Mátalé at the date when this inscription was recorded.

TRANSLATION OF INSCRIPTION.

"At the completion of 1281 years of the glorious era of Saka,* in the fifteenth year of (the reign of) Sree Praakramabahoo, on the third day of the waning moon, in the month Unduwap, three or four hundred years since (the tract of land called) Kirilla-motaawa, of ten ammonams (in extent), had reverted to forest; on Sunday, (the moon's location being then) in the constellation Poosé, the work was commenced; and this field being reclaimed, and sown with corn, was, for merit's sake, dedicated to the holy dental relic.—May I be one who (shall have) attained the rewards of Swarga!"

* 1281 of Saka+78=A.D. 1359.

*** The words within parentheses are added to complete the sense in an English form.

TRANSLATION OF INSCRIPTIONS,

WITH AN INTRODUCTION

BY THE HONOURABLE GEORGE TURNOUR, ESQ.

SINCE the publication of the "Epitome of the History of Ceylon" in the Almanac of last year, I have received from Captain Forbes the historical inscriptions engraven on the stone slabs at Mihintele and Pollonnaroowa, and on the rock under which the great temple of Dambulla has been built; and, as I am requested to contribute for the Almanac of next year such further illustrations of general interest as will serve to corroborate that sketch of the local history, I have had translations made of those inscriptions. in elucidation of which I offer the following observations.

I cannot, however, avail myself of the materials obtained through Captain Forbes' researches, without again acknowledging the obligations I am under to him for the unreserved access he has allowed me to have to the results of his successful exertions to verify the authenticity of the native annals. More than seven years have elapsed since I first imparted to him the discovery I had then recently made, that the despised records of this island contained a connected history, extending back to so remote a date as nearly six centuries before the birth of Christ. Shortly after this I commenced the translation of the Maha Wanse, which I only carried to the tenth chapter, when I heard that that task had been already achieved in

England, and that the work was ready for the press; which made me relinquish (as I have already stated) the project I had then embarked in. I consequently merely took a few notes in the course of my subsequent reading of the remainder of that work. This accounts for my having borrowed (limited as I was as to time) so much more from the less authentic Singhalese works, in compiling the Epitome, than from the Maha Wanse itself. Since my removal to Kandy, more than five years ago, from want of leisure, I have scarcely referred to a native book. During the whole of this period, Captain Forbes has been zealously engaged in his researches. In the course of his inquiries into the portion of the history of Ceylon anterior to the Wijayan dynasty, and connected with the Budhas of this *kulpa*, who preceded Gautama (which I left wholly untouched), he has ascertained that many satisfactory data connected with the history of that still remoter period may yet be gleaned from the native annals; and he has succeeded in defining and establishing several interesting, but hitherto disputed points, as to the locality of the scenes and acts recorded in the fragments of the Ramayana, which are extant, or orally traditional, in Ceylon, by having identified, in various parts of the island, the places named in the account there given of the flight of Seeta. I have recently met with an unexpected corroboration of the correctness of his opinions, in the narrative of the travels of a Fakeer * in the middle of the last century, published in the fourth volume of the Asiatic Researches. I make the following extract from that paper, as it moreover confirms the native report, that there is another plain called the Bhoput Talawa, near Nowera-Elliye, still unexplored by Europeans; and as it invests that popular convalescent station with additional interest, from its having been ascertained by Captain Forbes that the "Seeta Koond" is situated

* The testimony of this Hindu is the more valuable, as the identification of Ceylon with Lanka is not admitted by the Indian Pundits; or rather, to use Tod's words, it is "an idea scouted by the Hindus, who transfer Lanka to a very distant region."

in the neighbourhood of Nowera-Elliye, and that some of the other incidents of interest narrated in that poem also occurred in that vicinity:—

"From Jaggernauth our traveller returned by nearly the same route to Ramisher,* whence he passed over into Silan, or Ceylon, and proceeded to its capital, which some, he observes, call Khundi (Candi), and others, Noora, but that Khundi Maha Rauje is the Prince's designation: and that further on he arrived at Catlgang,† on a river called the Manic-gunga, where there is a temple of Cartica, or Corticeya, the son of Mahadeo, to which he paid his respects, and then went on to visit the Sreepud, or 'the divine foot,' situated upon a mountain of extraordinary height;‡ and on one part of which there is also (according to this Fakeer's description) an extensive miry cavity, called the Bhoput Tank, and which bears also the name of the Tank of Ravan, or Raban (the *b* and *v* being pronounced indifferently in various parts of India), one of the former Kings of this island, well known in the Hindu legends for his wars with Rama, and from whom this tapu, or island, may probably have received its ancient appellation of Taprobane (*i. e.* the isle of Raban). But, however this may be, our traveller states that, leaving this tank, he proceeded on to a station called Seeta Koond (where Rama placed his wife Seeta, on the occasion of his war with her ravisher Ravan), and then reached at length to the Sreepud, on a most extensive table or flat, where there is, he observes, a bungalow built over the print of the divine foot; after worshiping which, he returned by the same route."

To revert to the historical inscriptions.—They verify the chronology developed in the Epitome with the utmost precision which could have been expected from them. Although Mr. Upham has been misled into the assertion (History of Budhism, page 31), that the Maha Wanse contains "dates most carefully affixed to every transaction of the missions or promulgation of Budha's doctrines," there are but few dates given, either in that

* Ramisseram. † Kattragam. ‡ Adam's Peak.

work or in the Singhalese histories. No other mode, therefore, of adjusting the chronology of the native history could be had ecourse to, than that of adding successively the number of years each sovereign has reigned, to any one of those given dates. As the fractional parts of the year are not generally specified with respect to the term of each reign, a progressively increasing error must necessarily accumulate from one given date to another, when an opportunity is at last afforded for correcting the series of anachronisms. I consequently consider these apparent defects in the chronology of the native histories to be one of the most convincing proofs of their genuineness and authenticity; as they establish, beyond all possibility of doubt, the absence of any attempt to adjust the individual or collective terms of the reigns of the several Kings comprised between any two given dates, to the full period embraced between them.

On many accounts I have considered it desirable that these inscriptions, which are composed in the abstruse idiom and phraseology employed in regal and sacred documents, should be translated by a person who possessed a thorough knowledge, not only of that idiom, but of the doctrines, rites, and ceremonies of Budhism: I therefore placed them in the hands of Mr. Armour, of Kandy; who, both from his attainments as a Singhalese scholar, and from his long intercourse with the Kandian priests, was the best qualified of any person I am acquainted with to execute the task. It is to him I owe the following able translations, which are rendered as nearly verbatim as the subjects treated of would admit.

The inscriptions at Mihintele bear no date. They must have been recorded about the year of Budha 805, A.D. 262. From the inscriptions themselves, and on reference to the Maha Wanse, I find that three Princes of the Cshestria tribe, descended from Okkaaka, and connected with the Laimini branches of the royal family, whose domains were near Mayanganna in Bintenne, repaired to the court of the reigning sovereign, Weja Indoo, in A.D. 241. They were received into favour, and appointed to the highest offices in the state; of which they availed themselves in the course of a few months to conspire against their benefactor, and to put him to death. One of these Princes, Sangatissa, ascended the throne; and retained the other two, Sirisangabo and Golooabhaa, in their high stations. Sangatissa was carried off within four years by poison, which was secretly administered to him in a jambo fruit by the inhabitants of the western villages, to which the King was in the habit of making excursions, when he probably subjected those people to the extortions inseparable from the royal progresses of the olden times. Sirisangabo succeeded him in A.D. 246, who was a rigid devotee, and had taken the vows of the order *atta sill;* the ordinances of which, together with the observance of many rules of devotion and acts of self-denial, totally prohibited the destruction of animal life. It may readily be conceived that the feebleness of a Government administered by so bigoted an enthusiast soon led to anarchy. Crimes of the greatest enormity, committed with impunity, rapidly increased in all parts of the kingdom. When the malefactors were brought to the prison of the capital, as the King's vow precluded the possibility of their being executed, they were secretly released at night after condemnation; and the corpses furnished by the usual casualties of a populous city were exhibited at the place of execution, on gibbets and impaling poles, as the victims of the violated laws. "By these means," says the Budhist historian, "a pious King successfully repressed crime, and yet gave the criminal time and opportunity to reform." The result, however, as might have been expected, was precisely the reverse of that representation. The whole frame of society was disorganised; and a famine, with its usual concomitant a pestilence, combining with these public disorders, Golooabhaa, who then held the office of treasurer, easily wrested the sceptre from the weak hands which then swayed it. Sirisangabo offered no resistance. "He privately left the city, taking with him," observes the historian, "nothing but his 'preankada' (water-strainer), which is used by all the devotees, from the *pan sill* to the *atta sill* orders, to prevent the destruction of the lives of the animalculæ which they would otherwise imperceptibly swallow in drinking unstrained water." The Maha Wanse briefly closes the history of this King by stating that, in his wanderings as a hermit, he met with a peasant who shared his scanty repast with him. Wishing to reward this act of charity, and having nothing else to bestow, Sirisangabo, by the supernatural power he had acquired by his life of piety, "*detached*" his head from his shoulders, and presented it to the peasant, desiring him to produce it to Golooabhaa; which he did, and received his reward.

The subsequent writers of the Singhalese histories, and the expounders of those histories to Europeans,* have unsparingly used their usual privilege of exaggeration and embellishment in their accounts of the life and death of this idolized sovereign of Ceylon. They represent that the usurper Golooabhaa set a high reward on the head of Sirisangabo; and that many heads, obtained by murder and assassination, had been produced before the usurper by persons who successively forfeited their own heads for the imposition they had attempted to practise. Sirisangabo, hearing of these enormities, resolved to put an end to them by sacrificing his own life. In this frame of mind, he met with a peasant who had fled from his home horrified at the suggestion of his wife, of destroying the King. He revealed his distress to his disguised sovereign. In order that the reward might be secured to this man, the King avowed himself, and with his own hands severed his head from his body. The head was produced to Golooabhaa, and the bearer of it was about to suffer as another impostor, when it sprung up, and, self-poised, in the air, addressed the usurper, proclaiming itself to be the head of King Sirisangabo. The peasant is stated to have received his reward; and the head was buried with great pomp at Attwanagala, over which the usurper raised a daagoba, which is still standing.

* Philalethes, page 33.—Davy, page 299.

This tissue of mystery and miracle admits of being explained in a few words: Golooabhaa, on his accession, found himself opposed by the all-influential priesthood, who were naturally enough attached to the deposed bigot. It became necessary, therefore, for the safety of the usurper, that he should finally get rid of the dethroned sovereign, and at the same time dispose of him in a manner least obnoxious to the priesthood;—hence the private murder in the wilderness, and the subsequent pompous interment, conferred on the plea of the miracle performed at his death. Golooabhaa, however, notwithstanding these expedients, and though he performed many acts of ostentatious piety, failed in his efforts to conciliate the church; in which, unhappily for him, a furious schism raged at that period. He continued consequently so unpopular with the priesthood, that his son Makalan Detootissa, who attempted to pacify that schism, (the record of which pacification is contained in this inscription,) omits his name entirely, and dates the record in question from the 10th day of the 16th year *after* the accession of Sirisangabo. For the purpose of defining his relationship to the royal family, he is compelled, in consequence of this omission of his father's name, to record that of his younger brother and successor Maha Sen. This pacification, however, only endured while Detootissa was sovereign. The devastations committed by the revival of the Wytooliya heresy are recorded in ample detail in the reign of his successor. Without this explanation, the Mihintele inscriptions might justly be considered rather to impugn than to corroborate the correctness of the dates and facts given in the Epitome. The inference drawn from this inscription would naturally have been that Sirisangabo's reign extended to at least sixteen years, and that Detootissa and his younger brother Maha Sen, were contemporary rulers of separate portions or of subordinate principalities of Ceylon; whereas Sirisangabo was dethroned two years only after his accession, in A.D. 248, by Golooabhaa, who was succeeded, after a reign of thirteen years, by his son Detootissa: consequently, "the sixteenth year after the accession of Sirisangabo was A.D. 262, the second year of Detootissa's reign, and the fourteenth after the expulsion of Sirisangabo from the throne." Maha Sen was a prince who, in early youth, gave promise of the great reputation he subsequently acquired, and had already in his brother's reign assumed a position of prominence in the eyes of the nation; which readily accounts for Detootissa's reference to his name, when state policy precluded the record of that of his father.

The other inscriptions are four in number: three recorded by the King Kirti Nissanga, two of them at Pollonnaroowa, and one at Dambulla, all which must have been engraven between A.D. 1187 and 1196; and one by King Saahasamallawa in A.D. 1200 at Pollonnaroowa.

The last of these inscriptions dates the accession of Saahasamallawa in the year of Budha 1743, A.D. 1200, while in the Epitome I have brought the period down to Budha 1748; an anachronism which I should have attributed without the slightest hesitation to the imperfection, explained above, as inherent in the chronology of the native history. On referring, however, to the Maha Wanse, to ascertain the justness of Kirti Nissanga's claim to the extravagant praises lavished on him both as a sovereign and a warrior, I find that I have mis-stated the term of the reign of the regicide Mihindoo the Fifth, or Kitsen Kisdaas, whose short-lived power lasted only *five days*, and not *five years*. The Maha Wanse, in three verses, describes his contemptible existence as a sovereign for those five *days*, in language too decisively descriptive of his unrecognised usurpation, to leave any doubt as to the correctness of substituting *days* for *years*. From which work I also learn that the individual whom Wejayabahoo the Second had "selected as his successor" was not Kitsen Kisdaas, but Kirti Nissanga.

These inscriptions, also, though valuable as defining the genealogy of those sovereigns, and exhibiting the national opinions of that period as regard the principles of good government, are nevertheless, without proper explanations, as much calculated to distort facts and disguise historical truth, as the Mihintele inscriptions are calculated to mislead in regard to the chronology of that earlier period of the native history.

It must now remain for ever a matter for conjecture, whether it was the personal vanity of the *Kaalinga* sovereigns, or the policy of the party which invited them from the continent, and seated them on the throne of Ceylon, in the hope of their becoming the founders of a long line of sovereigns, or both united, which have invested them with the high character they bear in these inscriptions. The history of the period at which they reigned was compiled, within little more than half a century after their demise, under the auspices of Praakramabahoo the Third, a descendant of the original royal family, which had then been restored to the throne. The *Kaalinga* Princes consequently receive no greater meed of praise from the historian patronized by the former dynasty, than might have been expected from so reluctant a panegyrist. There could, however, have been no want of authentic data to establish what is claimed for them, if they really merited the eulogies they have received in the inscriptions; and there certainly are no collateral circumstances, connected with the history of that period, which justify the boundless pretensions to good government advanced by Kirti Nissanga in particular. The term of his reign is apparently too short, in the disordered state of the country at that epoch, to have realized his proud boast, similar to that of Alfred, "that gold bracelets hung up near the highways should remain untouched;" followed by precepts not unworthy of the memorable sentiments preserved in the same British sovereign's will, "that it was just the English should for ever remain as free as their own thoughts." It appears also to be quite certain that Kirti Nissanga was not involved in any foreign war. The fame of his prowess in arms, set forth in these inscriptions, must consequently have been earned in his visits to his royal relations on the continent of India, in pompous Asiatic pageants, like the renown of our eighth Henry in "the field of the cloth of gold."

The manner in which he is recorded to have put down robbery (by bribing the thieves) is one of the most curious, and certainly most questionable, among his political measures; but during the time that a considerable portion of the population was composed of migratory foreigners, stray bands of robbers, whom it was impossible to extirpate, might very probably have established themselves among the fastnesses of the mountains; and we may pardon the Singbalese monarch for yielding to a course of doubtful policy, which the want of energy and union even in European governments have rendered it necessary for the traveller to adopt in comparatively modern times.

Taken altogether, the view thus presented of the internal government of Ceylon during the twelfth century is such as may well excite the curiosity of the antiquary, encouraged as he must be by the certainty that the pursuit will be rewarded by the discovery of important historical facts, characteristic of the principles of Asiatic government. We find the royal charity ostentatiously recorded, after the oriental custom; but at the same time we perceive the head of the state anxious to relieve, or at least to acquire the reputation of having relieved, distress, and promoted the prosperity of his subjects, by reducing taxation and constructing works of public utility. As, however, all improvements under a despotic government must depend upon the character of one individual, it is not surprising that the isolated efforts of a few rulers should have had so little *permanent* effect upon the general welfare; nor that the people who could appreciate the good qualities of a patriotic sovereign should have relapsed into comparative barbarism beneath the yoke of subsequent weak and imbecile rulers.

The preservation of the institutions of the land, and the maintenance of the agricultural prosperity of the country (on which the welfare of the inhabitants chiefly depended), were both of a character which equally required the unremitting exercise of the powers of an energetic ruler; and it will have been seen by the events recorded in the Epitome, that the condition of the country throughout the period embraced in that sketch, wholly depended on the individual character of the reigning sovereign, or the minister to whom the government of the kingdom may have been intrusted.

No. 1.

THE INSCRIPTION AT MIHINTELE.

On the 10th day of the 16th year *after* the regal canopy had been elevated by Siri Sangabodhi Abhaya Maha Raja, who was born unto Abhaha Sala Mewan Maha Raja, an illustrious Cshettry, of the dynasty of Okkaaka, which is the pinnacle of the glories of the Cshettrya race, in the radiant womb of Queen Dewoogon Bisauw, who was of the same race,—who having held the dignities of aipaa* and mahapaa, in proper course succeeded to the kingly office, and illuminated Lakdiwa† with the effulgence of his majesty; the sovereign lord, the brother of the eminent Maha Sen, voluntarily made a covenant with the select of the priesthood of Saigiri wihare, and of Abhayagiri wihare, to the effect that the Abhayagiri wihare shall conform to the anciently established institutes of the Saigiri wihare; and that the same regulations shall be in force respecting the priests of this wihare, as well as the workmen, the servants, the offices, the receipts,

* Aipaa or aadipaada, and mahapaa or mahaadipaada, principal officers of state.

† Lakdiwa or Lanka dweepa, the island of Lanka or Ceylon: from the root lanka, signifying "adorned, elegant, beauteous."

and the expenditure thereof, and consequently made the following ordinance:—

That the Bhikshu* priests, resident at this wihare, shall make it a constant practice to rise at the dawn, meditate on the four preservative † principles, perform the ablution, and then having attired themselves with the cheewera (or yellow garments) in the manner prescribed in the (book) Sekhiyawe, they shall resort to the Etweherra, and, having there performed the religious offices, afterwards partake of conjee and rice, and shall duly administer to the priests who could not attend, on account of sickness, such things, at their respective cells, as the physicians had prescribed.

That to the expounders of the Abhidharma ‡ pitake shall be assigned twelve cells; to those who preach from the Soottraa ‡ pitake, seven cells; and to such of the resident priests who read the Wineye ‡ pitake, five cells; with food and raiment.

That when donations are made of acceptable gifts unto the priesthood in general, the same shall be duly delivered unto them, and shall not be appropriated otherwise.

That all the lands which belong to this wihare, and the products thereof, shall be enjoyed by the priesthood in common, and shall not be subdivided and possessed separately.

That when orders are issued to the dependants or retainers, or when any of them are to be dismissed, it shall be with the concurrence of the whole community of priests, and not by the will of an individual.

The Bhikshu priests, resident at this wihare, shall enjoy,

* Bhikshu; priests of the superior order of Upasampada.

† The four preservative principles, viz. Meditating on the virtues of Budha; wishing unto all beings deliverance from woe; reflecting on the impurity of the substances which constitute the corporeal frame; and the contemplation of death.

‡ The Abhidharma pitake, the doctrine of metaphysics, consists of the discourses or sermons of Budha, addressed to the gods. The Soottraa pitake comprises the lessons inculcated for the benefit of all beings in general; and the Wineye pitake consists principally of laws, &c. for the observance of the Budhist priesthood.

in such manner as is sanctioned, the products of the fields, the orchards, &c. which appertain to the Etweherra; but none of them shall expend them in places not appertaining to the Etweherra.

Priests that infringe these rules shall cease to dwell in this wihare.

The priests who act as supervisors of the Nikaayas (or subsidiary associations), and those who superintend the various offices, the overseers of the villages, the cooks, the writer (of accounts in the wihare,—he that takes account of the incomes), and the receiver of the incomes,—all these persons shall be under the general control of the community of Abhayagiri, whose residence shall be stationary at Etweherra, and who will conduct the internal and external services, and manage the receipts and disbursements in unity and concord.

Persons shall be appointed to furnish necessaries, and assist those whose business is to receive and to issue provisions; and, if any of the dependants or the priests of this wihare should act contrary to the regulations, they shall be dismissed, after what was due from them has been recovered, and entries made thereof; but those whose business it is to recover and collect the incomes shall not be dismissed.

The servants of the *daagey* * shall have charge of whatever is brought to it.

Those who have services and offices allotted to them, shall attend duly at their respective places, excepting those who may have gone on wihare service to a distance: those who must attend at the place where rice is issued, and at the place where rice and conjee are prepared in the morning, will not be allowed to be absent.

Nothing that accrues to the Etweherra and the daagey shall be given away; nor shall anything be purchased from the servants.

* Daagey; a house built close to a daagoba, for the purpose of offerings.

The servants of the wihare shall not exact services from the people belonging thereto, nor shall the people be sent out to work for others.

The officers of the Etweherra shall take care of the five yaalas* dedicated to the Katoomaha Saeya, at Damgamuwa, for the purpose of keeping it in repair; and they shall repair the said daagoba† accordingly; and the two Kiriya‡ (eight ammonams) granted from Elgamiya for maintaining the Kiribad pauw shall be expended on its preservation.

The daagey, the Magoolmahsalapilemegey (or house of the great stone image), the Mahabogey,§ the Nayadae, the shrine of the Princess Mininaal dewi, the Katumaha Saeya, the Kiribad pauw daageb, the daagobas of Etweherra, situate on the upper hill and on the lower hill,—the offerings collected at all these places, together with the one hundred kalam || of gold from Etweherra, with the ten yaalas of paddy, shall be annually expended for the purpose of repairing the daagobas of this temple and the other edifices.

If the servants attached to the daagey and the pilemegey embezzle or squander the offerings rendered thereat, laborious work shall be imposed on them.

One-third of the (village) Gassagaessi belonging to Kiribad pauw with the Sangawaelle thereof, the land contiguous to Manaa Wewa, the land contiguous to the upper and the lower lakes of Lahinipauw and the Sangawella thereof, the ground around the lake Pahadewila, and the ground surrounding the

* Yaal, a score; twenty ammonams' extent of land, or twenty ammonams of grain, or twenty head of cattle.

† Daagoba, *i. e.* Dhatu-garba, a womb or receptacle for a relic; a monument containing either a corporeal relic of or an utensil which had been used by, Budha.

‡ Kiriya; two ammonams.

§ Bogey; a house built at the foot of a bo or pippal-tree, for the purpose of receiving offerings: when furnished with images of Budha, the daagey and bogey are also called Pilemegey, or Image house, and Budugey.

|| Kalam, or kalanda, is the weight of twenty maditi or manjishta seeds, or of forty olinda seeds.

lake Porodeni Pokuna,—what is derived from these places may be appropriated to the wihare.

It being proper (or a matter of course) to take land-fees from the occupiers of temple lands, the same may be levied, but not from such as are the slaves and menials of the wihare.

Those who have only assumed the yellow vestments, but engage in traffic inconsistently therewith, and destroy life (by following the chase, killing poultry, &c.) shall not be permitted to dwell around the mount.

None but proper persons shall be employed as servants at the wihare. The lands belonging to this temple shall be allotted for services to itself, and shall not be assigned for any other purpoes.

Only the regular services shall be exacted, and not any extra labour, on account of *poya** festivals, &c.

Lands belonging to the Etweherra may be allotted to the labourers and to the wihare slaves in lieu of wages; but neither fields nor orchards, &c. shall be transferred in parveny † nor given to them in mortgage.

The raw rice which the dependants of the wihare must furnish according to the ancient custom, shall alone be received, and victuals shall not be taken from the other inhabitants. Fees shall not be exacted from the cultivators, nor shall their cattle be seized by the domestics, for the purpose of employing the cattle to labour their (the domestics') fields.

The hereditary service fields shall not be resumed even in cases of disobedience; nor shall damage be done to the gardens, nor the trees or plants be cut down.

Throughout the domains of this wihare, neither palm-trees, nor mee-trees, ‡ nor any other fruit-bearing trees, shall be felled, even with the consent of the tenants.

* Poya days are those of the new and the full moon; the first and the last quarter.

† Parveny signifies hereditary or ancestorial, and also heritable.

‡ Mee-tree; the Madhudruma: a description whereof is given in the first volume of the Asiatic Researches.

If a fault be committed by any of the cultivators, the adequate fine shall be assessed according to usage; and, in lieu thereof, the delinquent shall be directed to work at the lake in making an excavation (not exceeding) sixteen cubits in circumference, and one cubit in depth; if he refuse so to labour, the assessed fine shall be levied.

After paying the allotted wages to those who are entitled thereto, the rest of the revenues of the lands belonging to this wihare shall be entered in books by the proper officers, so that the same may be under inspection.

The daily expenditure on account of the Maha Patra,* and the hired servants and the repairs, shall be written in books, and accounts kept of the contents of the store-room by the appointed persons respectively: every month these accounts shall be collected into one account; and, at the end of each year, the twelve months' accounts shall be formed into one lekam, or register, to be produced before the assembled priests and there disposed of. Any of the servants who should infringe this regulation shall be fined, and dismissed from the service.

No. 2.

ON THE SECOND ROCK.

To the priest who has the superintendence of the several nikaayas (or associations), one naeliya † of rice daily for the bana ‡ at the wass season, § one kalenda and four

* Maha Patra, or the great bowl: a well-endowed wihare is furnished with a patra, or bowl of a large size, which is filled with offerings of rice and other eatables on particular occasions.

† Naeliya; a measure containing four chundoos.

‡ Bana; speech, discourse, sermon.

§ Wass; the rainy season, commencing with the day of the full moon in the month of Essela, *August*, and lasting three months, during which the Budhist priests are enjoined to remain stationary.

akas* of gold; and for the bana at the conclusion of the wass a like quantity.

To the superintendent of a village, wages of five kiriyas, and a daily allowance of one naeliya of rice; fifteen kalendas yearly for flower money. The cook, the wihare writer, the rajakariya writer, the receiver of the revenues, and the principal attendant, shall each have five kiriyas; a waiter shall have one kiriya and two payas,† with two adamanaas ‡ of rice; a number of watchmen at the rate of two payas, with one adamanaa of rice; a manager of the festivals, one kiriya, with a farm in Damiya, and three kalendas, two akas yearly as flower money; an attendant on the officiating person, one kiriya and a farm in Damiya.

For cloths for the great Budhist festival called Somnas, one kalenda.

To a plasterer one paya, with two patas § of rice; to a scavenger, and to a maker of sandals, each one kiriya and two payas, with two adamanaas of rice; to one who spreads cloths (for the ceiling) to the roof, two payas, with a farm in Damiya; for cloths used at the great Budhist festival called Roovanasoon, one kalenda; to him that spreads cloths on the floor, two payas, and a farm in Damiya; to the person employed in whitewashing, two payas, with one adamanaa and one pata of rice; to each of the eleven persons who furnish lime, two payas, and a farm in Damiya.

To each of the four Wattanaawaeri, one adamanaa of rice, with two payas as diwel.||

It is proper that when the Bhikshu priests of this wihare receive garments according to their stations, that he who is provided shall make a distribution of such garments amongst those who are in want thereof.

* An aka is equal to two and a half manjadies, or manjishta seed: in weight eight akas make a kalenda.

† Paya; a paela, or quarter of an ammonam.

‡ Adamanaa; a naeliya or measure.

§ Pata; a handful.

|| Diwel; hire-wages.

To each of the two receivers of the revenues, two payas, with one adamanaa and two patas of rice.

To a warder of the granary, two payas, with one adamanaa and two patas of rice.

To the yetamawa, one paya, with one adamanaa and two patas of rice.

To the warder of the banagey,* one paya, with one adamanaa and two patas of rice.

To the person who communicates orders to the menials, two payas; and to the twenty-four inferior menials, one paya each, with a kalenda for clothing annually.

To an attendant on the priests, one kiriya, with one adamanaa of rice; one kiriya and two payas from the village Nalologama to each of the twelve cooks; to the head servant, one adamanaa and one pata of rice; to each person who dresses victuals, and also procures the fuel, three adamanaas of rice; to one who supplies fuel, but does not cook, and to one who is employed on errands, two adamanaas of rice each; and to one who only cooks, but does not fetch the fuel, one adamanaa of rice; to the chief thatcher (or tiler), two payas, with one adamanaa and one pata of rice; and to each of the eleven inferior thatchers (or tilers), two payas, with one adamanaa of rice; to each of the five potters, who furnish daily five chatties, one kiriya; to a patra manufacturer, who supplies every month ten patras and ten water-pots, two kiriyas, with two adamanaas of rice; to the person who furnishes a water-strainer monthly, one kiriya and two payas; to a physician, a regular allowance, with a farm in Damiya; to a surgeon, two payas; to a madonwa, one kiriya and two payas, with a farm in Damiya.

The village of Karedeygama allotted as diwel (or in lieu of wages) to the receiver of the dues of the daagey, to the overseer of the tenantry, to the writer of the accounts of dues and service, and to the three superintendents of works.

* Banagey; a house wherein the bana or sermons of Budha are preached.

Four farms or homesteads in Damiya to the persons who furnish rosin or incense; and an allowance from this village for furnishing oil to the daagey: also two kiriyas in this village to the two persons who supply flowers for offerings at the daagey, and who sweep away the withered flowers; also a farm in Damiya: two kiriyas in the village Sapoogamiya to the cultivator of lotus-flowers for supplying one hundred and twenty flowers monthly; and two kiriyas to a painter; one naeliya of rice to the warder of the daagey.

The village Gooneygama to the six persons who supply incense for the Mahabudugey, to the preacher of bana, to the schoolmaster, and to six devotees; two payas from this village to the person who supplies flowers for the Mahabudugey, with a farm in Damiya; two farms in Damiya to the suppliers of incense at this village; to the person officiating at the shrine of the great stone statue (of Budha), and to his assistant, two payas, with one adamanaa and two patas of rice.

To the suppliers of oil and strainers for the daagey, and the like for the pelemegey, and to an examiner, one kiriya and two payas, with two adamanaas of rice each.

To the chief builder * * and to two master carpenters, and eight inferior carpenters, and two braziers, the village Wadoodeweygama; one kiriya to each of the two stonecutters, and three kiriyas to each of the two goldsmiths; to each of the two blacksmiths one kiriya; to the lime-burners, the village Soonooboldeweygama; to six carters, the village Dunumugama; two payas as diwel, with one adamanaa of rice, to each of the twelve labourers; and to their overseer employed in effecting the repairs, one kiriya, with one adamanaa and one pata of rice.

Two payas to each of the three warders of the three sacred edifices, Nawagoona Maha Saeya, Nettewiya Maha Saeya, and Ambulu Daagoba. A farm in the village Damiya to each person employed in keeping clean and in good order the different daagobas at Etweherra, on the upper hill and on the lower hill.

Thus are servants appointed to attend at the daagey, the pilemegey and, the banagey; and, moreover, two washers have been appointed to wash the cloths, the vestments, and the bed linen; three kiriyas being allotted to each of them in the village Magoolwewa.

The services and dues from all the lands belonging to this wihare shall be regularly obtained; there shall be concord, and no contention, so that the institution may prosper. According to the supply of water in the lake, the same shall be distributed to the wihare lands in the manner formerly regulated by the Tamuls. None of the lands belonging to this wihare shall be transferred in parveny, nor mortgaged; those who have thus gotten any thereof shall not be allowed to retain possession, but the same shall be resumed for the wihare. To insure prosperity to the institution, these regulations shall be strictly obeyed.

No. 3.

THE INSCRIPTION ON THE GREAT TABLET AT POLLONNAROOWA.

Adoration to the Saakya-Lion (*i. e. Budha the Lion, or noblest individual of the race of Saakya*).

WEERA NISSANKHA MALLA, the perfectly-conversant with the sublime religion, the lamp which illumineth the whole world, the protector of the earth, and the fountain of renown, was conceived in the womb of the Queen Paarwati Maha Devi unto the King Sree Jaya Gopa, the glory of the dynasty which reigned in the city of Singhapura, in the kingdom of Kaalinga, on the continent of Dambadiva,* which is the birth-

* The insular continent, whereof Ceylon is one of the appurtenant islets.

place of Budha,* Bodhi-Satwayo,† and Chakkrawartees;‡ and, having grown up amidst regal splendour, was invited by the King, who was his senior kinsman, to come and reign over his hereditary kingdom of Lakdiva. Consequently he departed from his native city, and landed on this island in great pomp and state, in the year 1700, after the period when Wijaya Raja, a descendant of the aërovolant sovereign Kaalinga Chakkrawartee, of the illustrious and virtuous race of Okkaaka,§ landed on the island of Lakdiva, which, by the command of Budha, was placed under the tutelary care of the gods, and, having extirpated the *Yakshas*,‖ made it an abode of mankind; and, having been installed in the office of Aipaa (viceroy or prime minister), enjoyed the luxuries of regality; and having been accomplished in the art of war, as well as in all the other branches of knowledge which form the circle of the arts and sciences, he in due order of regal succession received the sacred unction; and, being then crowned, was installed King. At the festival of his coronation he was invested with a glory which filled the firmament, and overpowered all beholders; and with such daring courage, that, when he was taking diversion in a forest, a furious she-bear having rushed towards him, he laid her and her whelps dead at his feet. When he traversed a dry desert, and wished for water, an unexpected cloud instantly poured down an abundant shower. His royal prowess was such, that, like the spring of the noble lion, nothing could withstand it. When he went to enjoy the bath, and a huge polonga approached him there, he turned aside and said (to the snake), "Thou knowest what thou deservest;" whereupon the snake stung

* One who has attained perfection of wisdom.

† One who is in the course of attaining perfection; a Budha *in petto*.

‡ Sovereign of the whole world.

§ Okkaaka, also called the Saakya Wangsa, and Manu Wangsa, the descendants of Vaiwaswata Manu, who was appointed at the first social compact—the Maha Sammata, or Grand Congress,—to rule over mankind; hence his title of Maha Sammata Rajjuruwo.

‖ Yakshas; demons.

itself, and sacrificed its life. His irresistible majesty was such, that the state elephant no sooner saw him than he roared the shout of triumph, and took the King on his back. His glorious presence gladdeneth all beholders. Thus glorified, his majesty the great King Sirisangabo Kaalinga Praakramabahoo Weeraraja Nissanka Malla Apprati Malla dispersed his enemies as the sun over the summit of Udaagala (dispelleth darkness); and causing the smiles of the countenances of his people to expand with gladness, exercising power and enjoying regal delights like another Sekkra Dewindra,† in benignity resembling the full moon, in firmness the mountain Meru,‡ in profundity (of knowledge) the great ocean, in patience the earth, and occupying his station like a Calpa Wurksha § produced by the merits of his subjects, his majesty considered thus, "The malice of some people, and the anxiety of others to maintain the rights of their respective families, have been heretofore, and may prove hereafter, the source of danger to our dynasty;" and, being moved with benevolence towards the people, he confirmed to them the privileges appropriate to the different families, and relinquished the revenues of five years. He reduced the rate of taxes on arable lands imposed in former reigns, and fixed the Otoo || duty at one ammonam, three pelahs for every one ammonam's extent * * * * * * * * He relinquished the tax on the dry grain produced on chenas, the cultivation of which is attended with distress; and ordained that such tax should cease for evermore. He quenched the fire of indigence with showers of riches, consisting of gold coin, copper, bell-metal, gold, silver, pearls, precious stones, vestments, and jewels,

† Sekkra Dewindra, *i. e.* Sekkra the lord of gods—Indra; whose mansion is on the summit of Sumeru, and who governs this nether world, and the two lowest of the Diwa Lokas, or Divine worlds, viz. the Chaaturmaha Raajike, and Taawatingsa.

‡ Meru, Sumeru, Sineru; the mountain in the centre of the Sakwula or world, analogous to the north pole.

§ Calpa Wurksha; a tree which gives all that is desired.

|| Otoo: a unit; a tithe or tenth.

He appointed ministers and others, whom he provided with lands, slaves, cattle, houses, and various other riches in abundance: he re-constructed the embankments of great lakes, watercourses, and weirs, which had remained neglected many years in the *three** kingdoms *(or cantons of the island)*, all which he restored to prosperity, and granted to the inhabitants thereof the boon of security and other gifts. He appointed judges in many provinces to remove injustice; and, considering that robbers committed robberies through hunger for wealth, he gave them whatever riches they desired, and thus relieved the country from the dread of thieves; and by establishing order amongst the dwellers in forests, and the dwellers in villages, he removed the thorns (of annoyance). According to the sacred injunctions of the doctrine of Budha, he also expelled the unrighteous from the religious communities, and thus freed the country in general of the thorns (of evil-doers). He provided the four requisites † for the comfortable maintenance of the holy priesthood; and every year caused priests to be ordained, and bestowed gifts of Katt'hine, &c.;‡ and, as in former times, assigned extensive estates and lands of lesser extent (to the wihares).

Having greatly promoted the interests of the doctrine,§ and advanced the same, as well as the sciences, by bestowing suitable gifts on professors of the religion, and on professors of the sciences; and considering that the continuance of the religion and of the sciences depended on the royal dynasty, he sent to the country of Kaalinga, and caused many Princesses of the Soma, Surya Wangsa (Luni-solar race), to be brought hither; married the royal virgins to his son the exalted Weera Bahoo, and increased the royal family.

His majesty wearing the crown, and being decorated with

* The three kingdoms or divisions of the realm; Roohoona, Maayaa, Pihitti.

† The four requisites, viz. raiment, victuals, lodging, and physic or such delicacies as the aged and infirm require.

‡ Katt'hine; yellow garments bestowed after the wass season.

§ The doctrine: Soesana; the tenets inculcated by Budha.

the royal ornaments, caused himself, as well as the chief Queens Kaalinga Subhaddra Maha Devi, and Gangaa Wansa Kaalinga Maha Devi, his son the aforesaid and exalted personage, and his daughter Sarwaanga Soonderee, to be weighed in a balance every year; and by bestowing five times their weight (of goods) on the priests and Brahmins, the blind, the lame, the dwarfish, and the deformed, and other destitute and friendless people who thronged from the ten regions, made them happy, and caused a constant supply of rain.

All the people who were interested in the cause of the religion, and in the welfare of the country, were therefore affected with the most submissive fidelity, and devoted their lives to his majesty; who, having attained the acmé of virtue, daily performed acts of merit, and Kaalinga * * the tileka † of Pulastipura.‡ * * * * * *

No. 4.

INSCRIPTION ON THE SAME TABLET AT POLLONNAROOWA.

HAVING gladdened the people with showers of riches when he visited the villages, towns, and cities, and explored the fastnesses, and the strongholds, and secure places on mountains and in forests, at the time he made the tour of this island; he built wihares in every part of the country, and also the great Meyangoona wihare; and having caused the sitting and the erect images in the cave of Dambulla to be gilt, at the cost of a sum of 10,000;§ and having made offerings of valuables, worth a sum of seven lakshas, to the great Ruanweli Saeya at Anooraadhapoora; he caused statues to

† The tileka; an ornamental circlet of sandal, &c. on the forehead.

‡ Pulastipura; the city of Pollonnaroowa.

§ 10,000; supposed to mean so many kaarshaapana or pagodas.

be made of the Dewetas, who rejoiced at the said puja, and had the same gilded and placed in proper situations. Having thus restored to its ancient condition the island of Lakdiva, the receptacle of the efficacious doctrines of Budha, * * * * * apprehending evil, to Dambadiva (he proceeded), attended by a completely organized army, (composed of squadrons of horses, elephants, chariots, and foot-soldiers,) and consistently with his cognomen of the Dauntless and Irresistible Warrior, * * * he proclaimed his royal prowess, * * and appointed champions to go and challenge battle * * whereupon each, declaring that he was able to accomplish it alone, prepared to go forth to the fight. * * * "Let only our lives be spared * * * * it shall be even as thou shouldst vouchsafe to command" * * * With many gifts (rendered in token of inferiority of prowess), and a great multitude of people from the Sollee country, * * and having formed friendly alliances with the peaceably disposed Princes of the countries of * * Carnata, Nellooroo, Gowda, Kaalinga, * * Having thus daunted them by his energy, he brought the gifts which he had received from the different countries to Ramesswera;† he caused himself to be weighed in a balance * * and as a lasting memorial, he there built a dewalle, to which he gave the name of Nissankeswera * * * In compliance with the supplications of the Kings of Dambadiva to relieve them from fear, he returned with the said army to Lakdiva, and making this reflection, "In this world I have no enemies, therefore I shall apply myself to the conquering of enemies (of the next world)," he proceeded to build the three alms-houses, which were called Nissankha Daana Saalaa, and many others, in his own and in many other countries; and furnished each of them with utensils of gold and of silver, and with abundance of victuals, so as to vie

† Ramisseram

with a Calpa Wurksha; and in order to witness in person the rejoicings of the mendicants who received food thereat, he built another alms-house, which he called Nissankha Daana Mandape. He dedicated his son and his daughter to the Paatra and the Dalada relics, and afterwards redeemed them by offering up in their stead a daagoba of solid gold and other valuables. He caused to be built of stone a Dalada temple with a covered terrace around it, and an open hall decorated with wreaths and festoons, and likewise gateways and walls; and the whole of such exquisite workmanship, that beholders should be delighted, and thereby merit Swarga † and Moksha. ‡ He then caused another structure to be formed to shelter under its roof the daagoba and the principal temple; he also caused a Ruanweli daagoba to be constructed on the north side of the royal dwelling, of eighty cubits in height, and surrounded it with walls having gateways, and with cells for the residence of priests: thus he ensured the prosperity of the religion and the country. Moreover, Lanka * * being sacred ground, and possessing sacred qualities beneficial to sentient beings, he enjoined the preservation * * * exhorted them to abstain from those evils * * to preserve the honour of their respective families * * to be loyal * * * considering that when Princes award penalties for offences, they only act as physicians who prescribe remedies for diseases of the body, and exercise their power in order to restrain from crime, and so prevent falling into hell * * to understand that conspiracies are invocations to bring on death; to have a sense of gratitude, * * * to be assiduous in their exertions for the maintenance of the regality, inasmuch as these things owe their subsistence to Kings and

† Swarga; that state of happiness which consists chiefly in the exquisite gratification of the five senses.

‡ Moksha: *i. e.* extrication; salvation from the trammels of existence; annihilation: this is the Budhist idea of Nerewana, and thus differs from the Hindu notion of Moksha, which is the dissolution of individuality and absorption into the Divine essence.

Princes * * * Therefore having received from them titles, offices, and riches * * * ought not to be. Now some of the Gowi† tribe * * * * * * * * it is proper to conserve the kingdom, even by placing in the seat of royalty the sandals worn by a former sovereign * * Enemies to the doctrines of Budha ought not to be installed in Lakdiva, which is appropriate to the Kaalinga dynasty, for that would be like substituting a poison-tree for a Calpa Wurksha; but if Princes of the Kaalinga Wangsa, to whom Lakdiva has been peculiarly appropriate since the reign of Wijaya Raja, be sought for and brought hither, they will prove worthy rulers, and preserve the religion and the country. Aspire to attain the felicities of both worlds, reflecting that virtue doth conquer the universe. Future sovereigns are thus affectionately exhorted by Kaalinga Nissankha, King of Ceylon. This engraved stone is the one which the chief minister Unawoomandanawan caused the strong men of Nissankha to bring from the mountain Saegirriya at Anooraadhapoora, in the time of the lord Sree Kaalinga Chakkrawarti.

No. 5.

INSCRIPTION ON THE DAMBULLA ROCK, A.D. 1200.

THE sovereign lord of Lanka, Praakramabahoo Chakkrawarti, of the dynasty of Kaalinga, (surnamed) the Heroic and Invincible Royal Warrior; gloriously endued with might, majesty, and wisdom, and, like the placid moon, radiant with cheering and benignant qualities; the liege lord of Lakdiva by right of birth, deriving descent from the race of Wijaya Raja, who

† Gowi, or agriculturist.

extirpated the demons and peopled Ceylon, and was an object of veneration to the other royal dynasties of Dambadiva, whose renown extended over the whole world; having dispersed his enemies, as the brilliant orb of the sun over the summit of the mountain of the morn dispelleth darkness; and having extended the canopy of his dominion over the whole island; enriched the inhabitants, who were become impoverished by inordinate taxes, and made them opulent by gifts of lands, cattle, and slaves, by relinquishing the revenues for five years and restoring inheritances, and by annual donations of five balanced weights (equipoises of the King's person), consisting of gold, precious stones, pearls, silver, &c.; and from an earnest wish that succeeding Kings should not again impoverish the inhabitants of Ceylon by levying excessive imposts; he ordained that the revenue should be at the rate of five pelahs with a madarang * of four ridies, or one ammonam, three pelahs with a madarang of a pagoda for each ammonam (of land according to the fertility thereof); and considering that those who laboured with the bill-hook in (clearing) thorny jungles (for cultivation), earned their livelihood distressfully, he ordained that they should be always exempt from the tax. He also made it a rule that when permanent grants of land may be made to those who had performed meritorious services, such behests should not be evanescent like lines drawn upon water, by being inscribed on leaves, a material which is subject to be destroyed by rats and white ants; but that such patents shall be engraved on plates of copper, so as to endure long unto their respective posterities.

Thrice did he make the circuit of the island; and, having visited the villages, the towns, and the cities, and having explored the places difficult of access, the fastnesses surrounded with water, the strongholds in the midst of forests, and those upon steep hills, he had as precise a view of the whole as if

* Madarang at present signifies a fine paid by a cultivator to a proprietor of land on receiving it for cultivation.

it were an amlaca * on the palm of his hand; and such was the security which he established, as well in the wilderness as in the inhabited places, that even a woman might traverse the country with a precious jewel and not be asked, What is it? When he had thus insured safety in this island, he longed to engage in war, and twice dismayed the Kings of Paandu; and having accepted the royal maidens, and also the elephants and horses, with other tributes of homage which they sent him, he formed friendly alliances with such of the Princes of Choda, of Gowda, and of many other countries as duly appreciated his good will, but by his personal valour struck terror into those who esteemed not his friendship; and he caused Princesses to be brought unto him from each of those countries, with other tributes of homage: and, as then there remained no hostile Kings throughout Dambadiva to wage war against him, he tarried at Rajameswara, † where he made donations of balanced weights, consisting of valuables; and thus enriched the poor, and satisfied the needy. He then caused obelisks of victory, formed of stone, to be set up as lasting monuments; and, having built a dewalle consisting of five divisions, departed thence with his army, composed of four regular bodies, and returned to Ceylon. Then reflecting that, albeit he had no enemies here, he might possibly encounter enemies hereafter, he caused alms-houses to be erected at many places in Dambadiva, as well as in this island, and caused alms to be distributed constantly. He also caused gardens and fields to be cultivated, and dwellings for priests to be formed upon the hill Rankohokalooheenne, wherein is situate the cave of Dambulu Lena. Having a perfect knowledge of the doctrines of Budha, he promoted the cause of religion, and also the interests of science; he restored the ruined fanes, and the roads, which were destroyed in consequence of the calamities which had befallen the land during

* A precious stone, which, if held in the hand towards any quarter, every object in that direction becomes visible; a kind of prism.

† Ramisseram.

former reigns, and (re) built the wihares in the city of Anooraadhapoora, in Kelaniya, Mewoogone, and many other places: he expended vast riches, and within this wihare he caused to be made seventy-two statues of Budha in the recumbent, the sitting, and the standing posture; and having caused them to be gilt, celebrated a great puja at the cost of seven lacks of money; and, as is thus recorded upon this stone, gave (to this cave) the name of Swarna Giriguhaaya.*

No. 6.

ENGRAVEN ON A TABLET FORMED ON A ROCK AT POLLONNAROOWA.

Saahasa Malla, of the illustrious race of Kaalinga, having been brought over from the country of Kaalinga and installed King of Ceylon by the fortunate chieftain, has rewarded him with extensive lands and other riches; which, being the sacred gifts of gratitude, ought to be guaranteed unto him.

After the demise of Nissankha Malla, who formerly reigned in Ceylon, and subsequent to the immersion (of the ashes) of a number of Kings who succeeded him, and had, like so many diminutive stars, twinkled after the sun had gone down; when Ceylon, being without a ruler, was as a dark night without a dawn; Kooloondoottetti Abo-nawan, a chieftain of lon, who bore a great affection for his country, and was endowed with wisdom, virtue, honour, and other qualities befitting a statesman, advised with his old and constant friend Kumbudal-nawan, another patriotic chieftain, and saying, a kingdom without a King, like a ship without a steersman, cannot prosper, and is as cheerless as a day without sun; and the religion of Budha has nothing to depend upon for sup-

* *i. e.* Cave of the golden mountain.

port in the absence of the discus of domination,—Wijaya Raja having extirpated the Yakshas from the island of Ceylon, converted it as it were into a ground-plot free of roots and stumps, and therefore the Kings of that dynasty protected this country with great assiduity,—they resolved, saying, "We shall send to the country of Kaalinga, and have the younger brother of Nissankha Malla Śwamy, who formerly reigned here, to be brought hither, and so we shall preserve the religion and the country;" and, in pursuance of their resolve, they dispatched thither the loyal and accomplished chieftain Mallikaarjuna to invite the Prince, namely, Sirisangabo Kaalinga Wijayabahoo Raja, surnamed Saahasa Malla because of his surpassing prowess, who was born at Singhapura of the Queen Laka Maha Devi, to the King Sree Gopa Raja, a descendant of Kaalinga Chakkrawarti, who was sovereign of the whole (of this) Sakwela, and was of the illustrious race of Okkaaka. The Prince was accordingly conducted with great pomp to the town of Kahakonde Pattanama in the Sollee country, where he was attired in rich vestments and jewels, and was served as became one who was expected to fill the royal office. The malcontent chieftains,—who, hearing of this, caused tumults with the design of establishing themselves in power, and who hated monarchs because they inflicted punishments and granted rewards, thereby to protect the country and promote religion, —were subdued within two years; and then as it were the elevating and displaying of the full moon, they brought forth the Prince, and having embarked him at an auspicious moment, and during a fortunate stellary coincidence, conducted him in safety over the sea and over the land; and the triple kingdom being brought under the shelter of one regal canopy, he received the sacred unction at an auspicious moment, and under a fortunate asterism, on Wednesday the 12th day of the increasing moon, in the month Binera, at the completion of 1743 years and twenty-seven days of the era of Budha.

In reward of this transcendent exploit, he, in the very first year of his reign, invested the said chieftain with the badge of the dignity of Senewirat, and appointed him prime minister; and, because the mother of such offspring deserved to have much rendered unto her, he conferred on the said chieftain's mother the title of Lanka Tileke Devi, and caused her to be invested with a girdle of gold, and bestowed on her many valuable gifts.

Inasmuch as it is a duty incumbent on Kings to reward and protect those who have done exploits in their service, it is enjoined, and thus recorded on stone, that future Kings shall not resume the lands, and the retinue, and other riches which have been granted to this chieftain, Lak Wijaya Senewi, to last so long as the sun and the moon should endure; but that they shall guarantee the same on these terms, and so perpetuate their own dynasty.

If, seeing this, ministers and others entrusted with the administration of the government, should yet arrogate these things to themselves, or confiscate them for the King, they will be as subverters of the kingdom, they will be as outcasts, and they will be like unto dogs and carrion crows. Therefore, let those who are really loyal, and desirous of guarding their sovereign lord, secure unto this person all the wealth which has been bestowed on him.

The rewards conferred by the King Saahasa Malla, of the Kaalinga dynasty, on the fortunate Ceylonese chieftain who was steadfastly resolved on preserving the kingdom, ought to be guaranteed to him by future sovereigns, so that the Kaalinga dynasty may endure as long as the sun and the moon; and also by persons in authority, so that the rewards of their loyalty may be likewise ensured unto them.

Sirisangabo Weera Raja Nissankha Malla, of the race of Kaalinga, and Chakkrawarti (sole sovereign of this kingdom), having established order in Ceylon, and brought the whole country under one canopy; having relinquished the revenues of five years, and thereby relieved the people of Ceylon from the distresses occasioned by the exactions of former Kings; having distributed yearly five times his own weight of valuables, and bestowed titles and lands, slaves and cattle, gold, precious stones, vestments and jewels, and various other riches, and thereby caused gladness * * ; having caused places of shelter to the necessitous to be constructed in other countries, as well as in his own kingdom, and abundance of alms to be dealt out thereat; having surveyed the whole country, and explored all the strongholds, and established the prosperity of the country and of the religion; having then, through a vehement desire of engaging in war, proceeded to Dambadiva, followed by an army complete in all the four constituent hosts; and challenged to battle, and meeting with no opponent, but seen the gifts of homage, consisting of royal virgins, gold, &c. which were presented by the Princes of Paandu * * * ; and having then set up the staff of victory; he returned to Lakdiva, and reigned in accordance with the ten precepts of government, during which period he caused the Ruanweli daagoba to be constructed, and beheld the work from the rock whereon this is inscribed.—Success!

[N.B. *The words in parentheses have been interpolated in order to explain more clearly the sense of the original.*]—Ed.

THE END.